Oratory in the Old South
1828-1860

*Prepared under the auspices of the
Speech Association of America*

LOUISIANA STATE UNIVERSITY PRESS *Baton Rouge*

Contents

Oratory
in the
Old South
1828-1860

EDITED BY WALDO W. BRADEN

with the assistance of J. Jeffery Auer

and Bert E. Bradley

Dedicated to
Dallas C. Dickey

Library of Congress Catalog Card Number: 78–103128
SBN 8071–9024–X
Manufactured in the United States of America by
Thos. J. Moran's Sons, Inc., Baton Rouge, Louisiana
Designed by Jules B. McKee

Preface

The book was originally conceived and initiated by Dallas C. Dickey of the University of Florida. More than any other person Dickey called our attention to southern public address as a field of study. He spent many years discussing the subject and encouraging his graduate students to investigate southern figures. In fact, some of the essays included here were first conceived as theses and dissertations directed by him. However, the untimely death of Dickey denied him the pleasure of carrying the project to fruition. The present editor, as a member of the original committee established by the Speech Association of America, has brought the work to completion.

The volume is the eighth one published under the auspices of the Speech Association of America. The editor wishes to express his appreciation to the association and to numerous persons who in various ways contributed to this project.

WALDO W. BRADEN
Louisiana State University

Oratory in the Old South
1828-1860

Introduction

WALDO W. BRADEN

"It is doubtful if there has ever been a society in which the orator counted for more than he did in the Cotton Kingdom," observes William Garrott Brown.[1] He is not alone in this belief. Many agree with W. J. Cash that an overriding characteristic of the Southerner prior to the Civil War was his passion for politics and oratory.[2] They further assert that prevailing at hustings and camp meetings, and in courtrooms and legislatures was a rhetorical flourish that took the form of grandiloquent language, vibrant voice, and impassioned action. For these persons southern oratory was in a class by itself almost without equal anywhere else. But like similar concepts, modified by the word "southern," this notion is most difficult to tie down, to describe, and to analyze. As popularly conceived, it may be little more than a myth or legend that confuses emotion and substance, fancy and fact.[3]

The present volume of essays seeks to reveal the flesh-and-blood speakers of the Old South during the period from 1828 to the Civil War. Concentration upon several occasions of this

[1] William Garrott Brown, *The Lower South in American History* (New York, 1902), 125.

[2] W. J. Cash, *The Mind of the South* (Garden City, 1941), 52.

[3] Waldo W. Braden, "The Emergence of the Concept of Southern Oratory," *Southern Speech Journal*, XXVI (Spring, 1961), 173–83.

3

thirty-two-year span, when Southerners were fraught with challenges from within and without, should provide the critics with sufficient source materials to locate and isolate the genre.

Because of limitations of space the contributors concentrate mainly upon political speakers: Nullifiers, Anti-Nullifiers, Whigs, Moderate Democrats, Know-Nothings, Fire-Eaters, and Unionists. In main, each writer attempts to describe, analyze, and evaluate the peculiar rhetorical characteristics of a group of speakers and to discover how they used their public address as a means of political influence. Exceptions are the essays on John C. Calhoun, the master orator and strategist, and the one on Southern Commercial Conventions. Interwoven in many of these essays are brief descriptions of significant speakers as they operated in the public forum. The resulting overview of the major rhetorical movements brings to light many less-known, as well as prominent, orators.

Making no attempt to force the essays into a pattern or mold, the editor has left the choice of critical method to each contributor; consequently, some writers are more historical than rhetorical in their treatments, and each one varies in the elements he considers important. Not striving for a complete view of all speaking from 1828 to 1860, they provide an appraisal which is kaleidoscopic, throwing light upon different groups and varying occasions as they come to prominence. Obviously there are gaps and omissions. No doubt some readers will be disappointed not to find a particular speaker treated here at length.

At the outset the reader should understand how these writers think of the terms "rhetoric" and "rhetorical criticism." In this context the word "rhetoric" is used in its broadest historical sense to imply the theory and practice of persuasive discourse and not to imply the use of language alone or a course in sophomore English. The use of the term here is consistent with the definition of Marie Hochmuth Nichols: "the theory and the practice of the verbal mode of presenting judgment and choice, knowledge and feeling." [4]

Rhetorical criticism, in common with other types of criticism, strives to describe, analyze, appreciate, and, most important, evaluate. For a similar volume J. Jeffery Auer observes:

> Historical studies must, of necessity, investigate rhetoric, identify persuasive appeals, and examine the causative factors influencing men's minds, impelling them to act in one way or another. Historical events do not take place in a vacuum; a people's behavior develops from their reactions and adjustments to the forces playing upon them. Economic circumstances, social pressures, cultural heritages, political developments, and the very geography and aerography of the environment create the psychological forces that set off reactions and motivate decisions.
>
> Decisions, however, do not bloom unaided in the minds of men. It is the function of rhetoric to give form to economic, social, and political problems, and to establish alternative solutions. Most of the alert citizens of the United States, for example, had done a good deal of thinking about the issues of antislavery and disunion in the critical years before the Civil War. But public speakers crystallized commonly unarticulated notions into hardened opinions.[5]

Setting the tone of this collection of essays, Ralph Eubanks characterizes southern public address during these vital years as a rhetoric of desperation, meaning of course that each group which came forward was ultimately frustrated and in the end smothered by the complexity of the issues, the emotionalism, and the gradual drift toward repression. Loyal to southern agrarianism and saddled with a slave economy, these spokesmen were incapable of or unwilling to develop or to debate lines of argument of sufficient dimension to accommodate local demands, adjust to changing economic developments, and at the

---

[4] Marie Hochmuth Nichols, *Rhetoric and Criticism* (Baton Rouge, 1963), 7.

[5] J. Jeffery Auer (ed.), *Antislavery and Disunion, 1858-1861: Studies in the Rhetoric of Compromise and Conflict* (New York, 1963), v-vi.

same time maintain national bonds. Yet regardless of their affiliations most southern speakers repeatedly gave voice to their loyalties to the Constitution and the federal system. What Calhoun and men like him sought were checks on the power of the general government, methods to safeguard and preserve the plantation system based upon a slave economy and an aristocratic culture.

Many historians agree that the decade before 1830 marked the beginning of what has been called a southern nationalism or consciousness of regional pride.[6] The struggle between the Nullifiers and Unionists in South Carolina from 1828 to 1833 serves as a fitting introduction for this period. The passage of an objectionable tariff forced South Carolinians, aristocratic and conservative, to weigh their economic and political futures within the federal system. Beset at home with unpleasant and disturbing economic developments, two well-educated groups tested in vigorous controversy the desirability of resisting the power of the general government. The prospect of becoming a permanent minority and the possibility of being forced to contribute to the economic well-being of other states, particularly in the North, stirred numerous oratorical exchanges and lengthy argumentation.

Through his analysis of the Nullifiers (the affirmative), Eubanks exposes dominant southern attitudes, sentiments, and ideologies. Influenced by Kenneth Burke,[7] Eubanks discusses context, strategies, and idioms, or what he terms "valuative and axiological grounds." Seeking to understand the southern mind, he isolates deftly, as fundamental values, liberty, honor, and eloquence. The first two, he thinks, were commonplaces or

[6] See Charles S. Sydnor, *The Development of Southern Sectionalism, 1819–1848* (Baton Rouge, 1948) and Avery O. Craven, *The Growth of Southern Nationalism, 1848–1861* (Baton Rouge, 1953), Vols. V and VI of Wendell Holmes Stephenson and E. Merton Coulter (eds.), *A History of the South* (10 vols.; Baton Rouge, 1947—).

[7] See Kenneth Burke, *A Rhetoric of Motives* (New York, 1953).

sources from which speakers drew arguments, and the third they prized also for its own sake as the means. He emphasizes that the basic issue concerned the "equitable adjustment of power" between the national government and states or, more specifically, how the citizens of a state could remain loyal to the Constitution and the Union and at the same time protect its institutions from the whims of the absolute majority.

The Nullifiers looked to the guidance of John C. Calhoun who sought "a strictly legal or Constitutional method of getting rid of an unsatisfactory law." [8] As a master rhetorician and political philosopher he invented arguments for lesser men to discuss in the public forum. Hence, Thomas Cooper, James Hamilton, Jr., Robert J. Turnbull, William C. Preston, James Henry Hammond, Robert Y. Hayne, George McDuffie, William Harper, and Robert Barnwell Rhett became the agents to advance the Calhoun concepts of state interposition and nullification. As the campaign progressed, Eubanks finds that the Nullifiers became less logical, more revolutionary, and more impressionistic. In the style of a good Burkeian, Eubanks denies that these vigorous men possessed rhetorical excellence because they rested their case "on a grudging definition of liberty" and sought to sustain "a decaying order of privilege." But he provides little support for the popular image of the southern orator.

The Nullifiers met stiff opposition from an able coterie of Unionists (the negative), now sometimes forgotten or passed over. From a different vantage point Merrill G. Christophersen offers a running account of how these Anti-Nullifiers matched their opponents move for move. In his opening pages he sets the stage with a particularly revealing discussion of how the young blades of Charleston were groomed for eloquence in their homes, schools, literary societies, and conversational clubs. Motivated by an intense desire for oral excellence, these men

[8] Avery O. Craven, *Civil War in the Making, 1815–1860* (Baton Rouge, 1959), 41.

perfected their oratorical talents, often seeking oratory for oratory's sake, and developing it as "an end and as an instrumentality." As a result, an unusual number of extremely well-qualified speakers resided in Charleston to argue interposition and nullification.

Opposing the theorizing of Calhoun and the oratory of Preston and Rhett and their like, were Hugh S. Legaré, William Smith, William Drayton, Thomas Smith Grimké, Daniel and Alfred Huger, Joel R. Poinsett, Benjamin F. Perry, David Johnson, Mitchell King, and James L. Petigru. Firm in their stand for the Union and the Constitution, these men argued that nullification was revolutionary. Pursuing a shrewd strategy, they successfully answered the affirmative case at public meetings, in the legislature, on the stump, and in the courts. By their fervor and sincerity they also demonstrated that a strong Union sentiment persisted in South Carolina.

In addition Christophersen discusses how these leaders carried their persuasion in behalf of their cause into neighboring states. Through conversation and private counsel they stiffened the Union support throughout the region. Not a majority in South Carolina after 1830, the Unionists nevertheless held the Nullifiers in check and, according to Christophersen, postponed the war thirty years.

Interestingly, they did not answer Calhoun's line of argument concerning the threat of the national government to a state and the "peculiar institution" of the South. Placed on the defensive, they produced no convincing answers to the South's dilemma or no new positions from which to argue. They found their strength in the realm of manipulation and skillful use of existing institutions.

Following the first two essays which concern the years from 1828 to 1833, Robert Gunderson's essay on the Whigs bridges the gap from the early thirties to the Compromise of 1850 and the demise of the Whig Party. Through realignment of political factions the Whigs sought to pull together a party which could gain political dominance. Varying in motivation from state to state, individuals left Democracy for a variety of reasons: dislike of Andrew Jackson, fear of rising frontier democracy, petty quarrels, and incompatibility with other Democrats. Beneath the announced reasons were deeper and more intense sentiments, often undefined and undeclared. From its birth, the continued effectiveness of the party hung precariously on loose alliance and upon sidestepping the slavery question which divided northern and southern Whigs.

Aware of these loose ties, the Whig orators, often at the local level bypassing fundamental arguments, exploited emotionally charged polemics to carry the day. Gunderson observes, "Compounding Whig ideological confusion was a romantic hallucination of aristocracy." He suggests that the elections of 1840 and 1848 reveal the sterility of their *inventio*. The log cabin and hard cider campaign of 1840, the antics of Davy Crockett, the reign of violence at meetings, the selection of military heroes for standard bearers—men popular but unskilled in government—and flamboyant excesses suggest the poor quality of their appeals and the futility of their position. Whig oratory, which on the national level often was characterized by "conservatism and moderation," was marked at the local level by demagoguery, avoidance of main issues, equivocation, and attacks on scapegoats. At least in this sense it qualified as a rhetoric of desperation.

It may seem strange to include in this collection an essay devoted to the Democrats, for in fact almost all the principal figures discussed in this book were, at one time or another, Democrats. First Democrats, some Whigs returned to the fold with the demise of their party. The Fire-Eaters of course were Democrats. In his essay Lindsey S. Perkins discusses speakers who "occupied an essentially middle-of-the-road position," selecting as typical moderates: two Virginians and two

Georgians, James McDowell and Herschel Vespasian Johnson, Alexander H. Stephens, and Robert Toombs.

These four men, as did many Southerners, recognized the fallibility of slavery, opposed breaking federal ties, and were not easily stirred to violent action. Perhaps it is significant that they came from Virginia and Georgia, states not as subject to the intensity and hysteria of the day as South Carolina. Johnson and McDowell were lifelong Democrats. Stephens and Toombs for a time strayed into the Whig Party, later attempted to form their own Constitutional Unionist Party in Georgia. Finally, with some reluctance, the two reunited with the Democratic Party in the last years of the troubled fifties. On many occasions they demonstrated that they were not afraid to stand forth in public debate and argue their positions. In the end, however, like many other Southerners, Robert E. Lee for example, these leaders, when forced to decide between national and state loyalties, sided with their states and gave their allegiance to the Confederacy.

The first four writers hint at the role of John C. Calhoun. For example, at one place Eubanks says: "Consultations with Calhoun at his Fort Hill home, by personal conference and correspondence, produced the general outline of a dialectical position on remedy as well as a plan for tactical maneuver." Within South Carolina, Calhoun served as strategist, adviser, counselor, and, yes, dialectician and rhetorician. He seemed to prefer remaining aloof from local encounters. On the national scene he revealed himself most clearly as a speaker when he matched wits with Daniel Webster, advanced an apologia for slavery, and exerted his influence upon other southern leaders.

Rhetorically, what was his stance? J. L. Tarver and B. E. Bradley examine how Calhoun handled expository persuasion to justify human slavery. Similar to his posture in private conference, he resorted to expository discourse to advance his apologia, but Bradley and Tarver say "his speeches were singularly deficient in appeals for action." In their analysis Bradley and Tarver are certainly consistent with the notion that Calhoun was the master dialectician—perhaps even regarded as a kind of father figure. They suggest how he reinforced this impression: he explained and elaborated upon his interpretations, letting others become emotional and anxious about these positions at the local level. But above and removed from the fray, the father figure hovered over each encounter, carefully following and on occasion directing the little men in their polemics. As the position of the South changed, Calhoun was forced to argue that slavery was a positive good. Limited by his value system and his loyalty to South Carolina, Calhoun could not see that he "was blind to the flaws of his own thinking and thus not master but the victim of his metaphysics." The tragic stance of this great mind in rationalizing human slavery, so thoroughly condemned outside the South, is another evidence of the rhetoric of desperation.

The essay on the Southern Commercial Conventions represents a shift in method and theme from the earlier chapters. To add to the mosaic of the book Owen Peterson reviews the speaking of sixteen meetings which assembled periodically between 1837 and 1859 to see what new insight they throw upon southern public address. At these affairs the central motivation was the growing sectional sensitivity to the South's economic and political problems. Peterson says: "Harboring the suspicion that their northern competitors flourished at their expenses Southerners began to seek measures to offset the North's economic superiority." The participants were mainly business and commercial leaders but also present were politicians, editors, preachers, professors, railroad and steamship promoters. Convention speakers included John C. Calhoun,

Alexander Stephens, Judah P. Benjamin, Albert J. Pike, Robert Barnwell Rhett, William Lowndes Yancey, Henry S. Foote, Hugh S. Legaré, Pierre Soulé and many others.

The drift of these sixteen meetings followed the changing attitudes of the region. The first four (1837–39) mainly considered direct trade with Europe. Between 1845 and 1852 the focus shifted to internal improvements, particularly with reference to promoting railroads to the west. The remaining ten (1852–59) adopted "a belligerent stance and simply denounced" the federal government. During these last meetings the Fire-Eaters appeared to make strong pleas for southern unity, for combatting northern expansion, and at last for actual disunion. Expressing sectional consciousness, the radical leaders demanded southern education, native southern teachers, southern publishing houses, southern teachers' colleges, "buy southern," and even "vacation southern." At the final two conventions—at Montgomery, 1858, and Vicksburg, 1859—disunionists openly came out for resumption of the slave trade and separation from the Union.

What do these occasions reflect about southern oratory? Peterson indicated that delegates failed to come to grips with key issues, to perfect an influential pressure group, and to develop a unified program for the South. He does not find the speaking exceptional or penetrating, distinctive or distinguished.

The final decade of the period under study represents significant changes in the public address of the South. Open conflict between the North and the South was narrowly averted in 1850 through a compromise that settled almost nothing related to equitable adjustment of power between the national and state governments. During the final decade debate turned on whether a reasonable alternative to sectional conflict could be found. The Know-Nothings, the Fire-Eaters, and the Unionists all gave different answers.

Most clearly the rhetoric of desperation was manifest in the strategies and maneuvers of the Know-Nothing Party. Donald W. Zacharias concentrates on how representative Know-Nothing orators gave "symbolic value to select issues." He further considers "the role of special occasions for speech-making in promotion of the movement and the characteristics of the language employed to express Know-Nothing appeals."

He shows how many persons of substantial stature in the South flirted with bigotry and demagoguery. Much like the Whigs they sparred with straw men in order somehow to avoid becoming entangled in a discussion of the "peculiar institution" and the South's real problems. They found themselves adrift; they no longer had the Whig Party; they could not find congenial companions in the Democratic Party and were frightened by the abolitionists and Republicans. By the manner of their speaking they reflected the hopelessness of their cause.

Attracting many leaders of the defunct Whig Party the southern wing of this so-called American Party directed its persuasive strategy toward "preserving the Union—with slavery." But like the Whigs in their search for ways to get around the decisive issue of slavery, they concocted vitriolic appeals against the foreign born and Catholicism. Where expedient they shifted positions to concentrate upon local reforms in order to woo the support of Catholics. In frenzy and near hysteria they expended their energies in ratification conventions, barbecues, public debates, flag raisings, street preaching, parades, and fireworks. Much like a religious or fraternal order they played with secret codes, patriotic fervor, and ritualistic responses. In evaluating the efforts of these men Zacharias says: "They can be commended for their unselfish devotion to the South, but they must be judged harshly for the strategies they used in winning support for the movement. Harsh language in Know-Nothing speeches betrayed the orators' desperation. . . . Certainly the reasoning in their public rallies was superficial and specious." Like others before them they found no way to forestall the impending crisis.

Of all the speakers of the Old South, the so-called Fire-Eaters provide the rhetorical critic with the knottiest problem. H. Hardy Perritt provides an insight into this paradoxical group through a case study of four leading figures: Edmund Ruffin of Virginia, John A. Quitman of Mississippi, Robert Barnwell Rhett of South Carolina, and William Lowndes Yancey of Alabama. To protect agrarian slavocracy against encroachment by the expanding industrialism of the North, these four men and other leaders like them pushed the arguments of Calhoun to their logical conclusion arriving at the position that the *only* solution was separation from the Union and the creation of the Confederacy. While others equivocated and attempted to avoid the slave issue, these men came out openly for the extension of the institution and for its protection. Contrary to what superficial examination might suggest, Perritt argues that these men were not demagogues or opportunists. When secession came they were denied leadership in the Confederacy. Having fought so violently for their position they stirred damaging attacks upon their characters and ethics, thus sacrificing personal advancement for principles. Subsequently the Fire-Eaters have suffered at the hands of historians and rhetorical critics because they were on the losing side and stood for a position which war and reconstruction obliterated.

The final essay discusses the southern Unionists, who were to be swallowed up in the onrush toward war. It is, of course, sometimes forgotten that in every southern state a sizeable body of opinion held firmly to its loyalty to the Union and sought until the last to avert secession. James Golden adds dimension to this study of southern public address through his penetrating characterizations of six conservative political leaders, so unlike in appearance and approach, but dedicated in their devotion to the Union. He leads the reader to appreciate and sympathize with bantam-like, fiery Henry A. Foote of Mississippi; erudite, polished, and friendly John J. Crittenden of Kentucky; "elegant, commanding, and courtly" Henry W. Hilliard of Alabama; "well-proportioned" Benjamin F. Perry of South Carolina; "violent, denunciatory, and distrusting" John Minor Botts of Virginia; and eccentric and emotional Sam Houston of Texas. These leaders were fearless in their opposition to the Fire-Eaters and the secessionists, and they had the courage to carry their campaign to preserve the Union into the northern states. In 1860 they divided in their support between Bell and Douglas and were critical of Breckinridge and Lincoln. In the words of Robert Gunderson, "Southern extremists silenced moderates by hysterical accusations of 'abolitionist' or 'submissionist.' "

Emerging from various political affiliations and diverse backgrounds these men agreed on "the preservation of the American Union, the protection of southern rights and adherence to the Constitution." Expressing their sentiments Henry W. Hilliard succinctly said: "The Constitution is the strength of the government and the bulwark of personal liberty; it must be upheld. He who violates it is false to his country, to himself, and to his race."

All that Golden claims for these Unionists is that they kept discussion open and that "they played no small part in delaying secession." In a final evaluation he observes: "Thus in a period when fresh analysis and new rhetorical strategies were urgently needed in evaluating the South's peculiar institution, they chose instead to eulogize the Constitution as a panacea. This unimaginative and simplistic solution was by late 1860 too sterile and evasive to blunt the abrasive attacks of the secessionists." Like earlier speakers of the South they were unable to free themselves from lines of thought prevalent for thirty years and crystalized in the writings of John C. Calhoun. These advocates of the status quo were placed in an indefensible position in their efforts to preserve state rights in order to protect a "grudging definition of liberty" and "a decaying order or privilege." They found that "stereotyped appeals to the Constitution were no more effective in putting down cries for disunion than the demagogic tactics of the Whigs and Know-Nothings."

What conclusions do these essays suggest? A recurring emphasis throughout the series is expressed in Eubank's phrase, "a rhetoric of desperation." As various groups took their turns at deliberating and debating they met frustration and oftentimes disappointment. They found no ways to resolve the conflict between national loyalties and state interests. The Nullifiers of South Carolina, counseled by John C. Calhoun, proposed interposition and nullification as a solution, but they were frustrated before putting it to a crucial test. Although the Anti-Nullifiers delayed confrontation, it was probably the threat of the federal government, the determination of Andrew Jackson, and the failure to muster support of neighboring states that forestalled action. The Whigs sought an answer through realignment of political factions, but they maintained their tenuous bonds by sidestepping the slave issue. To maintain their unity they resorted to demagoguery and dramatics, particularly within the South. One group who might have gained a favorable hearing, the moderate Democrats, could do no better than repeat a stereotype to the effect that abiding by the Constitution would solve all problems. This answer was no solution to the growing tension between the North and the South. The business and professional leaders assembling at the Commercial Conventions were stymied in producing an economic program for the region because they could not free themselves of bickering and biases. Continuing the practices of the Whigs, the Know-Nothings attacked straw men and expended their energies in making scapegoats of

Catholics and foreigners. Sadly, otherwise responsible men cheapened themselves by emotional histrionics. The Fire-Eaters advanced secession as a solution to meet the impasse which had tormented Southerners for thirty years, arguing that protection of slavery could be maintained only in a separate nation. Often their arguments and proposals were met with attacks upon their personalities and characters, but not by sound arguments. In face of the rising tide of revolution, the best the Unionists of the late fifties could advance was the tired old stereotype that there was nothing to fear if all parties would simply abide by the Constitution. This was no better as an answer to the proponents of secession than it had been thirty years earlier when it was used as an answer to nullification. At a moment when new leadership with new solutions to the problems of slavery was needed, the conservative Unionists, honorable but insensitive to the irrationalism of the time, were helpless and ineffective. Did the Fire-Eaters win? In spite of the triumphing of their course of action—secession—they had fought so hard that they destroyed their own ethos and hence were all but forgotten when the Confederacy sought leadership.

The essays give evidence that the speakers of the South in the thirty years prior to the conflict do not fall into a common pattern. Motivated by a great variety of forces, these speakers did not think alike and certainly did not orate alike. No genre of southern oratory appears. Gunderson thought that he noted its elements in the Whigs' appeal to the ignorant voters. Perkins named one speaker who seemed to possess the attributes associated with southern oratory. It is true that some speakers on occasion soared in oratorical flights and seemed to enunciate sweeping idioms. But the elements of commonality actually developed from generally held tenets which served as the bases for many speeches—a desire to preserve

17

state rights, slavery, and an agrarian aristocracy. But likeness in method of speaking—in use of language, voice, and bodily action—failed to appear. These essays help to destroy the myth of a southern orator.

I

The Rhetoric
of the Nullifiers

RALPH T. EUBANKS

In pure identification there would be no strife. Likewise, there would be no strife in absolute separateness. . . . But put *identification* and *division* ambiguously together, so that you cannot know for certain just where one ends and the other begins, and you have the characteristic invitation to rhetoric.*

The austere transformation of the Old South from a spirit of American to one of southern nationalism between the years 1820 and 1850 quite overshadows many another significant feature of nineteenth century American history. The full measure of that transformation emerges from two contrasting rhetorical statements of the period. The first is from a speech delivered by John C. Calhoun in the United States House of Representatives three years before the Missouri question arose. Agitated by the specter of sectionalism, Calhoun cautioned: "We are under the most imperious obligation to counteract every tendency to disunion. . . . Let us then bind the Republic

---

* Kenneth Burke, *A Rhetoric of Motives* (New York, 1950), 25. (Italics supplied.)

19

together with a perfect system of roads and canals. So situated, blessed with a form of government at once combining liberty and strength, we may reasonably raise our eyes to a most splendid future. . . . [But] if we permit a . . . selfish, and sectional spirit to take possession of this House, this happy scene will vanish. We will divide, and in its consequences will follow misery and degradation." [1] The second statement was made in 1850 by the elder Langdon Cheves. Addressing the assembled delegates at the Nashville Convention, Cheves appeared the incarnation of southern nationalism. Cried he, "What is the remedy? United secession of the slaveholding States. Nothing else will be wise—nothing else practicable. Unite and you shall form one of the most splendid empires on which the sun ever shone, of the most homogeneous population, all the same blood and lineage, a soil the most fruitful and a climate the most lovely." [2]

The span of years between these two contrasting utterances represents an epoch dominated by meticulous debate on: *"What the constitution is."* [3] On courthouse lawn, in legislative chamber—even in the church sanctuary—speakers by the thousands grappled with the basic issue and the countless related questions. Put simply, the basic issue was the ancient one of *unrestricted power to rule.* Or, as more commonly phrased in the debates of the period: the equitable adjustment of power between the central and the state (or colonial) authorities. On this root problem American debate had actually

1 *Annals of Congress,* 18th Cong., 2nd Sess., 851–58.

2 Cited in Rollin G. Osterweis, *Romanticism and Nationalism in the Old South* (New Haven, 1949), 7.

3 Senator Bell of New Hampshire is reported to have used the phrase in a discussion with Daniel Webster on the question of what rhetorical strategy the latter should use in his "Second Reply to Hayne." See Edward K. Graham, "The History of Southern Oratory During the Federal Period, 1788–1861," in J.A.C. Chandler *et al* (eds.), *The South in the Building of the Nation* (13 vols.; Richmond, 1909–13), IX, 30.

started with the Stamp Act. It would hardly be ended with Lee's signature at Appomattox.

Between 1830 and 1860 the problem resolved itself for most Southerners into an elemental consideration: preservation of the integrity of southern culture. The very survival of the South's "peculiar institution," as well as its values and ideals, its customs and its mores, were presumed to be at stake. Out of this long, feverish debate there issued what may be termed a Rhetoric of Desperation. Passionate and inexorable, this rhetoric consumed the energies of some of the most cultivated minds of the Old South.[4]

A crucial phase in the development of this rhetoric was the well-known nullification controversy—a political struggle that brought South Carolina close to war with the Union, and even her two opposing factions to the brink of civil conflict. Inquiry into the rhetoric of the Nullifier faction provides a clearer understanding of the critical first stage of the rhetoric of that generation of southern speakers which arose between William Lowndes and Jefferson Davis.

The object of this essay is to characterize and evaluate the rhetoric of the Nullifiers, those leaders who between the years 1828 and 1833 advocated "state interposition" as the proper solution to the economic ills suffered by the staple-producing southern states as a result of the federal protective tariff laws.[5] Inquiry is directed into three topics: (1) the sociopolitical context of the Nullifiers' rhetoric; (2) the pattern of their rhetorical strategy; and (3) the nature of their rhetorical idiom.

[4] Reynolds has demonstrated that this rhetoric, having finally depleted the purely dialectical resources available to it, resorted to the nonrational resources of "sectional bitterness and romanticism." William Reynolds, "Deliberative Speaking in Ante-Bellum South Carolina: The Idiom of a Culture" (Ph.D. dissertation, University of Florida, 1960), 236–39.

[5] Only so-called "avowed" Nullifiers will be discussed in this paper; those who stopped short of open advocacy of the doctrine will be excluded.

21

Representative speakers and occasions are examined as they serve to illuminate the unfolding pattern of rhetorical strategy.

What was the nature of the "mediatory ground," using Kenneth Burke's phrase, on which the rhetorical battle of nullification was waged? To answer this question we must identify the major sociopolitical "divisions" between the northern and the southern states. In 1819 these differences lay under the surface, held down by more compelling pressures of "identification," which were synthesized in the ideal of American nationalism. These divisions, powerful and ominous, later touched off the desperate struggle. Realizing their potency, many political leaders skirted them in public discussion. The most critical were represented in the tension between federalism and republicanism, between agrarianism and industrial capitalism, between seaboard and frontier, between the aristocratic and the plebeian ways of life, and between slavery and freedom. In South Carolina these national divisions, appearing in microcosm, established the mediatory ground on which the nullification debate was waged.[6]

Yet the ground on which the Nullifiers and their opponents clashed in 1828 was not altogether untrodden; it had been reconnoitered in the Sixteenth Congress (1819–21) during the debates on the Missouri question and the protective tariff bill. These issues, resonant with sectional self-interest, proved strong enough to strip away the mask of apparent unity between North and South. The resulting argument threw into bold relief the growing strength of northern industrialism and the waning strength of southern agrarianism. Again, these congressional debates disclosed a growing willingness to ac-

[6] After 1830, as the great constitutional debate matured, these divisions polarized in two opposing ideals which Parrington has termed "equalitarian idealism" and "economic realism." See Vernon Louis Parrington, *The Romantic Revolution in America, 1800–1860*, Vol. II of Parrington, *Main Currents in American Thought* (3 vols.; New York, 1927–30), 4.

cept what John M. Anderson has aptly termed "*a misidentification of the political order with a part of the social order*." [7] Above all, these debates defined motives: they drew out the cleavages in purpose and value that would lead finally to the deep alienation of a "house divided against itself." [8]

The tariff question which generated the nullification controversy was but one manifestation of an emergent economic nationalism. Under the aegis of this national trend the federal government assumed the power to alter radically certain aspects of the economic life. Led by the Old Republicans, southern congressmen opposed the new philosophy and the various protective tariff measures presented between the years 1820 and 1828. Together the Old and Young Republicans developed a rich fund of negative argument—a fund upon which both Nullifier and Anti-Nullifier would later draw. The rhetorical situation during the first stage of the nullification debate appears more intelligible when considered as an extension of these congressional tariff debates. For by 1828 the need issue had been fully explored.

The protective tariff movement arose—as such sociopolitical movements often do—from an emergency situation. The War of 1812 brought the birth of a number of new manufacturing enterprises, most of which were located in New England. Desiring to shield them from foreign competition, Congress saw fit in 1816 to invoke the protective principle. The panic of 1819 inspired the manufacturers to seek even greater protection. In 1820 and again in 1824 Congress considered bills calling for an

[7] John M. Anderson (ed.), *Calhoun: Basic Documents* (State College, Pa., 1952), 15. (Italics added.)

[8] Sydnor has suggested: "Perhaps it is anachronistic to speak of Southerners at the beginning of the year 1819. The sense of oppression and the sectional patriotism that were soon to appear had not yet become visible." Charles S. Sydnor, *The Development of Southern Sectionalism*, 32. Cf. C. Vann Woodward, who says, "The South was American a long time before it was Southern in any self-conscious or distinctive way." "The Search for Southern Identity," *Virginia Quarterly Review*, XXXIV (1958), 338.

extraordinary increase in the duties on iron, lead, glass, cotton bagging, and woolen goods.[9]

The agrarian-industrial division shaped the tariff debate in both Congresses. Taken together, these several debates covered the pro and con arguments that Nullifier and Anti-Nullifier would later adduce on the protection issue. Proponents, representing New England, the middle states, Kentucky and Tennessee, focused upon relative advantage. By 1824 they had developed the so-called home market argument: the contention that protection would stimulate the demand for agricultural products which, in turn, would fully compensate for the rise in retail prices on articles of American manufacture. The southern opposition, fearful that these increases might prompt England to seek a non-American source of raw cotton, denied the validity of the home market theory. In the 1824 debates southern speakers, turning to the constitutional issue, argued that since Congress had power only to raise revenue, the protective tariff was clearly a violation of the Constitution.[10]

By 1824 the industrial interest had gained political ascendancy over the agrarian interest. The 1820 bill passed the House, yet failed by one vote in the Senate. But with the help of the congressional reapportionment of 1823 and the first full-blown lobby to appear in Washington, the protectionists passed a strong tariff law in the Eighteenth Congress. The tariff of 1824 demonstrated clearly that protectionism rested not upon national but upon sectional interest. Before the next contest on the tariff, New England became solidly protariff; a part of

[9] Edward Stanwood, *American Tariff Controversies in the Nineteenth Century* (2 vols.; Boston and New York, 1904), I, 181–84.

[10] *Annals of Congress*, 16th Cong., 1st Sess., 1954; 18th Cong., 1st Sess. 649, 1918, 1983–85, 1994, 2009–25; Stanwood, *American Tariff Controversies*, I, 182–91. As the great constitutional debate developed, Southerners came to depend more heavily upon the topic of legality for rhetorical leverage. Reynolds has observed, for example, that "after 1836, the stock [South] Carolina approach to all bills in Congress was first to test their constitutionality." Reynolds, "Deliberative Speaking", 223.

the Middle belt, both North and South, through political alliances, shifted to an antitariff position. Only Pennsylvania, of the northern states, along with the South held fast to their 1824 position.[11]

Between 1824 and 1828 the protective movement grew ever stronger. Though the Woolens Bill of 1827 failed, the 1828 "Tariff of Abominations" dramatized the growing disposition to identify the political order with a particular part of the social order. Supporting the 1828 bill were New England and the North, together with Kentucky and western Virginia. Opposing it were the South and the Southwest. In the eyes of the Cotton Kingdom the tariff was not designed to raise revenue, nor was its object to regulate foreign commerce. Rather, it was calculated to promote domestic industrialism. Of the 1828 bill Katherine Coman has written: "The prohibitory duties on the coarse cottons and woolens with which the slaves were clothed, on sugar, salt, and iron manufactures, gave the planters no choice but to buy of domestic producers at prices averaging 40 per cent higher than in foreign markets." [12] Without question the protective tariff, as the Nullifiers were soon to maintain, contributed to the economic decline suffered in South Carolina during the closing years of the decade.[13]

Southern antitariff remonstrances poured from legislative chambers, newspapers, and the hustings. The legislatures of Virginia, Georgia, Alabama, North Carolina, Mississippi, and South Carolina issued protests. Mississippi, in typical phrase, resolved: "That the Tariff of 1828 is contrary to the spirit of the Constitution of the United States; impolitic and oppressive

---

[11] Taussig terms the tariff of 1824 the "first and most direct fruit of the early protective movement . . . ." F. W. Taussig, *The Tariff History of the United States* (7th ed., New York and London, 1923), 74–75.

[12] Katherine Coman, *The Industrial History of the United States* (rev. ed.; New York, 1910), 196.

[13] David Duncan Wallace, *South Carolina: A Short History* (Chapel Hill, 1951), 388–89.

in its operation on the Southern States, and ought to be resisted by all constitutional means." [14]

No other state of the Cotton Kingdom developed so ardent and united an opposition to protectionism as did South Carolina. Long before the Tariff of Abominations became law, antinationalistic feeling had swept the state. As early as 1825, the legislature had approved a set of antitariff resolutions. [15] But not until the summer of 1828 did nullification emerge from the antitariff controversy. Immediately after passage of the tariff act of 1828 the nullification movement entered what Leland Griffin has called the "inception period." [16] At this stage, as Chauncey Boucher observes, "The people saw remonstrances proving futile and began to think of the next necessary step." [17] Thus, in terms of the rhetorical procedure of deliberative debate, the controversy fell under domination of the stock issue, "What is the proper remedy for existing ills?" The best rhetorical efforts of southern congressional delegations had failed to halt protectionism. Nor had the solemn protests of state legislature and the antitariff meeting achieved results. In a nutshell the overriding question now was, "What remedy *beyond* remonstrance will cure the ills?" From the assertions and denials developed the movement of nullification.

During the six-year debate the affirmative and negative orators confronted each other on all of the "status questions" of

---

[14] See Herman V. Ames (ed.), *State Documents on Federal Relations: The States and the United States* (Philadelphia, 1906), 152–58.

[15] Chauncey S. Boucher, *The Nullification Controversy in South Carolina* (Chicago, 1916), 1–3.

[16] This phase of a rhetorical movement Griffin has defined as "a time when the roots of a pre-existing sentiment, nourished by interested rhetoricians, begin to flower into public notice, or when some striking event occurs which immediately creates a host of aggressor rhetoricians and is itself sufficient to initiate the movement." Leland M. Griffin, "The Rhetoric of Historical Movements," *Quarterly Journal of Speech*, XXXVIII (April, 1952), 186.

[17] Boucher, *The Nullification Controversy*, 6–7.

deliberative controversy: *ill, reformability, remedy,* and *cost.*[18] The most hotly disputed were, "Whether the proposed remedy will be effectual" and "Whether the remedy will cost too much." Yet the prior questions of the extent of the ill and its reformability were at no time during the long controversy dead issues. Indeed, long after the need issue had been exhausted, the two latter questions were at times potent enough to give direction to the contest.

Before the actual inception of the movement in the summer of 1828, the public was prepared for the presentation of far less conservative remedies than remonstrance and protest. Most critical to the strategy of the Nullifiers were two rhetorical maneuvers of 1827—one from the pen and one from the stump. The first was a series of articles written for the *Mercury* by Robert J. Turnbull under the pseudonym, "Brutus." Believing as early as 1827 that the ill was reformable only through drastic action, Turnbull wrote in one essay: "Should we even be subjugated, what then: We shall have the proud consolation of not having submitted without a struggle. . . . There is not an atom of disgrace in being vanquished. But there is meanness in submission." [19] One other spokesman took an extremely advanced position on remedy, suggesting that the choice lay between submission and disunion. In one of the most crucial utterances of the nullification debates, Dr. Thomas Cooper, a South Carolina College professor, developed that position. On July 2, 1827, at a Columbia meeting called to protest the Woolens Bill, Cooper counseled that both human nature and economic history would soon force upon the South the alternatives, submis-

---

[18] Hultzén's application of the ancient theory of *status* to deliberative speaking is useful in explaining in broad terms the rhetorical structure of the nullification movement. Lee Hultzén, "Status in Deliberative Analysis," in *The Rhetorical Idiom,* ed. Donald C. Bryant (Ithaca, 1958), 109–10.

[19] Phillips, *The Course of the South to Secession: An Interpretation by Ulrich Bonnell Phillips,* ed., E. Merton Coulter (New York, 1939), 130.

sion or disunion. Cooper well deserves the title sometimes given him, "The Father of Nullification." Described by his biographer as "a philosophical materialist, Unitarian, and political revolutionist," who "[valued] the union too little because he loved liberty too well," Cooper phrased the South's dilemma with genuine eloquence.[20] Arguing from the central moral axiom, "Equality is equity," Cooper reasoned:

> By and by we shall be driven to adopt some decisive measure *when the power is gone from us*. Wealth will be transferred to the north, and wealth is power. Every year of submission rivets the chains upon us, and we shall go on remonstrating, complaining, and reluctantly submitting, till the remedy now in power will be looked up to in vain. . . . It is vain that the force of argument is with us; the hand of power is against us and upon us . . . and nothing but determination and decision can prevent our being prostrated. . . . I have said, that we shall 'ere long be compelled to calculate the value of the Union; and to inquire of what use to us is this most unequal alliance? By which the south has always been the loser, and the north always the gainer? Is it worth our while to continue this union of states, where the north demand to be our masters and we are required to be their tributaries? Who with the most insulting mockery call the yoke they put upon our necks the American system! The question, however, is fast approaching the alternative, of submission or separation.[21]

Prescient and militantly eloquent, Cooper's speech was too advanced for public acceptance in or outside the state. Andrew Butler, speaking in the South Carolina house in December, charged that Cooper's speech was tantamount "to rebellion against the Constitution which we are all sworn to support." [22]

---

[20] See Dumas Malone, *The Public Life of Thomas Cooper, 1783–1839* (New Haven, 1926), for an objective assessment of Cooper's public career. Also useful is C. F. Himes, *Life and Times of Thomas Cooper* (Carlisle, Pa., 1918).

[21] The full text of Cooper's address is given in *Niles' Weekly Register*, XXXIII (September, 1827–March, 1828), 28–32.

[22] Charleston *Daily Courier*, December 21, 1827.

Hezekiah Niles, defender of Clay's American System, suggested that "the distinguished and learned gentleman" had "more indulged his feelings than exerted his powers of argument." [23] Yet Cooper reasoned in fact from clear rational principles on the issues of ill and reformability, keeping himself anchored in "the nature of things." And the course of later events certified his prophecy. Still, his premature analysis of remedy and his cavalier handling of cost disclose a view of society inimical to the ways of democratic deliberation and action. Though he had nothing to do with the final events of nullification, yet Cooper was extremely influential in getting the movement started. Malone holds that "no man more than he deserves to be termed the schoolmaster of state rights and the prophet of secession." [24]

We have surveyed the political and rhetorical origins of the nullification controversy. We are now in position to focus upon the valuative or axiological ground of the Nullifiers' rhetoric. Our task is to identify the leading *values* or conceptions of "the desirable," by which the nullification spokesmen conducted their rhetorical transactions.[25] In order to discover these critcal symbols of identification, we must examine the nature of the culture to which the Nullifiers appealed for support.

The plantation society of South Carolina's coastal plain (the Low Country) governed largely the cultural patterns of the rest of the state—the Middle and the Up-Country. This militant aristocracy was composed for the most part of the planting

---

[23] *Niles' Weekly Register*, XXXIII (September, 1827–March, 1828), 17.

[24] Dumas Malone, "Thomas Cooper and the State Rights Movement in South Carolina, 1823–1830," *North Carolina Historical Review*, III (April, 1926), 184–97.

[25] I am distinguishing here between "mere likings" (the "desired") and rationally secured human preferences, between the *de facto* and the *de jure*. Genuine "value" comes into being through the exercise of judgment and has to do with the "ends and purposes of human effort." See the discussion in Harry Girvetz, et al, *Science, Folklore, and Philosophy* (New York, 1966), 463–69. See also Talcott Parsons and Edward A. Shils (eds.), *Toward a General Theory of Action* (Cambridge, Mass., 1951), 422.

and professional classes. Originally an aristocracy of family, it became after the 1830's an "aristocracy of mind." Rosser H. Taylor has described this culture as a "mud-sill civilization"— a culture resting upon the exploitation of labor. The Negro slave was the "mud-sill." Not equipped to rise above a servile state, so the theory ran, the Negro was intended to serve the well-born intellects, who would thus be in position to bear finer cultural fruit.[26] It was indeed, as Chapman Milling suggests, the labor of the Negro slave that "made possible the golden age of the Low Country." [27]

As frontier conditions fell away and as cotton culture spread, the way of the mud-siller became more nearly the way of the Palmetto State. The mud-siller's institutions and values were particularly influential on the independent farmers, merchants, small tradesmen, teachers, artisans, and mechanics. According to Taylor, "The artisans, mechanics and tradesmen were confined largely to the towns and Charleston; while the farmers, a much larger group, were confined almost entirely to rural districts, with a preponderance in the Up-Country." [28] Even the poor white yeomanry of the coastal pinelands, sandhills, and remote corners of the Up-Country districts did not escape the influence of the coastal gentry. In the main, however, the Up-Country economy created a more democratic social order.

Among the patents of nobility of the gentry was the right to rule the state's affairs. Of this ruling minority were the leading Nullifiers: Thomas Cooper, James Hamilton, Jr., Robert J. Turnbull, John C. Calhoun, James H. Hammond, Robert Y.

26 Rosser H. Taylor, "The Mud-Sill Theory in South Carolina," *Proceedings of the South Carolina Historical Association*, IX (1939), 35.

27 Chapman J. Milling, *Beneath So Kind a Sky* (Columbia, S.C., 1948), 5. For an incisive analysis of the economic foundations of this culture, see Henry Hardy Perritt, "Robert Barnwell Rhett: South Carolina Secession Spokesman" (Ph.D. dissertation, University of Florida, 1954), 3ff.

28 Rosser H. Taylor, *Ante-Bellum South Carolina: A Social and Cultural History*. The James Sprunt Studies in History and Political Science, XXV (Chapel Hill, 1942), 75.

Hayne, George McDuffie, William C. Preston, Robert Barnwell Rhett, and William Harper.[29] Some were planters; all were acute legal minds; all were able political leaders of the Jeffersonian persuasion. Together with the Anti-Nullifiers, their political antagonists whose sympathies lay largely with federalism, these men managed the state's affairs both at Columbia and in Washington.

The chief "good" of the mud-sill society was *liberty*. From the "Po' Buckra" of the pine lands to the affluent gentry of Charleston, liberty was a value term to conjure with. The Nullifier prized liberty more than Union. In his famous response to Jackson's toast at the Jefferson Day Dinner in Washington, Calhoun declared: "The Union: Next to our liberty most dear." The Anti-Nullifier, prizing liberty no less than the Nullifier, believed like Webster that liberty and union were "one and inseparable." To the South Carolina Nullifier liberty meant above all else a condition of individual sovereignty among freemen. Its opposite was submission to the coercive will of another, whether the British Crown, the Industrial North, or a Chief Executive like King Andrew Jackson. Speaking in the South Carolina lower house in 1829, Robert Barnwell Rhett uttered the battle cry of the Nullifiers when he exclaimed: "Our watchword is the glorious name of Liberty, not yet a bye [*sic*] word of pity and contempt." [30]

Next to liberty in the mud-siller's hierarchy of values was *honor*. Fed by the concept of Norman chivalry, this value was institutionalized in the *code duello*. John Hope Franklin contends that nothing was more important than honor to the man of the antebellum South. "Indeed," writes Franklin, "he placed it above wealth, art, learning, and the other 'delicacies' of an

[29] Beyond South Carolina's borders the leading Nullifiers were George Poindexter of Mississippi, Augustin S. Clayton of Georgia, Dixon H. Lewis of Alabama, Samuel Carson and Samuel Sawyer of North Carolina.

[30] Quoted in Perritt, "Robert Barnwell Rhett: South Carolina Secession Spokesman," 53.

31

urban civilization and regarded its protection as a continuing preoccupation." [31] In the code of the duel, the Southerner asserted his sense of personal sovereignty, believing the "Iron Law" both an incentive to rectitude and "a shield of personal honor." [32]

Yet another leading "good" of the mud-siller's life was *eloquence*, which served both as an end (conception of "the desirable") and as an instrumentality of public service. Of rhetoric in the Old South, W. J. Cash has written: "[It] flourished far beyond even its American average; it early became a passion—and not only a passion but a primary standard of judgment, the *sine qua non* of leadership." [33] Another southern historian wrote, "It is doubtful if there ever has been a society in which the orator counted for more than he did in the Cotton Kingdom." [34] In no other southern state, perhaps, was rhetoric cherished as in the Palmetto State. A South Carolina College president said of his state's passion for oratory: "No people make such a constant demand upon the *viva voce* as our own, and among none is the facility of public speaking so indispensable to success in every walk of life." [35] From the ranks of the South Carolina mud-siller came what William G. Carleton has aptly termed the "pure orator," i.e., "the orators for oratory's sake." Argues Carleton, "To them oratory was an art superior to politics, party management, and perhaps even statesmanship." [36] Amongst both the Nullifiers and the Anti-Nullifiers

[31] John Hope Franklin, *The Militant South, 1800–1861* (Cambridge, Mass., 1956), 35, *passim*.

[32] "A Defense of Duelling," in Charleston *City Gazette*, January 8, 1822.

[33] Wilbur J. Cash, *The Mind of the South* (Garden City, 1954), 63–64.

[34] William Garrott Brown, *The Lower South in American History* (New York, 1902), 125.

[35] James H. Thornwell, "Semi-Centennial Address, December, 1856," quoted in Reynolds, "Deliberative Speaking," 13.

[36] William G. Carleton, "The Celebrity Cult a Century Ago," *Georgia Review*, XIV (Summer, 1960), 137.

were a number of these men—men like William C. Preston and Hugh S. Legaré.[37]

Eloquence in South Carolina was considered the handmaid of liberty and honor. William C. Preston, "The Inspired Declaimer," voiced the commonly held view when he declared: "Liberty and eloquence are united in all ages." [38] To the South Carolinian the relationship between eloquence and honor was equally intimate. He used both bullets and words to vindicate his honor. No question: the code of the duel was consummated not always by "pistols at ten paces," but sometimes by deadly utterance. Yet eloquence meant even more to the public stewards of the mud-sill culture. It was an aesthetic good besides. Preston, for some years a professor of rhetoric and *belles-lettres* at South Carolina College, declared: "Eloquence is an argument alive and in motion—the statue of Pygmalion, inspired with vitality." [39] In the same spirit Hugh S. Legaré spoke of eloquence as "poetry subdued to the business of civic life." [40] There is indeed a sense in which rhetorical attainment was the very signature of the mud-sill society.

In fine, the values of liberty and honor were the crucial commonplaces of the nullification debate. Eloquence was the chief efficient means by which these symbols of command were put into play and the total engagement carried out. In our exposition of rhetorical strategy, we shall see how the rhetorical maneuvers of both the Nullifiers and their opponents were ultimately accomplished in terms of conceptions of "the desirable."

[37] For an examination of the mythical side of the tradition of "Southern Oratory," see Waldo W. Braden, "The Emergence of the Concept of Southern Oratory," *Southern Speech Journal*, XXVI (Spring, 1961), 173–83; Braden, "Southern Oratory Reconsidered: A Search for an Image," *Southern Speech Journal*, XXIX (Summer, 1964), 303–15.

[38] William C. Preston, *Eulogy on Hugh Swinton Legaré, Delivered at the Request of the City of Charleston, November 7, 1843* (Charleston, 1843), 6.

[39] *Ibid.*

[40] Cited in Carleton, "The Celebrity Cult," 137.

In broad outline the rhetorical strategy of the Nullifiers (affirmative) was to acquaint the people with the theory of state interposition, to identify this doctrine as an efficient remedy with the values of liberty and honor and to meet with counter argument and Anti-Nullifiers' (negative) objections on the stock issue of cost. The rhetorical strategy of the Anti-Nullifiers, characterized broadly, was to convince the people that the tariff ills were not as oppressive on the South as commonly believed, that remonstrance and the ballot (the constitutional means of resistance) would ultimately prove an efficient remedy, and that nullification was equivalent to secession—as "fatal" to liberty as complete federal consolidation.

In the fulfillment of their strategy the rival factions strove to use well not only the intrinsic powers of the speaker but also the resources of newspaper, pamphlet, and club.[41] Again, each faction sought to reinforce its verbal persuasions with nonverbal ones. The Nullifiers invoked the common symbols of state sovereignty and liberty: the palmetto tree, the image of the coiled rattlesnake (with motto, *Noli me tangere*), and the wounded Revolutionary War veteran. The Anti-Nullifiers drew upon these symbols to some extent, but they also made capital of the Flag and the Eagle of the United States—symbols of nationalism. Each party utilized to the fullest the persuasive potential of Independence Day ("the Sabbath of Liberty"), carrying out in every district the standard ritual of parade, prayers, orations, "original odes," and the feast.

At these annual celebrations political partisanship was reflected in both toast and oration. Typical of the toasts were those offered in 1830 at Columbia: *"The Constitution of the United States.—It gives no power to oppress."* ; *"The Union.*

---

[41] Burke warns that "often we must think of rhetoric not in terms of some one particular address, but as a general *body of identifications* that owe their convincingness much more to trivial repetition and dull daily reenforcement than to exceptional rhetorical skill . . . ." Burke, *A Rhetoric of Motives* (New York, 1953), 26.

—Dearer than life, but not dearer than liberty."; "*State Rights.* —The rallying point of the Republican Party." [42] As an additional source of persuasion both factions employed the prestige of public figures, historical and living. The Nullifiers invoked the names of three revered Virginia state righters: Patrick Henry, Thomas Jefferson, and James Madison. Until their delusion was shattered in July, 1831, the Nullifiers also claimed President Jackson.[43] But they lost Jackson's support, and Madison's as well.[44] In the thrust and counterthrust neither side yielded quarter. Gaillard Hunt observes: "Their difference was no ordinary difference. The Carolinian was a man of intense convictions and impatient of opposition, and while it is doubtless true that the . . . nullifiers [were] the more violent and intolerant of the two [parties], the Unionists, on their side, were fully prepared to support their opinions at all hazards." [45]

The leaders of the loosely-organized state rights group, alert to the advantages of a more favorable public opinion, evolved a strategic plan in the summer and fall of 1828. From this plan came the affirmative maneuvers of October and November that precipitated the debate. Consultations with Calhoun at his Fort Hill home, by personal conference and correspondence, produced the general outlines of a dialectical position on remedy as well as a plan for tactical maneuver. In a revealing letter from Calhoun to William C. Preston, representative from Richland District, the strategy and its sources were pictured clearly. Preston, the letter shows, had asked Calhoun to prepare a document for the guidance of the state rights orators in the forthcoming legislature. This document, the famous *Exposition,*

[42] Columbia (S.C.) *Southern Times,* July 5, 1830.
[43] Boucher, *The Nullification Controversy,* 150.
[44] Frederic Bancroft, *Calhoun and the South Carolina Nullification Movement* (Baltimore, 1929), 89–90; Ralph L. Ketcham (ed.), "Jefferson and Madison and the Doctrines of Interposition and Nullification," *Virginia Magazine of History and Biography,* LXVI (April, 1958), 182.
[45] Gaillard Hunt, "South Carolina During the Nullification Struggle," *Political Science Quarterly,* VI (1891), 236.

contained a set of propositions on both ill and remedy. Promising to "commence a draft immediately," Calhoun requested of Preston certain information on the question of ill. Preston had earlier suggested nullification as the proper remedy, for Calhoun wrote: "Your views appear to me to be perfectly correct. . . . The remedy you refer to [state interposition] is the only safe and efficient one, and is abundantly adequate. *I speak with confidence. It alone can save the Union.* The only question is the mode and time." [46] Counseling his lieutenants on "mode and time," Calhoun was conservative and wise. Said he: "*All moves aiming at reform and revolution as ours is, must, to be successful, be characterized by* [sic] great respect for the opinions of others." Putting the last touches to the strategy, Calhoun advised: "It seems to me all that can be done at present is an able report, fully exposing our wrongs, and unfolding our remedies, *but to abstain for the present from applying it,* on grounds of respect for others and a sense of moderation, with the adoption of such measures as may produce harmony of opinion among the oppressed States."

Following Jefferson and Madison, Calhoun formulated a set of propositions for the Nullifiers' oratory to work upon. The Constitution, he argued, was clearly a compact among independent sovereignties. It followed, therefore, under accepted principles of international law, that each party had a right to judge of infractions of the compact. Further, "in case of a deliberate, palpable, and dangerous exercise of power not delegated," each party had a right to interpose to arrest the patent violation.[47] The Nullifiers were now provided with a "kill-or-

[46] Calhoun to Preston, November 6, 1828, in David Rankin Barbee (ed.), "A Sheaf of Old Letters," *Tyler's Quarterly Historical and Genealogical Magazine,* XXXII (October, 1950), 90–92. The letter, belonging to a Major W. B. Lewis, was first published August 23, 1863, in the New York *Times.* The *Times* had received it from "a correspondent" in Nashville, Tennessee who signed himself "C.V.S."
[47] John C. Calhoun, *The Works of John Caldwell Calhoun* (6 vols.;

cure" remedy—one that went beyond the right of petition and the ballot in an effort to establish a third constitutional means of state intervention—nullification. They had assumed an incalculable burden on the issue of cost. And their restless, imperious natures made it impossible for them to follow Calhoun's conservative counsel.

For the first presentation of their position, the Nullifiers selected Walterboro, where in June, 1828, Robert Barnwell Rhett had presented his Colleton address urging "open resistance to the Laws of the Union."[48] The orator was James Hamilton, Jr., the archetypal Nullifier. Characterized by political opponent B. F. Perry as "the embodiment of chivalry," Hamilton was a man of action as well as a social philosopher, jealous of liberty and honor, patriotic, "kind and affectionate," imperious, and deadly in debate. To the nullification movement Hamilton lent both his administrative ability and his fluency. He established nullification clubs in every district of the state and in the fall of 1832 carried the elections in two thirds of the districts. "But for him," wrote Perry, "nullification would have fallen stillborn, or been crushed in its swaddling clothes."[49]

Hamilton, "a small man, quite handsome and prepossessing in . . . appearance," kept his appointment on October 21, 1828, with the audience of three to four hundred citizens of Colleton, though he was "enfeebled by a distressing malady."[50] In a two-hour speech, by turns analytical and romantic, he ex-

---

New York, 1851–56), VI, 60; Charles M. Wiltse, "Calhoun: An Interpretation," *Proceedings of the South Carolina Historical Association*, XVIII (1948), 30. Edward S. Corwin examines the foundations of Calhoun's doctrine in "National Power and State Interposition, 1787–1861," p. 546.

[48] Perritt, "Robert Barnwell Rhett: South Carolina Secession Spokesman," 43–44.

[49] Benjamin F. Perry, *Reminiscences of Public Men* (2nd series: Greenville, S. C., 1889), 143–47; *Dictionary of American Biography*, VIII, 187–88.

[50] The full text of Hamilton's speech was carried in the Charleston *Mercury*, October 30, 1828, and in *Niles' Weekly Register*, XXXV (September, 1828–March, 1829), 203–208.

amined the stock issues. First, he defined the ill in terms of a "despotic sectional majority," who appeared to "acknowledge no other canons" for the interpretation of the Constitution save "their own selfish and misguided interests." Was the ill reformable? In his judgment it was not. "When," cried the famous southern duelist, "have you known avarice to stay its cormorant appetite when it could sate it with impunity? When have you known profligate ambition to give up the certain means of accumulating power?" Arguing like his Columbia mentor, Thomas Cooper, from a cynical definition of human nature, he rejected out of hand the notion that a northern majority by "a generous exercise of power" would relieve the economic distress of the Cotton Kingdom.

Hamilton then climaxed his analysis of ill with a romantic interpretation of the South's economic plight. "Do you want the melancholy signs of our fast coming decay? " he began.

Look around through this once happy, this once prosperous land; see the wilderness retaining her empire. Look at those waste and desolate spots which once teemed with fertility and life, abandoned to the fern which rears its head amidst solitudes which were once blessed by the smiling industry of man. Where are now those beautiful homesteads and venerable chateaus which once adorned this land of our fathers . . . ? Gone, fallen into irreversible decay. On the very hearth stone where hospitality kindled the most genial fires that ever blazed on her altars, the fox may lay [sic] down in security and peace, and from the casement of the very window from which notes of virtuous revelry were once heard, the owl sends forth to the listening solitude of the surrounding waste her melancholy descant to mark the spot where desolation has come.

Hamilton turned next to the question of remedy. By the route of residues, he arrived at the doctrine of nullification. One by one he impeached the stock remedies—excises, nonconsumption, the establishment of southern manufactures—advising against any measure that would put the state on trial in a federal court. Invoking the honor-identification, Hamilton challenged: "Let our antagonist be a co-equal sovereign, and let us meet him on equal grounds." The appropriate remedy, he concluded, is "*a nullification* by the State either in its legislative capacity, or by a convention of the people in their sovereignty, of the 'unauthorized act.' "

Finally, Hamilton examined the question of cost. Nullification would leave three courses open to the general government: (1) submission to "our mode of redress," (2) appeal to a convention of the states for the purpose of obtaining a decision on the constitutionality of the measure, and (3) "direct coercion with the bayonet." In a sanguine piece of reasoning Hamilton—for three years recognized House leader of Jackson's opposition to the Adams administration—ironically rejected the third alternative.

With "dusk approaching," Hamilton concluded. To forestall the charge of disunion, he appended a toast: "Let us not abandon this work [the Constitution] of our fathers until the only alternative left is to abandon *it* or Liberty *itself*." [51]

Hamilton's address epitomizes the rhetorical strategy of the Nullifiers as well as their argumentative deficiencies and strengths. He associated the Nullifiers' cause with the values of liberty and honor. On the other hand, he slighted causal analysis on the question of ill and reasoned tenuously on cost. It is a tribute to Hamilton's powers of logical invention, however, that four more years of debate would contribute little to the basic analysis he had offered at Walterboro.

When the state legislature convened at Columbia in November, 1828, the Nullifiers put their case to the test of legislative debate. Divided among themselves as to the appropriate remedy, the affirmative committed tactical errors. Preston, the thirty-four-year-old Richland orator, led the so-called "action" wing of his party. Rhett, the true register of Calhoun's wishes, gave direction to the moderate wing of the state rights group. Hugh S. Legaré led the "union and peace" faction (negative) whose power was centered in Charleston. Calhoun, fearful lest a "want of caution" would "expose the State to the imputation of dangerous designs," hoped that the legislature would give the new administration time to apply "its wisdom and virtue" to the tariff question.[52]

But Preston ignored Calhoun's advice on the ground that "angry feelings" would be "engendered on both sides" if the debate were "protracted." [53] He immediately submitted a set of resolutions embodying the tenets of Calhoun's *Exposition*. His fifth resolution affirmed that *"interposition is now necessary."* [54] In what the *Mercury* termed "a truly eloquent, able, manly, and energetic Speech," the ex-Virginian argued the case for immediate action.[55] In support of his crucial fifth resolution he contended (1) that interposition was the only effective remedy; (2) that it was now necessary in order to prevent economic disaster in the South; (3) that the other staple-producing states would support South Carolina's action; and (4) that the people of the state were ready to try the method of interposition.[56]

For the Anti-Nullifiers Legaré, the Charleston legal scholar, led the attack. He meticulously examined Calhoun's propositions. A "juridical romantic," contemptuous of Jeffersonian

---

[52] Ralph T. Eubanks, "An Historical and Rhetorical Study of the Speaking of William C. Preston" (Ph.D. dissertation, University of Florida, 1957), 114–21; Merrill G. Christophersen, "A Rhetorical Study of Hugh Swinton Legaré (Ph.D. dissertation, University of Florida, 1954), 163–71; Calhoun to Preston, November 6, 1828, in Barbee (ed.), "A Sheaf of Old Letters."

[53] Columbia (S.C.) *Southern Times and State Gazette*, August 9, 1830.

[54] Journals of the South Carolina lower house, December 2, 1828.

[55] Charleston *Mercury*, December 16, 1828.

[56] Eubanks, "An Historical and Rhetorical Study of the Speaking of William C. Preston," 119. Preston's arguments were summarized from sketchy accounts carried in the *Mercury*.

principles and political theorizing,[57] Legaré sought to shatter the "Carolina doctrine" with legal argument. He granted the right of secession (revolution) "in a case of extreme necessity"; he denied the Nullifiers' claim that interposition was a constitutional mode of protecting a state's "residuary powers." [58] Most damaging of all to the affirmative's case was his disquieting position on cost which he climaxed with a presentment of the probable "consequences" of civil strife between state and federal powers.[59]

A leading argument on cost advanced by the Anti-Nullifiers was that a state convention, called for the purpose of considering the tariff laws, might undertake to alter the balance of power between the Low Country and the Up-Country. For the Nullifiers Rhett refuted this argument, contending that the Up-Country majority could change the balance at will.[60]

Moderate counsels prevailed. The legislature approved a compromise resolution calling for a "solemn protest" to be "entered on the journals of the senate of the United States" and requesting the other southern states to cooperate with South Carolina "in such measures as may be necessary for arresting the evil." [61] One Up-Country editor believed that the legislature had agreed "to forbear a *little longer*" in order "to avoid the possibility of the most disastrous catastrophe." [62] But the growing action wing of the State Rights Party was disappointed. At the Fourth of July celebration in Walterboro one of their number offered the following toast: *"Our State Legisla-*

[57] Parrington, *The Romantic Revolution in America*, 109–19.
[58] Legaré's arguments are summarized in Christophersen, "A Rhetorical Study of Hugh Swinton Legaré," 163–71.
[59] See Preston, *Eulogy on Hugh S. Legaré*, 7.
[60] Perritt, "Robert Barnwell Rhett: South Carolina Secession Spokesman," 52–53.
[61] Charleston *Courier*, December 20, 1828.
[62] Columbia (S.C.) *Telescope*, quoted in *Niles' Weekly Register*, XXXV (September, 1828–March, 1829), 309.

ture of 1828—The People asked it for bread and received a stone." [63]

Yet to the Nullifiers it was clear that arousal of a favorable public opinion was a rhetorical assignment of the greatest magnitude. So divided was opinion that South Carolina was "by no means a unit even as to the doctrine of state rights." [64] Rhetorically, the Nullifiers perceived their task as twofold: (1) removal of the "disunion" stigma from their doctrine; and (2) enlightenment of the public as to the merits of nullification in South Carolina and in the South at large. For the next two years these objectives shaped the rhetorical activity of the Nullifiers.

Available evidence suggests that the Nullifiers based their campaign of education upon a set of empirical guides. One leading principle was derived from a widely held view of the southern temper. Following the 1828 legislative session, Preston wrote his friend, Waddy Thompson: "There does not seem to have been a single heaving of a wave since the storm has passed by. The state is exhausted by its paroxysm of excitement and must be left to recover strength before it can go thru another. This is always the way with Southern people. They lack perseverance and can only effect their object by a *coup de main* .... In a few days our *Exposition* will be published which will perhaps be the signal for recommencement." [65]

A second guide was clearly in line with the "persuasion-conviction dualism" theory of Campbell and Blair which held that the orator must establish a stable conviction of the understanding before attempting to move the will. That the

[63] Charleston *Mercury*, July 10, 1829.

[64] Boucher, *The Nullification Controversy*, 42.

[65] Preston to Thompson, January 23, 1829, in Waddy Thompson Papers, South Caroliniana Library, University of South Carolina, Columbia. The Nullifiers' educational campaign had actually begun with the legislature's approval of a proposal to print for distribution 5,000 copies of the *Protest* and the *Exposition*.

Nullifiers understood this dictum and sought consciously to apply it appears evident in certain letters of Francis Pickens of Edgefield. Nominal leader of the campaign of enlightenment and author of the widely read "Hampden" essays, Pickens wrote, for example, to James Hammond of Columbia in March, 1830: "I think it idle to attempt to rouse a community to act before you inform them where they are and what they stand on." [66]

The Nullifiers' strategy was not confined to oratory. It included also the rhetoric of the newspaper editorial and the pamphlet. On the coastal plain the Charleston *Mercury* daily challenged the people to rely upon their Revolutionary heritage of liberty and honor. From Columbia the *Southern Times*, edited by lawyer James Henry Hammond, carried the Nullifiers' cause into the remote regions of the interior. [67] Not content with the Nullifiers' editorials, Pickens urged extensive use of the pamphlet to supplement oration and newspaper. "We are negligent of one thing," he wrote to Hammond, "and that is that we do not take pains enough to spread information in any easy way and in such a way before the people that they would read it. . . . The people will not read in the newspapers so well and with as much impression anything, as if it were in a pamphlet before them." [68] One index to the effectiveness of the Nullifiers' address to the understanding is a letter to the *Southern Times* editor from Benjamin F. Whitner: "I have had repeated conversations with many of the plain but intelligent [Up-Country] farmers . . . , and I find the apprehension universal that the friends of convention do not propose it as a peaceful

[66] Pickens to Hammond, March 8, 1830, in James Hammond Papers, Library of Congress, Manuscripts Division.
[67] Elizabeth Merritt, "James Henry Hammond, 1807–1864," in *Johns Hopkins University Studies in Historical and Political Science*, XLI (Baltimore, 1923), 347–61; Robert C. Tucker, "James Henry Hammond, South Carolinian" (Ph.D. dissertation, University of North Carolina, 1958), 223–54.
[68] Pickens to Hammond, June 26, 1830, in Hammond Papers.

remedy. But in every instance where I had an opportunity to explain and illustrate the right of a state to this exercise of sovereignty . . . I have found the people in favor of convention." [69]

An important event in the Nullifiers' campaign to achieve "conviction of the mind" was the famous Webster-Hayne debate which, incidentally, does not at all appear to have been so planned. For the Nullifiers it was a "mixed blessing." In his so-called first reply to Hayne on January 20, 1830, Webster, seeking to forestall an antitariff alliance between West and South, maneuvered Hayne into a defense of the Carolina doctrine. As Wiltse has observed: "The method he chose was a variation of the *argumentum ad hominem*: to discredit the South by crying 'Treason.' " [70] Webster delivered an encomium to "the consolidation of our Union, in which is involved our prosperity, felicity, safety, perhaps our national existence." Then he suggested sarcastically that Hayne could never be numbered among those who disparaged the federal government and urged that it was "time to calculate the value of the Union." [71]

Unwisely, Hayne permitted his antagonist to choose the battleground. Matching arguments with Webster, the great constitutional lawyer, Hayne began his second speech on January 20 and finished it on January 25. He had prepared himself with care over the weekend.[72] In the words of one eye-witness: "For two hours . . . he bore down in a strain of eloquence, alternately grave, indignant, and witty, upon the Senator from Massachusetts, the like of which I have never witnessed, and which, as I thought, completely demolished him. Mr. Webster

[69] Whitner to Hammond, September 11, 1830, in Hammond Papers.

[70] Charles M. Wiltse, *John C. Calhoun: Nullifier, 1829–1839* (Indianapolis, New York, 1949), 57. Wiltse's analysis of the "Great Debate" (53–66) presents a perceptive analysis of the dialectical feature of Webster's and Hayne's rhetoric in this contest.

[71] *Register of Debates*, 21st Cong., 1st sess., 41.

[72] Robert Y. Hayne, *Defence of the South: General Hayne in Reply to Mr. Webster* (Charleston, 1830), 20.

evidently suffered. He seemed uneasy in his seat; sometimes he took notes—then audibly dissented, anon assented, and occasionally leaned back in his chair." [73]

The burden of Hayne's reply rested in the topic of "majority-minority relations." Through careful constitutional reasoning he developed the thesis that nullification was nothing more nor less than the "good old Republican creed of 1798" which, short of armed conflict, was the best hope against a despotic majority.

In reply to Webster's imputations against South Carolina's recent actions, Hayne reminded his listeners that South Carolina had "kept steadily in view the preservation of the Union, by the only means by which she believes it can be preserved—a firm, manly, and steady resistance against usurpation." Invoking the memory of the Revolutionists' struggle, Hayne concluded as a true Nullifier: "The south is acting on a principle she has always held sacred—resistance to unauthorized taxation.... Sir, if acting on these high motives—if animated by that ardent love of liberty which has always been the most prominent trait of the southern character—we should be hurried beyond the bounds of a cold and calculating prudence, who is there, with one noble and generous sentiment in his bosom, that would not be disposed, in the language of Burke, to exclaim, 'you must pardon something to the spirit of liberty.' " [74]

As Wiltse observes, Webster argued "from precedent that

---

[73] Charles G. De Witt, "The Great Webster-Hayne Debate," *Olde Ulster*, IX (November, 1913), 335. This little-known source characterizes Hayne as a "slightly young man" with "full, round face, without whiskers—light brown hair, which he wears in the *exquisite* style . . . small grey eyes, weakened, perhaps, by study . . . wide mouth, glib tongue—rather delicate in his person, though by no means ghostly. His voice has more volume than [Thomas Hart Benton's] . . . and he pours forth his arguments in a torrent of impetuous eloquence that always commands attention and seldom fails to convince. While speaking he is full of action—stepping incessantly backward and forward between his desk and the bar, near which he sits."

[74] *Register of Debates*, 21st Cong., 1st sess., 58.

his view was the law of the land." On the other hand, Hayne's state rights view rested on strong historical ground. "The framers of the Constitution," observes Wiltse, "had not meant to create a power state and had intended to leave local sovereignty as a check against the kind of arbitrary authority that had brought on the Revolution in the first place." [75] This was the ancient, yet unresolved, question of unrestricted power to rule.

Yet the doctrine of nullification was virtually untenable on either theoretical or practical ground, as the debates demonstrated. Of the doctrine A. H. Kelly and W. A. Harbison have written:

At best the idea was extraconstitutional and rested upon a tenuous and overelaborate argument as to the nature of the Union and the Constitution. . . . A more serious consideration was that nullification in practice would have paralyzed the entire constitutional system. . . . Finally, the . . . theory disregarded the fact that forty years of constitutional growth had evolved a very different and quite workable method for the settlement of constitutional disputes. . . . As of 1832 the [Supreme] Court's right to act as arbiter of the Constitution was accepted by the great majority of American statesmen, lawyers, and common citizens.[76]

The great debate helped and hindered the Nullifiers' crusade for a government so checked and balanced that the interests of the minority would be safe. First, it gave the Carolina doctrine a national forum, providing for the first time nation-wide publicity for the southern state rights view. Second, the newspaper war between North and South on the relative merits of the protagonists' cases served to enhance the Nullifiers' honor-identification in South Carolina and in the South at large. Still, many concluded from the debates that the Nullifiers were treasonable opponents of Union. And the inference made difficult

[75] Wiltse, *Calhoun: Nullifier*, 65.
[76] Alfred H. Kelly and Winfred A. Harbison, *The American Constitution: Its Origins and Development* (rev. ed.; New York, 1955), 310–11.

their rhetorical task of vitiating the force of the Anti-Nullifiers' cry of "disunion."

Dedicated to their cause and resourceful in their deliberative and extradeliberative planning, the Nullifiers strove to carry the state elections on the convention issue. Early, the leadership in Columbia decided to narrow the struggle to South Carolina. In February Preston again wrote to Thompson: "I have never calculated on the cooperation of the other [southern] states until we have taken some definitive step. They will not join us 'til circumstances compell [*sic*] them to take one or the other side, and then they must of necessity take ours. . . . For the slave question will be the real issue. . . . So. Carolina is strong enough by herself to do right [?] or perish in trying—this is my creed." [77]

Preston's creed became the creed of the State Rights and Free Trade Party. The Nullifiers also revised their rhetorical strategy for their summer campaign. On the question of ill they moved to what they believed stronger moral ground. Habitually, the Nullifiers had approached ill through economics instead of constitutionality. Perceiving now an opportunity to snatch another rhetorical grace for the Nullifiers, Hammond suggested in an editorial: "We go upon higher ground. We are struggling for principle. We demand an abandonment of the power which Congress has assumed to pass the [tariff] law. If the law be constitutional [he argued], what right have we to speak of resistance?" [78] Hammond was, in fact, simply bringing the debate back to the question of arbitrary exercise of power. The position was an old one that had been lost to sight. Earlier opponents of protectionism had held that the Constitution authorized Congress to levy duties *only* for the purpose of raising revenue. Thus, the principle to which Hammond refers is the

---

[77] Preston to Thompson, February 14, 1830, in William Campbell Preston Papers, South Caroliniana Library.

[78] Columbia (S.C.) *Southern Times*, February 22, 1830.

right use of power. It follows that he was denying the authority of the Supreme Court to serve as final arbiter of the Constitution.

The Nullifiers climaxed their campaign to win the yeomanry of the interior with a state rights meeting in Columbia on September 20, 1830. Candor and moderation appear to have been perceived as the leading criteria of presentation for this important meeting. In advance of the gathering at Columbia, Whitner had cautioned: "I do hope that those who may figure as public speakers on that occasion may be conciliating and plain, stir up no angry passions, nor excite prejudice and ill will by aspersing the motives and questioning the patriotism of those who differ with them [and] who are timid and slow to adopt any cause that may unnecessarily jeopardize the peace and union of the states." [79]

To the Nullifiers Judge William Harper of Columbia seemed a natural choice to keynote the proconvention case. Characterized by Perry as "a great logician, but an unpleasant speaker," Harper was known as a legal genius whose only vices were tippling and devouring "the literary trash of the day." Though the tall, disarming chancellor was halting in vocal delivery and "ungraceful" in bodily action, he "was regarded next to Calhoun in expounding the new political doctrine." [80]

In one of the ablest constitutional defenses of the compact theory of government produced by the Nullifiers, Harper sought to demonstrate that nullification was "a peaceful, safe, and efficacious" remedy.[81] Placing ill on high ethical ground, he contended it could no longer be gainsaid that the South was in "a permanent minority" with a "*sectional* majority against it—a majority of different views and interests and little com-

[79] Whitner to Hammond, September 11, 1830, in Hammond Papers.
[80] Perry, *Reminiscences of Public Men*, 35–38.
[81] *Proceedings of the State Rights' Meeting, Columbia, S.C., on the Twentieth of September, 1830* (Columbia, 1830), 46 pp. The text of Harper's address was also printed in the Charleston *Mercury*, October 20, 1830.

mon sympathy." Would the sectional majority reform itself? Said Harper: "A despotic majority is the only despot exempted from all responsibility." He developed a statement of the constitutional right of nullification, calling both upon authority and argument from definition. Since the Constitution was a compact, the parties to it had the right to judge of infractions and to interpose their own original sovereignty whenever the joint agreement was violated through an unauthorized exercise of power on the part of the general government. In a style devoid of figure, the Columbia chancellor argued that the Supreme Court was not the final arbiter in cases of violation:

The truth is, as observed by Mr. Jefferson, that the Constitution no more commits the interpretation of the Constitution to the Judiciary, than to any other department of the Government. Each is bound by the Constitution, and each, in the exercise of its powers, must determine for itself, incidentally, what the Constitution is. Indeed the *Constitution* no more commits the interpretation of itself to the Supreme Court than to the Courts of the States. The words are, "the Judicial power *shall extend* to all cases in law and equity, arising under the Constitution, the laws of the United States"; and does not the jurisdiction of the State Courts extend to cases arising under the Constitution and laws of the United States? . . . It is true that this authority has been peculiarly arrogated to the Supreme Court . . . by means of that *law* which declares that there shall be an appeal from the courts of the last resort of the several states, to the Supreme Court.

Harper described the Nullifiers' convention plan, then turned to cost. Arguing feebly from probability, he asserted that since the state rights formula was a peaceful remedy, no President would have the courage to resort to violence. Asked Harper: "Shall the states be deterred from using their lawful and Constitutional privileges, for fear that it shall provoke others to lawless and unconstitutional violence?" He then offered assurance of the ultimate cooperation of South Carolina's "sister states." Such were their circumstances, he reasoned, that they would necessarily take their places beside South Carolina. Addressing himself now to the will, he challenged: "But if anything could retard the desired co-operation, it would be that South Carolina should shrink from the course she has marked out for herself." Harper closed on a conciliatory note, inviting the Anti-Nullifiers to join with the Nullifiers in "resistance to tyranny."

The state rights speeches that followed were far less expository and more hortative than Harper's. For the Unionists Judge Richardson attempted to refute Harper. The Nullifiers left their "address to the will" in the capable hands of Rhett and Preston. Night had fallen when the vote was taken on the resolution for convention. "Upon a division," observed one reporter, "there appeared against the resolution only EIGHT! "

The Nullifiers were determined to test their strength. In the 1830 legislature they touched off a full-scale debate on the convention issue. For the convention group Preston assumed the burden of debate. Before an audience consisting of "the [South Carolina] College, House, and all who could get near enough," Preston spoke almost four hours, beginning on December 10 and finishing the next day. A grandnephew of Patrick Henry and a member of the First Families of Virginia, Preston had cultivated the arts of oratory and politics from youth. He had already achieved national stature as an orator and was perhaps the most compelling speaker amongst the nullifying faction. Preston covered all the status questions, blending refutation and constructive argument. To him, whose Senior oration had been "The Life and Character of Jefferson," the basic issue was whether the legislature was willing to permit the "Constitution of '89 to be superseded by a substitute." Both his style and his invocation of liberty were befitting to this great nephew of Patrick Henry. The sandy-haired Richland orator was at his best on remedy, drawing applause for his moral justification of the South Carolina doctrine:

The right of *nullification* is in fact the right of self-preservation. . . . If the right of resistance is destroyed the right of tyranny is established. . . . We cannot properly be asked whence we derive the right of *nullification?* The true and only question is, where is it prohibited to us? Has anyone answered this question? The only argument against it is that such a check upon the general government would be very inconvenient. All checks upon power are inconvenient to those who wield that power. Anarchy is the cry with which despotism frightens the timid into its toils.[82]

B. F. Perry, editor of the unfriendly Greenville *Mountaineer*, wrote of Preston's effort: "His speech, from beginning to end, was a most powerful and eloquent one. . . . Never did I listen with a more thrilling effect to the speech of anyone. Col. Preston is certainly an able debater, and would be distinguished in any legislative body in the world." [83]

After the 1830 debates the Nullifiers readjusted their rhetorical strategy. Although unable to carry their Convention proposal because of division in their own ranks, they did pass a resolution recognizing the right of a state to apply the doctrine of nullification.[84] The logical course was a return to the questions of ill and reformability. This the Nullifiers in fact did: they then sought with vigor to convince the state (1) that the tariff laws were partial and oppressive on the economy of the South, and (2) that hope of redress from Congress was un-

---

[82] *The Debate of the South Carolina Legislature, December, 1830, on the Reports of the Committees of Both Houses, in Favor of a Convention, &c* (Columbia, 1831), 191–203; Eubanks, "An Historical and Rhetorical Study of the Speaking of William C. Preston," 119–23.

[83] Greenville (S.C.) *Mountaineer*, December 17, 1830, quoted in Lillian A. Kibler, *Benjamin F. Perry, South Carolina Unionst* (Durham, 1946), 102.

[84] Columbia (S.C.) *Southern Times and State Gazette*, December 17, 1830.

grounded. If these issues could be won, then the state stood pledged to action. Some nullification orators abused the strategy, however, contending falsely that the state was "unanimous" on the question of ill and differed only on remedy. But they could not so easily discharge half the affirmative burden; the Anti-Nullifiers were quick to label the sharp tactic.

The rhetoric of the Nullifiers was to be for the next two years largely an address to the will. Encouraged by their successes within the state and convinced of the ultimate support of sister states, the party leaders now leaned as never before upon the master symbols, liberty and honor. Upon these values they premised their appeals to action which, as the controversy progressed, became more openly revolutionary. Their style grew more staccato. Their figuration assumed a more martial quality. Their structuring became more impressionistic. They depended less upon logical argument, more upon stratagem. Like the Anti-Nullifiers, they resorted more to "dyslogistic terms" of the *ad hominem* variety in an effort to vitiate opposing ethical appeals. Their opponents became "submission men" and "weaklings"; they, in turn, were branded "Jacobins" and "disunionists." Worst of all, the Hotspurs of the State Rights and Free Trade Party grew more intolerant of opposing views and more thoroughly persuaded of their own rectitude. Turnbull, for example, proclaimed at the Fourth of July celebration in Charleston in 1831: "It is . . . no longer left, as I humbly conceive, to the discretion of any citizen, whether he will or will not support these [state rights] principles, solemnly adjudged by the collected wisdom of the state . . . to be the only principles in which the safety of the republic is to be found." [85]

We may indeed characterize this final stage of the Nullifiers' rhetoric—using Burke's terminology of rhetorical design—as

[85] *Speech of R. J. Turnbull, Esq. at the Celebration of the State Rights and Free Trade Party of Charleston on the Fourth of July, 1831* (Columbia, 1831), 4.

"agonistic." That is, rhetoric ruled by the motive of gaining advantage. Translated into the value-terms of the mud-sill culture, their rhetoric fell under control of the demand symbol of honor—preservation of the personal honor of the Nullifiers and of the honor of the Palmetto State. This view is supported not only by the Nullifiers' public but by their "private" rhetoric, i.e., the rhetoric of their private conferences and correspondence. The period of agonistic rhetoric extended from May, 1831, to November, 1832, the period of campaigning to win a legislature for the call of a nullification convention.

George McDuffie, one of the younger leaders of the State Rights Party, opened the campaign on May 19, 1831, at a Charleston dinner given in his honor. The party had followed so far the conservative counsel of Calhoun, who had kept in the background. It had insisted that its remedy was constitutional. At the same time, it had disavowed revolution and disunion. Public opinion had cooled; the administration had not reformed the tariff; Great Britain was threatening to place a retaliatory duty on cotton. Besides, the party's honor was in peril.

Hamilton and McDuffie met in Charleston and sketched the broad outlines of the new agonistic rhetoric.[86] In their struggle for advantage they seized upon the element of surprise, deciding to shift to the ground of revolution. For this assignment McDuffie was the ideal choice. Nullification he had always thought justifiable only as a revolutionary measure. A man of humble birth who by talent and drive had made his way into Carolina's baronage, McDuffie was popularly regarded as one of the best speakers of his region. He was a ready debater and a stirring orator as well. Yet his deficiencies of presentation were notable: a tenor voice, with undistinguished pitch control; only "one gesture, a sledge hammer blow" of the right

[86] See Hamilton to Hammond, Charleston, May 3, 1831, in "Letters on the Nullification Movement in South Carolina, 1830–1834," *American Historical Review*, VI, 745.

arm; and a tendency to be "rude, overbearing, and insulting" in debate. Except for his scraggly Roman haircut, he might never have been recognized as a Carolina river baron. In demeanor he was rustic and impersonal. "He was not," as William J. Grayson observed, "what Dr. Johnson called a clubbable man." On the other hand, McDuffie had much to commend him to a Carolina audience in the 1830's. He spoke extempore from careful preparation. Again, he always created the impression of trustworthiness.[87]

McDuffie gave a three-hour speech at Charleston, fulfilling to the letter the newly revised rhetorical strategy of the action wing of his party. In the development of his well-known "Forty Bale" theory, he argued that the tariff laws amounted to a tax on the cotton grower or producer, in the amount of forty bales out of every one hundred produced.[88] He contended that all hope of redress from the majority was delusory. Finally, he insisted that the only remedy for the intolerable ill was the state rights formula which he placed unapologetically on the ground of revolution:

I believe this to be one of those great emergencies in human affairs, which imposes an imperative obligation upon the sovereign power of the State to take care that the republic receive no detriment. I will not moot the question of Nullification as a mere question of constitutional power, for I am aware of the efforts of our oppressors to make an issue upon that, in order to divert public attention from the true issue. I will readily concede that a State cannot nullify an act of Congress, by virtue of any power derived from the Constitution. It would be a perfect solecism to suppose any such power was conferred by the Constitution. This right flows from a higher

[87] Edwin L. Green, *George McDuffie* (Columbia, S.C., 1936), Chapter XII, "The Orator"; William J. Grayson Autobiography, MS. in South Caroliniana Library, 166.

[88] *Speech of the Hon. George McDuffie at a Public Dinner Given to Him By the Citizens of Charleston, (S. C.), May 19, 1831* (Charleston, 1831), 29. McDuffie "revised" the text of his address and had it published in pamphlet form for distribution "throughout the South."

source. All that I claim for the State, in this respect, necessarily results from the mere fact of sovereignty [i.e., the right of revolution].

McDuffie produced the expected "advantages." In placing the state rights cause on the ground of natural right, he gave the actionists moral superiority. Forcing Calhoun into open advocacy of nullification also delivered over to the Nullifiers the prestige of the Vice-President. From the young leader's point of view, the speech carried the advantage of shock. "Little Jimmy" Hamilton wrote to Hammond: "McDuffie . . . made a superb and gigantic effort which has struck a damp in the heart of our opponent." [89]

But advantage was defined in more conservative terms by Calhoun and Hayne, who sought to return the nullification movement to the constitutional ground Calhoun had staked out in 1828. This countermove began on July 4, 1831, at a mass party rally in Charleston where Hayne presented nullification as a "peaceful, constitutional" remedy. [90] Calhoun, Priest of the Nullifiers, soon added to the party's advantages the famed Fort Hill address, a cogent piece which was printed for distribution as a "peaceful, constitutional" remedy. [90] Calhoun, Priest of the conscious rectitude," the Great Nullifier developed the thesis that the only "solid and durable foundation of liberty" was a "strict accountability" of both maker and executor of the law

[89] Hamilton to Hammond, May 21, 1831, in "Letters on the Nullification Movement, 1830–1834," p. 746.

[90] See *Proceedings of the Celebration of the 4th of July, 1831, Charleston, S. C. By the State Rights and Free Trade Party: Containing the Speeches and Toasts, Delivered on the Occasion* (Charleston, 1831), 73.

[91] Wiltse, *Calhoun: Nullifier*, 113–14, contains a perceptive analysis of the Fort Hill address. For an appraisal of Calhoun's speaking career, see Herbert T. Curry, "John C. Calhoun," in *History and Criticism of American Public Address*, II (New York and London, 1943), 639–64. Among the better studies of Calhoun's political doctrines are August O. Spain, *The Political Theory of John C. Calhoun* (New York, 1951), and Charles M. Wiltse, "Calhoun's Democracy," *Journal of Politics*, III (May, 1941), 210–23.

"to those on whom the laws in reality operate." [92] Genuine liberty, Calhoun believed, could be attained only insofar as some organic law were derived to prevent excesses in the exercise of the majority will. For his pains he has become one of the most ambiguous political figures of his times. Lord Acton said of him: "Webster may have been the truest interpreter of the law, [but] Calhoun was the real defender of the Union." [93] At the opposite pole is the recent view of him as the "Marx of the Master Class," a legalistic weaver of words whose political doctrines were devised to undercut equalitarian idealism. [94] Penelope Davis Preston, the perceptive second wife of William Preston, came near the truth perhaps when she wrote that Calhoun, like most, was "a mixture of good and ill." [95]

Certainly John Anderson is correct: Calhoun "challenged the central tenets of the developing American political tradition, in particular its concept of a monolithic nationalism and of freedom." [96] To his credit was his resolute attack on the ancient issue of unrestricted power to rule. Yet to his discredit was his linkage of promising political theory to the cause of a slave aristocracy. His nullification rhetoric—inexorably logical (given his basic premise of state sovereignty), clear, unpoetic, and humorless—was at last a rhetoric of special pleading which, ironically, did untold damage to agrarian democracy.

[92] Calhoun, *Works*, VI, 59–123. Calhoun's two most important public speeches on the nullification question are contained in *Works*, II: "Speech on the Force Bill," February 15–16, 1833 (197–262), and "Speech on His Resolutions in Support of State Rights," February 26, 1833 (262–309).

[93] Cited in Richard M. Weaver, "Lord Acton: The Historian as Thinker," *Modern Age*, V (Winter, 1960–61), 19–20.

[94] Richard Hofstadter, *The American Political Tradition and the Men Who Made It* (New York, 1961), 68–92. Cf. Current's view that Calhoun "took Jefferson's liberal doctrine of State Rights and identified it with a policy of reaction." Richard N. Current, "John C. Calhoun, Philosopher of Reaction," *Antioch Review*, II (June, 1943), 223.

[95] The diary of Penelope Davis Preston (MS in South Caroliniana Library).

[96] Anderson (ed.), *Calhoun: Basic Documents*, 12.

The Rhetoric of the Nullifiers

During the final year of the controversy the rhetoricians of both sides turned occasionally from "agonistic" to a rhetoric of "proving opposites." Both factions argued rigorously on ill and cost. On the issue of ill, the Unionists appear to have been at their best in their claim that the Nullifiers had exaggerated the evil effects of the tariff. On the issue of cost, they sought chiefly to buttress an old contention: the claim that disunion—a highly probable result of nullification—would make the remedy worse than the cure. The Nullifiers argued with equal cogency on ill that the South could not expect relief from a self-interested majority. On the question of remedy, the Anti-Nullifiers had admitted that nullification was a revolutionary right. Therefore, when the new tariff law of 1832 made still more permanent the principle of protection, the Nullifiers could proceed to push the verbal war to its inexorable conclusion. With the chivalry on their side, they now spoke in bolder phrase. They admitted that nullification might not prove a peaceable remedy, and they invoked the demand symbols of honor and liberty with increasing fervor.[97]

By midsummer the campaign had reached a high emotional pitch. In his "Walterboro Manifesto" of July 4, Robert Barnwell Rhett referred to the tariff as an effort to "recolonize these Southern states," pronounced an encomium on revolution, and challenged his listeners to defend their rights by "effectual resistance." Shouted Rhett: "The spirit of '76 is not dead in Carolina. It kindles in the pine lands—it lights up along the swamps and our beautiful sea islands, and treads, with its blazing steps, on the tops of our mountains." [98] Manifestly, the time of reasoning, of attempting to "prove opposites," was past. According to Wiltse, "Intelligent men on each side thought

---

[97] Charleston *Mercury*, January 6, 1832; Greenville, S.C., *Mountaineer*, March 7, 1832; Charleston *City Gazette*, March 2, 1832.
[98] Charleston *Mercury*, July 6, 1832; Perritt, "Robert Barnwell Rhett: South Carolina Secession Spokesman," 69–74.

those on the other side bent on their destruction, and each side thought the other willfully, obstinately, and maliciously wrong." [99] The rhetoric of the Nullifiers, epitomized in Rhett's speech, was at this stage of the struggle a rhetoric of gaining advantage. Yet before the fall elections the Nullifiers had chastened their style considerably.

The Nullifiers were able to consummate their crusade. But the case for nullification was less compelling in the other "staple states." In August the *Mercury*—"chief of Nullifiers," as Niles termed it—predicted that "as surely as South Carolina *nullifies*, her position will be *supported by every other Southern state.*" [100] But most of the nullification orators were not so sanguine. William Preston had predicted in an 1831 address at Columbia that South Carolina would have to "look finally to itself alone." [101] The Old Dominion, mother of Patrick Henry, was a disappointment to the Nullifiers. The handful of simon-pure Nullifiers in Virginia—William H. Brodnax, James C. Bruce, and Vincent Witcher—could not sustain the issue of ill. So strong was Unionist sentiment in southwest Virginia that nullification was there "looked upon with horror." [102] Even the efforts of Virginia's fiery Governor John Floyd could not muster the needed support for South Carolina in the 1832 General Assembly. Floyd, a kinsman of Preston, wrote in his diary: "So ends the high character of the State of Virginia and such the end of liberty." [103]

[99] Wiltse, *Calhoun: Nullifier*, 135.

[100] Cited in article titled, "Going the Whole," *Niles' Weekly Register*, XLII (March, 1832–September, 1832), 405.

[101] Richmond *Enquirer*, quoted in Washington *National Intelligencer*, November 11, 1831.

[102] John Smith Preston to James H. Hammond, April 17, 1831, in Hammond Papers; Charleston *Mercury*, June 13, 1831; Claude G. Bowers, *The Party Battles of the Jackson Period* (Boston and New York, 1928), 261–62; William C. Preston to Hammond, December 31, 1832, in Hammond Papers; Washington *National Intelligencer*, December 20, 1831.

[103] Charles H. Ambler, *The Life and Diary of John Floyd* (Richmond, 1918), 200.

In Georgia nullification never commanded an organized, effective rhetoric. "Of all the other Southern States," writes Coulter, "Georgia was considered the best ground for the [nullification] doctrine to thrive and develop in." [104] And understandably so. Georgia's position on the Cherokee Indian question had been interpreted by some as outright nullification. Besides, in the Georgia discussion of the protective tariff laws, the question of *ill* was never a crucial issue. Yet there were also a number of factors to inhibit the growth of nullification rhetoric in Georgia. In the first place, many influential Georgians thought Calhoun a bitter enemy of their state. Also, some resented the rhetorical efforts of South Carolina leaders in the cities of Athens, Augusta, and Hamburg, efforts they felt were nothing more nor less than an intermeddling in the political affairs of another state. Finally, few Georgia political leaders had enough Jacobin blood to risk the label Nullifier. Almost single-handedly, Augustin S. Clayton, a popular state rights judge, pled the case for Georgia nullification. He was a leading figure in the rump antitariff convention at Milledgeville which took the state to the edge of nullification.[105] But Clayton was unable to move the Georgia legislature, which resolved "that we abhor the doctrine of Nullification as neither a peaceful, nor a constitutional remedy, but, on the contrary, as tending to civil commotion and disunion." [106]

The Carolina doctrine was no more popular in the other southern states. In North Carolina pro-Jackson sentiment

---

[104] E. Merton Coulter, "The Nullification Movement in Georgia," *Georgia Quarterly*, V (March, 1921), 3.

[105] Donald B. Sanger, "The Nullification Movement in Georgia," *Tyler's Quarterly Historical and Genealogical Magazine*, XI (October, 1929), 94–106; C. C. Childs, "The Struggle for Nationalism in Georgia," *Georgia Historical Quarterly*, XIV (September, 1930), 243; Stephen F. Miller, *Bench and Bar of Georgia: Memoirs and Sketches* (2 vols.; Philadelphia, 1858), I 139–65; *Proceedings of the Anti-Tariff Convention of the State of Georgia, Held in Milledgeville, 1832* (Milledgeville, 1832), 28.

[106] Ames (ed.), *State Documents on Federal Relations*, 181.

blighted the movement, and nullification was almost univer-
sally denounced as "the odious doctrine." [107] Still, a few
doughty figures like Samuel P. Carson and Samuel T. Sawyer
dared to bear the label, "enemy of the Union." The address of
both became little more than desperate defenses of their own
moral character. With bitterness Carson told one audience that
the Anti-Nullifiers, "under the guise of an unpopular name,"
were actually setting friend against friend.[108]

In Alabama the South Carolina cause got a lukewarm reception save in Montgomery District where the influence of
Dixon H. Lewis was strong. Lewis, a portly alumnus of South
Carolina College, concentrated his attack on what he termed
"the manufacturing aristocracy." Lewis' many addresses were
characteristically short, concise appeals which got their leverage from the liberty symbol. In a few instances, his speeches
amounted to a kind of lamentation.[109]

Mississippi also gave the Carolina remedy a cool reception.
Ill was not contested in the Mississippi debates for the protective laws were somewhat less oppressive here than in Georgia or South Carolina. In his address to the Mississippi General
Assembly in 1833, Acting Governor Hiram G. Runnels declared: "Indeed, is it not an anomaly in the affairs of all well
regulated governments, to see at the moment of general prosperity . . . that we should be brought to a pause by State dissensions [?]"[110] During the years from 1828 to 1833, as Cleo

[107] J. Carlyle Sitterson, *The Secession Movement in North Carolina.* The
James Sprunt Studies in History and Political Science, XXIII (Chapel Hill,
1939), 31.
[108] *Address to the Freemen of the Twelfth Congressional District of the
State of North Carolina* (1833 [?]). (Pamphlet in Southern Collection, University of North Carolina Library). Cf. Samuel T. Sawyer, *An Address to
the Freemen of Edenton, Declining a Poll* (Edenton, N. C., 1833), 7.
[109] Thomas M. Owen (ed.), *History of Alabama and Dictionary of Alabama Biography* (4 vols.; Chicago, 1921), IV, 1043–44; Wetumpka (Ala.)
Argus, June 15, 1842; Montgomery *State Gazette,* October 30, 1848.
[110] *Journal of the House of Representatives of the State of Mississippi of
the Seventeenth Session Held in the Town of Jackson* (Jackson, 1833), 56.

Hearon has observed, "the most important political and economic questions facing the state were removal of the Indians and the adoption of a land policy by the Federal government . . . that would be most favorable to the promotion of the speedy development of the State." [111] The state was supported on these issues by Jackson whose administration received, in turn, the zealous support of most Mississippians. It is equally true that some of the nullification minority in Mississippi were Nullifiers not so much because of their faith in the Carolina doctrine but rather because of their hostility to Andrew Jackson.

Leading the minority in Mississippi were John A. Quitman and George Poindexter, members of the Virginia school of strict construction.[112] Both men supported Calhoun in Mississippi with a rhetoric of "warmth or passion" which fulfilled Blair's requirement for "the highest order of eloquence." Poindexter represented the nullification faction in Washington; Quitman was the leading advocate in the state. Quitman, sometime Lutheran minister and classical scholar, urged the doctrine of interposition in "the solemnity of manner and measured enunciation" characteristic of his station as chancellor.[113] Poindexter, along with McDuffie and Preston, ranked as one of the ablest nullification orators. Virginia-born and schooled, he was a frail, "moody" man whose irritability and love of gaming kept him from attaining the highest success in public affairs. But he possessed at the same time certain qualities that won him esteem both at home and at Washington:

[111] Cleo Hearon, "Nullification in Mississippi," *Publications of the Mississippi Historical Society,* XII (University, Mississippi, 1912), 38.

[112] The point of view of both men is reflected in one of Poindexter's letters to J. F. H. Claiborne: "I go," he said, "for the Constitution as it is written on the strict observance of which, the very existence [?] and vital interests of the Southern States depend. . . ." Poindexter to Claiborne, March 26, 1832, in Claiborne Papers, Mississippi Department of Archives and History, Jackson.

[113] Jackson *Mississippian,* May 23, 1834.

a good legal mind, quick sympathy for the underdog, and plain grit.[114]

Poindexter's address in the United States Senate on Wilkins' Force Bill represents perhaps the most effective speech of his career; it was also one of the best of the nullification controversy. Certainly it overshadows the efforts of his colleagues in the debate on Jackson's explosive bill. Though Poindexter's rhetoric sometimes appeared too studied, it was on this occasion authentic and compelling. For more than three hours he talked, his lean frame tilted a little forward, his "keen and penetrating" eyes fixed on his listeners.[115] Poindexter spoke in direct, precise, and graphic phrase, weighing his arguments, not counting them.[116] The Force Bill he termed a measure "to repeal the constitution of the United States and to vest the President with despotic powers." For Jackson and Webster—to him symbols of the misuse of power—he had some sharp statements. For Jackson he suggested a message to be given the federal troops: "To arms, then, and vanquish these haughty sons of Carolina; let your watchword be tribute or extermination." Using *stylistic identification* with uncommon artistry, Poindexter compared his own political stand with Webster's: "The Senator from Massachusetts ranges himself on the side of power. I take my stand with those who seek to limit power within its defined boundaries. He supports the supremacy of laws; I defend the rights of the people." In the closing moments of his speech Poindexter linked liberty with the highest

114 See James D. Lynch, *The Bench and Bar of Mississippi* (New York, 1881), 27–34; untitled character sketch of Poindexter in Letters and Papers of George Poindexter, Mississippi Department of Archives and History; Dunbar Rowland (ed.), *Mississippi* (3 vols.; Jackson, 1916), II, 446–48.

115 *Biographical Sketch of the Honorable George Poindexter* (Washington, 1835), 58 pp. Green (p. 24) says of Poindexter's effort: "This speech enlarged and illustrated his reputation as a statesman and his capacity as a public debator in every quarter, and among politicians of every denomination."

116 *Register of Debates*, 22nd Cong., 2nd sess., 602–61.

rectitude and reiterated his central theme: "Resistance to tyrants is obedience to God."

He had achieved the end of his art; he had spoken well, using the rhetorical resources available to him. In Henry Clay's opinion, Poindexter had embodied "all which could be brought to bear on his side of the question." [117]

As Poindexter's effort suggests, the last phase of the Nullifiers' rhetoric became desperately competitive, an almost purely agonistic rhetoric. Jackson's Proclamation and Force Bill, the major extrinsic factors of the last stage of the controversy, did indeed open up new avenues of logical invention by which the argument could be carried forward. The core of this case was the charge of "executive usurpation of power." But Jackson created a crisis that prompted the Nullifiers to exploit more fully than ever the available means of persuasion.

In at least two ways, Jackson's maneuvers had created a psychology of urgency. First, they had given dramatic proof of the Nullifiers' miscalculation on cost. Second, they revealed the full dimensions of federal consolidation of power and faced the Nullifiers nakedly with the "greatest of all evils"—"submission to a government without limitation of powers." [118] In essence, Jackson had exploded the Nullifiers' basic premise of state sovereignty. The affront to their honor produced an atmosphere of urgency which stimulated a search for more effective means of getting at the public mind. Indeed, the final stage of the nullification debate illustrates what appear to be two fundamental laws of deliberative controversy: the greater the urgency of the oratory, the greater (1) "the profusion and vitality of the formal [rhetorical] devices," [119] and (2) the greater the reliance upon crucial conceptions of "the desirable."

[117] *Ibid.*, 811.
[118] See Governor Hayne's Inaugural Address of December 13, 1832, Washington *National Intelligencer*, December 21, 1832.
[119] Burke, *A Rhetoric of Motives*, 57.

In the following passage William Preston exemplifies the operation of both laws: "Who, and of whom, are we? Are we Russian *serfs,* or *slaves* of a Divan? Are we on the banks of the Bosphorus, or the Neva? Or is it on our *own free streams* that these things are proclaimed? Was *our high and well considered appeal* to congress and the states in this manner to be met by the blind fury and indecency of a man who thus vents upon the *liberties of the country,* his own personal animosities?" [120]

In their final partisan struggle with the Union men, the Nullifiers abandoned completely the "true advantage" of moral superiority. With local victory secured, they now sought to impose upon all state officials an oath of paramount allegiance to South Carolina. In short, the Nullifiers themselves became, ironically, an oppressive majority. The "test oath" was clearly a violation of freedom of conscience, a gross assault on human dignity. The rhetoric in support of it, though practiced in the best faith, could only be a base rhetoric which offered as real justice a perversion of justice.

We are now in position to conduct a closer inspection of the rhetorical idiom of the Nullifiers. This inspection will proceed from a view of rhetoric as "the discovery of and persuasion to right action." It will seek the answers to three related questions: (1) What were the purposes of the Nullifiers' rhetoric? (2) What rhetorical resources did they use in the fulfillment of these purposes? (3) What was the quality of these resources?

Inspection of purpose shows that a complex of motivations gave direction to the oratory of the Nullifiers. The immediate

---

[120] "Speech on Jackson's Proclamation," delivered in the South Carolina lower house, December 17, 1832. Versions of the speech are in Charleston *Mercury,* December 20, 1832, and Washington *National Intelligencer,* December 27, 1832. (Italics added.)

and overt aim of nullification was to cure an economic ill: to establish a constitutional remedy for the partial and oppressive operation of the federal protective tariff laws on the economy of the "staple states." The ultimate social purpose, verbalized with ever more forthrightness as the contest wore on, was the creation of a constitutional formula for preserving the integrity of the mud-sill way of life. Each major section was now maturing a philosophy to enable its own destiny. The South, gradually losing power in the young nation's councils, developed a defensive strategy of "particularism." The North, gradually acquiring more power in Congress, developed "a counter philosophy of nationalism created for its needs by northern capitalism." Contends Parrington: "The deeper purpose that lay behind the gesture of nullification was the [cultural] purpose of erecting in the slave states a civilization founded on a landed aristocracy that would serve as a sufficient counterweight to the mercantile and industrial civilization of the North."[121] But in the 1820's southern leaders certainly had no blueprint for a "slave empire."

The impulse of nullification was a defensive one. As a cultural impulse it was an expression of deep-lying anxiety for the future of the mud-sill way. Indeed, W. H. Freehling associates the movement directly with the slavery question. Freehling assumes the nullification episode to have been "above all else a highly revealing expression of South Carolina's morbid sensitivity to the beginnings of the anti-slavery crusade." [122] Thus the covert objective of nullification was to prevent the growth of an effective abolitionist crusade.

But in political terms the aim of the Nullifiers was to seek some clues to the dilemma of government as it applied to ma-

[121] Parrington, *The Romantic Revolution in America*, 64–66.
[122] William W. Freehling, "The Nullification Controversy in South Carolina" (Ph.D. dissertation, University of California, Berkeley, 1964), v; cf. Charles M. Wiltse, *The New Nation, 1800–1845* (New York, 1961), 115–16.

jority rule in a free republic. The same question prompted a puzzled American President to ask thirty years later: "Must a government, of necessity, be too strong for the liberties of its own people, or too weak to maintain its own existence." [123]

Let us now inspect the dialectical ground of the Nullifiers' rhetoric. Two questions shall guide our analysis: (1) What choices did they make from the available resources of persuasion? and (2) Were these choices sound ones? That is, to what extent was theirs "a good rhetoric?"

Whether the Nullifiers urged their listeners to "right action" is a question that involves an evaluation of the *substance* of their address. In other words, how sound were their dialectical choices? This question prompts consideration of the ethical ground of their opinions or, put another way, the cultural sources of their convictions. As we have seen, the Nullifiers based their inducements to action upon two major values, liberty and honor. Their devotion to these values was a natural product of the recent experience of the colonies' resistance to the oppressions of the British Crown and of the fierce independence of spirit fostered by the mud-sill way of life. The Nullifiers may not be challenged for their preference of liberty over Union—if the alternative truly lay between the two. On the other hand, their cardinal conception of the good reflected a parsimonious view of man's universal nature. That is, their definition of liberty was "particularistic," insomuch as it included only "freemen." And it gave to their case at last the color of special pleading.

The Nullifiers' essential conservatism was evident also in the "aspect" of their argument. As a group, they argued chiefly from definition, or from "the nature of things." They held, for example, that man is governed more by "self-interest" than by altruism. Similarly, they contended that it was in the

123 Philip Van Doren Stern (ed.), *The Life and Writings of Abraham Lincoln* (New York, 1940), 668.

nature of a "self-interested majority" to encroach upon the rights of the minority. To the Nullifiers, moreover, a written constitution was by nature "a compact among sovereigns." They argued further that the Constitution was by nature a device for "restraining" the majority. Again, the right of revolution they interpreted as a "natural right" with divine sanction. Even their appeal to the colonists' resistance to "vassalage" was in last analysis an argument from the nature of "our fathers." [124]

In their "address to the understanding" the Nullifiers also relied heavily upon argument from authority—another sign of their basic conservatism. The very nature of their remedy required that the "argumentative portion" of their speeches be largely devoted to an explication and defense of the state rights formula. Like a lawyer arguing a case, they proceeded with care, reasoning rigorously from the Constitution and citing the testimony of respected authorities. Chancellor Harper summed up the Nullifiers' argumentative credo: "But authority with most men weighs more than argument and our authorities are of the highest." [125] Harper was correct in his assessment of the quality of the Nullifiers' authorities. The state rights orators directed their appeals to the experience of the colonists and to the wisdom of the founding fathers as reflected in the Constitution and in the Virginia and Kentucky Resolutions. Yet the ethical ground of those appeals must be at last located in what J. Bronowski and B. Mazlish term the two "grand formative ideas" of the last five hundred years of western history—freedom and the right of dissent.[126] In short, the

[124] Cf. Hamilton's argument at the Hamburg Festival: "Would our fathers have compromised with Lord North, if he had agreed to reduce the duty on tea a penny, and to bring the stamps down to six pence?" Augusta (Ga.) *Chronicle*, June 7, 1832.

[125] *Proceedings of the State Rights' Meeting, Columbia, S.C.,* 28.

[126] J. Bronowski and Bruce Mazlish, *The Western Intellectual Tradition: From Leonardo to Hegel* (New York, 1960), 498–502.

Nullifiers' appeals to authority expressed "real hierarchy."

Let us now see how their argument was conducted within the four "status frames" of the debate. Ill was never sharply contested. The negative agreed that the policy of protectionism was harmful to the economy of the "staple states." But the question of the "degree" of ill sometimes became a part of the affirmative burden. In general, the Nullifiers were disposed to overestimate the harmful effects of the tariff laws on the southern economy. On the issue of reformability the Nullifiers were both at their argumentative best and worst. The immediate ill was a tottering economy, and the "melancholy signs of decay" were abundant. Yet the Nullifiers either could not or would not see that the causes were multiple. They refused to assess properly the economic weaknesses of the slave system. They ignored the shattering economic effects of the westward migration to the richer cotton lands of Mississippi and Texas. In fine, in their analysis of the causes of the ill they were far less realistic than the Anti-Nullifiers. On the other hand, the Nullifiers were more perceptive on the question of whether the manufacturing majority would abandon protectionism, that is, reform the leading cause of the ill. The Nullifiers' estimate of the "enemy" was made early and with uncanny accuracy.

It was on remedy that the Nullifiers met their chief opposition and reasoned with the greatest rigor. The strength of their argument rested in their accurate analysis of the historical ground of the state rights formula. The government established under the Constitution was not meant to be a power state. The framers, fully aware of power abuses that had spawned the American Revolution, had intended that local sovereignty be left as a check against arbitrary abuse of national power. But the Nullifiers had to wage their argument for the constitutionality of their remedy in the realm of tenuous legal meanings. The Virginia and Kentucky Resolutions were equivocal on most of the critical constitutional points. At the same time they did not contain a formal procedure for nullification. In addition, as worked out by Calhoun the doctrine was too abstruse for easy illumination. It is a tribute to the Nullifiers' powers of verbal illustration that they were able to make the doctrine intelligible to so many of the uneducated yeomanry of the Up-Country districts.

But on the status question of cost the Nullifiers managed their argument ineptly. As we have seen, they were signally deficient in their refutation of the negative charge that nullification was a "peaceable" remedy. The questions of cost were ultimately questions of value, and the masses of men had already ordained that "the Union" was more precious than the mud-sill conception of liberty. Still, the Nullifiers capitalized fully on the Carolinians' unique order of values. They managed with consummate skill to identify patriotism with "resistance to tyranny," and thus with both liberty and honor.

In "personal argument" the Nullifiers were compelling, for their character echoed the values that underlay their logical case. Among the ranks of the Nullifiers were some of the most respected men of the state's "chivalry." As a group these men loathed, above all else, "mean submission" to arbitrary rule. Both in word and in deed they upheld the Carolina code of honor during the nullification crusade. The Nullifiers also drew ethical strength from the nature of their campaign. They disregarded the traditional mud-sill view that the people should select leaders, not decide policy. In the manner of a Democrat, they carried out a popular, grass-roots crusade. In so doing, they gained an ethical advantage over their opponents. The Nullifiers bespoke a strong faith in the principle of popular majority rule. At bottom it exemplified both a belief in the right of the people to be consulted on public issues and faith in their ability to make sound policy decisions. The Nullifiers sought by every means of public enlightenment available to "convict the mind." They took a certain pride in their efforts. The Priest of the Nullifiers, in his "Speech on the Force Bill," said of the nullification debate: "Never was there a political discussion carried on with greater activity, and which appealed more directly to the intelligence of a community." [127] On the other hand, certain deficiencies of character marred the Nullifiers' personal argument. As a group they were intransigent, humorless in their public address, and uncharitable to those who differed with them.

The Nullifiers also drew rhetorical strength from able management of form. In their view good structure was achieved through adherence to the popular persuasion-conviction dualism. Typically, their introductions were brief, tactful responses to the toast of praise that ordinarily preceded the speech itself. There followed the carefully partitioned argumentative portion which, with its combination of reason and authority was designed to "convict the understanding." The next structural feature of their speeches was the address to the will which, though including the peroration, was relatively short. This structural formula was one that served well the aims of the Nullifiers. Its major flaw in practice was the unfortunate length of the address to the mind. Meticulously they tried the doctrine of nullification by the tests of both authority and reason. Their development was at times laborious and legalistic and, beyond question, exhausting to the yeoman.

The Nullifiers may be said to have fulfilled adequately Blair's requirements for effective language. Their style was, by the terminology of the times, "perspicuous." The Nullifiers' speeches were in many instances models of clear exposition. Lawyers all, the Nullifiers strove for a diction that faithfully represented their conceptions. They sought, in Preston's phrase, to use language that lay "beyond mistake or cavil." [128]

[127] Calhoun, *Works*, II, 214.
[128] *The Debate of the South Carolina Legislature, December, 1830*, 194.

Above all, they were able to maintain a remarkable stability of word reference, especially on key ethical terms such as "honor," "oppressive majority," "colonial vassalage," "solemn appeal," "an efficacious remedy," etc. When a Nullifier was short on perspicuity, the fault lay not in his diction but in his syntax.

The Nullifiers' tactics of figuration, like their habits of structuring, appear to have been under dominion of the persuasion-conviction dualism. Their address to the mind was singularly wanting in "figures of words," or tropes. A few speakers, most notably Calhoun and Harper, were little concerned with the doctrine of adornment. Others, Preston and Hamilton, for example, were genuinely adept in highlighting an idea through imaginative use of tropes. And with the possible exception of Rhett, none abused figuration.

In their address to the will, however, the Nullifiers made effective use of the trope to intensify an idea. As a group they showed a marked preference for metonymy, a trait that bespoke their sententiousness as well as their romanticism. Metonymy, with its substitution of a single suggestive detail for what is actually meant, was used on occasion with surety and skill to make compelling the address to the will. The following examples are characteristic: "The first tap of a drum [commencement of war] upon the borders of South Carolina would proclaim the dissolution of that government." (Preston); "With halters around their necks [enslaved], they fearlessly encountered the power of a mighty nation." (McDuffie). In short, figuration was functional in the style of the Nullifiers; it was in no sense "mere embellishment."

The Nullifiers addressed themselves resolutely to the human situation as they found it. With a strong sense of public stewardship, they raised their voices against the oppressions of a regnant majority. They spoke from fundamental principles

71

and in a style "bold, ardent, simple," as befit an orator who attended to "the proper language of the passions." A mere handful of men, they sustained one of the longest and most intense rhetorical crusades of American political history.

Their campaign for the support of Carolina was a model of rhetorical workmanship. The Nullifiers enjoyed a rare combination of rhetorical resources. And they used them imaginatively in their effort to identify the cause of nullification with the leading values of the mud-sill society. Hamilton's managerial brilliance and Calhoun's incisive essays were a faultless complement to Preston's and McDuffie's fervid oratory. Yet the Nullifiers failed to achieve the rhetorical excellence available to them in the moral philosophy and the rhetorical theory of their times. They grounded their case in a spurious definition of liberty—a definition that confined human dignity to the world of the "freeman." Further, in the presentation of their case they often argued feebly on the status frames of ill and cost.

In final assessment the rhetoric of the Nullifiers represents a continuation of western man's dialogue on justice. It was a rhetoric of dissent, of protest, carried out in behalf of the kindred causes of freedom of choice and cultural diversity. The rhetoric of the Nullifiers belongs therefore to the oratorical tradition of Demosthenes, Luther, and Henry. It was used indeed to sustain a decaying order of privilege. Yet paradoxically it bore within itself the true seed of the democratic polity. In this final fact lies the deeper significance of the rhetoric of the Nullifiers.

II

The Anti-Nullifiers

MERRILL G. CHRISTOPHERSEN

Pinched by the overburden of a cotton economy, by a sterile soil, and by the tariff, the people of the South turned easily to advocates who promised them quick relief. Men throughout South Carolina and the other southern states became more and more desperate as the economic jaws closed upon them. That desperation expressed itself in the struggle over nullification, on the one side in the oratory of emotional men who proposed action along the lines set down by John C. Calhoun, and on the other in the eloquence of equally emotional men who argued the precedents of the law. Though the Anti-Nullifiers ultimately had no authority louder than the common law to offer, they pleaded that the democracy which their forefathers had brought forth should be kept intact despite the oppressiveness of the tariff.

Hugh Swinton Legaré, William Smith, Thomas S. Grimké, Alfred and Daniel Huger, William Drayton, Joel R. Poinsett, Benjamin F. Perry, Judge David Johnson, Mitchell King, and James Louis Petigru were the Anti-Nullifiers and proved themselves able and brilliant in the controversy.

The two factions were thoroughly trained for their speaking assignments. All were sons of men who themselves had participated in those arguments and battles which had arisen during the formation of the new nation a generation earlier. Sons of such fathers had learned to speak publicly as a matter of course; they were trained in a twofold process seldom found in speech education today. As a guiding principle was this tenet: *The process of learning wisdom was at no time separated from the process of expressing that wisdom, either by pen or by tongue.* Associated with this principle went a corollary: *That as a man grew in learning and wisdom, he became the whole man speaking at all times, even when he spoke upon practical matters.*

Education, the gaining of and the expressing of that learning, was completely integrated. The process was continuous throughout life. South Carolina planters criticized their speakers, both in the families and in public, from their first utterances to the final phrases of their careers. And as a consequence the speakers sought to perfect themselves in eloquence throughout their lives.

The first and more obvious training for public speaking began in the home and continued through a boy's schooling. His speech training started before he went to school when his first audience was his family gathered in the parlor to read the weekly newspaper. The mother or a daughter might read aloud the advertisements on the first page and the arrivals at Charleston of ships and people on the third. The father, perhaps, then would read a political speech. After the older members had finished discussing political aspects of the speech (and a planter's wife was usually as political-minded as was her husband), the child might also read, perhaps as his first effort, a poem on page two. Then would come criticism from his father.

From the outset, therefore, speech training was a natural part of family life. It continued in the elementary schools, with the student reciting aloud, first in English, and then (as was the case with Legaré), at about the age of nine, in Latin, and later in Greek, the well-known speeches of the great orators, past and present.

At South Carolina College, for instance, which had educated most of the men engaged in the nullification controversy, the training in expression was much a part of the collegiate program. Each week, in whatever class he chose—varying his choice as he saw fit—the young student wrote a paper, pertinent to moral philosophy, mathematics, or chemistry. When completed, it was criticized by the professor of the class. The student then would memorize the final version and the following Saturday afternoon would deliver it as a speech before fellow students and a professor, on the College grounds (a Horseshoe which exists to this day).

Speaking, writing, and criticism, therefore, were complementary elements of the education which developed men well able to express themselves by the time of maturity. As they matured the young gentlemen became eloquent, better able to argue public questions persuasively.

The first phase of speech education was linked with a second learning, the art of private or conversational speaking. Such conversation was almost a sign of the southern gentleman. This too was a developing process, beginning in the home, when the young boy listened to critical discussions or the exchange of badinage among the older members. From the very start, moreover, the parents were careful to give a son every chance to voice his own thoughts, so that by the time he went off to school, he needed no coercion when asked to express his opinions.

The more formal part of training in conversation occurred in the college literary societies and, after college, in the literary societies of the larger cities, especially Charleston. In these groups public and private speaking were most important. Here were developed wit, exuberance, and pleasant liveliness.

Within the adult societies conversation became associated with the thinking of the time. Scientists, scholars in the humanities, visiting celebrities were invited to read papers. Afterwards, discussions lasted far into the night. Because the audience was as well informed as the speakers, the conversation was filled with pithiness and enlarged thought.

The final phase of conversational training ensued at the dining tables of Charleston and Columbia, as they existed between 1815 and 1840. There the final polish was placed upon the repartee of those already fluent in discourse. One observer testified that the "table was . . . a great center of attraction, and remarkable for the display of that courtesy and mutual respect without which it could never be a bond of enlightened intercourse." [1] For two generations the tables of the larger South Carolina cities encouraged conversational excellence. Each diner contributed a special flavor to the interchange of ideas. "Our own friends—our own peculiar set . . . [James R.] Pringle, . . . Impetuous, . . . hating as cordially and loving as devotedly as ever—Petigru, the same, noble, generous, witty, able, and delightful being. . . . [Joel R.] Poinsett has become domesticated among us, . . . [William] Drayton—the excellent—the pure—the disinterested." [2]

Poinsett gave weekly breakfasts, called "lessons in the art of conversation." It was reported that a "discussion led by him never flagged; he could always induce each guest to speak of that on which he spoke best." [3] At his evening parties Petigru entertained strangers from all over the world with talk that lasted until midnight. Among those who came to his home were General Winfield Scott, Edward Trelawny, Edward Everett, but most often Legaré, Benjamin and Daniel Huger,

[1] Charles Fraser, *Reminiscences of Charleston* (Charleston, 1854), 58.

[2] Mitchell King to Legaré, May 5, 1833 in Legaré Papers, South Caroliniana Library.

[3] Mrs. St. Julien Ravenel, *Charleston, The Place and the People* (New York, 1925), 431-32.

William Harper, and James Pringle, "The dinners were fired with wit, whether they took place at Petigru's or Judge Huger's, or Judge King's, or Pringle's." [4] Petigru by voice or jest, Legaré with classical allusion, pungent criticism, or sparkling illustration, Alfred Huger with sound Unionist doctrine, and William Harper with subtle analysis brought about rare exchanges and stimulation.

Because of their intense eagerness for information, many of these men carried their studies far beyond their college degree. Legaré and Preston enrolled in European schools. Petigru worked into the late hours in his own home. So it was with the others. Few political controversies have found so many brilliant and well-educated men engaged in the contest as did the battle over nullification.

Between 1824 and 1828, during the first days of opposition to the tariff in South Carolina, the idea of any action more radical than a protest to Congress was unthought of. Legaré, who framed the Protest, watched the state legislature move slowly towards measures which he knew would separate South Carolina from the American nation. To forestall such a drastic course, he used the full powers of his eloquence. When the ideas of nullification were urged, when emotional arguments advocated disunion, Legaré worked to unite supporters of the Union into a group which called itself the Union and State Rights Party, and soon came to be called Unionists.

In 1843 George Ticknor of Harvard said of Legaré that he was one of the great scholars of the country;[5] a century later Vernon Parrington agreed and went even further.[6] The Virginian, William Cabell Rives, saw him as a close friend with "an imperious sense of duty," who, with "burning eloquence"

[4] William J. Grayson, *James Louis Petigru* (New York, 1866), 102.
[5] Boston *Daily Advertiser*, June 30, 1843.
[6] Vernon Louis Parrington, *The Romantic Revolution in America* (New York, 1927), 114–15.

77

fought "the unworthy arts of the demagogue" throughout his life.[7]

To Legaré the greatest of demagogues was John C. Calhoun. When he was chargé d'affaires for the United States at Brussels, he said of the Nullifiers and of Calhoun:

I regard them without passion whenever I happen not to be inclined to ridicule. Nothing can be more ridiculous to one surveying them at a distance than their noisy, swelling self-conceit. . . . They, or rather Calhoun and a few of the ring-leaders, have been all along contriving to bring about their recent coalition with Clay, and these profligate *demagogues* have not scrupled to play at their political gaming table for the honor of the country, staking its very existence on a throw of the dice. When I think of the impudence with which they forced their absurdities down the throats of so many intelligent, good sort of people in South Carolina, I am disposed to despair of mankind.[8]

Again, in a letter to Isaac Holmes, who was later to become a Nullifier, Legaré wrote: "When I read your 'Ordinance,' I rubbed my eyes to be sure I was not in a dream. I could not believe it possible that such insolent tyranny was in the heart of any man, educated as and where I myself imbibed my detestation of all arbitrary power [Willmington Academy, near Abbeville, S.C., which both Calhoun and Legaré attended]." [9] Particularly odious to Legaré had been Calhoun's *Exposition* which William C. Preston attempted to push through the South Carolina house of representatives at its fall session in 1828. Preston urged that interposition of the powers of the state should be used to arrest the evil of the tariff. Legaré had countered with a set of resolutions of his own, the first state-

---

[7] William Cabell Rives, "H. S. Legaré, Late Attorney General of the United States," *Southern Literary Messenger*, IX (September, 1843), 570.

[8] Legaré to Mary Swinton Legaré, (his mother), May 10, 1833, in Legaré Papers.

[9] Legaré to Isaac Holmes, April 8, 1833, in Legaré Papers.

ment of the Anti-Nullifiers in South Carolina: (1) that protective duties are unconstitutional; (2) that the tariff of 1828 was unjust; (3) that the people of the state were not prepared for open rebellion without further argument and effort; (4) that another protest be sent to Congress, and that other governors be asked to join in the protest; (5) that no convention of the people ought to be called; and (6) that no act to nullify should be passed in South Carolina.[10] In these resolutions Legaré used the term "nullification" before Calhoun used it— the word does not appear in the *Exposition*.

In answer Preston offered the *Exposition*. The house as a Committee of the Whole went immediately into a week-long discussion. Shortly before the end of the debate, Legaré, in a long speech, carried the house. He summarized his previous arguments which he had used to advocate protests to Congress, but his chief attack was upon the *Exposition*.

"The states themselves formed the Union," he argued; "they vested certain powers in the Federal Government," but retained all "the residuary attributes." When the general government usurps some of these residuary attributes, "a court appointed by that very government decides in favor of the usurpation." There were, he stated, just two alternatives to be considered: "Either the state is bound by such a decision or she is not. If she is not, those who preach submission are cowards and slaves. If she is, she is bereft of all that is hers." To remedy the evil, he said, "a state may secede from the union in a case of extreme necessity," and the state "alone is the judge of that necessity. But no state has the constitutional right to call a convention in order to alter the constitution."

Legaré attacked the nullification premise as a peaceful remedy. If a state claim the right to obey a law, even though "our opponents say peace," he countered, "I say war, because the

[10] Charleston *Courier*, December 5, 1828; South Carolina Journal of the House, 1828 (Columbia, Historical Commission of South Carolina), 60.

constitution . . . is immediately dissolved." As for Calhoun's *Exposition* being a remedy which could avoid war, he stated: "The idea that for every political wrong there must be a legal, constitutional remedy is quite puerile. A government so contrived that it cannot go wrong is an invention yet to be found out."

Legaré had his solutions. "We have two remedies," he said, "for usurpation of a conceded power." The first "is a change of administration by election." The second "is revolution." The same two remedies he applied to the usurpation of a power not granted.

He pleaded with his audience: "Let us not complete our ruin by this rash effort to relieve ourselves from a temporary, however vexatious, evil." Because the people themselves gave power to the government, "it will be vain for the people to say they have a right to change their government as they please and as often as they please." To any such action the national legislature would answer: "You are a mob—a rabble—you are not the masters of the fold, because you have broken in through the windows and the back doors." [11]

Legaré's political adversary and personal friend, Preston, later summarized the final words in a eulogy: "Legaré depicted the possible consequences of a collision of the State with the Federal Government in a few glowing sentences—brother struggling with brother, parent with child, and the face of the land wrapped in conflagration and streaming with blood." [12]

The following day Legaré wrote to his mother telling her

---

[11] Charleston *Courier*, December 21, 1828; Charleston *South Carolina State Gazette* & Columbia (S.C.) *Advertiser*, December 8, 10, 17, 1828; Camden (S.C.) *Journal*, January 12, 1828. Calhoun wrote only the *Exposition*. Legaré wrote the *Protest*, which was the official document assented to by the South Carolina legislature in 1828.

[12] William C. Preston, *Eulogy on Hugh Swinton Legare; Delivered at the request of the City of Charleston, November 7, 1843* (Charleston, 1843), 28–29.

of his success: "I spoke almost two hours and a half to a deeply silent and attentive audience & with almost complete success." [13] That he received a two-thirds majority in the voting proved the truth of his words. The Charleston *Courier* reported that "the resolutions of Mr. Legaré go to instruct the Senators in Washington to enter a solemn protest on the journals of that body." [14]

Legaré and the Unionists thus staved off the movement to nullify, but they were effective only until the gathering discontent became stronger. By 1830 the Anti-Nullifiers lost their majority, both in the house and in the senate. Legaré resigned in order to become attorney general of the state. Two years later, when South Carolina nullified, he was in Europe, the first American chargé d'affaires in the newly created state of Belgium. His friend, James Louis Petigru, stepped into the vacated Unionist leadership.

Petigru gathered about him Daniel and Alfred Huger, both of whom loved the Union their fathers had made; William Drayton, idealistic, but an able senator in Washington, fighting for South Carolina and Unionism; Mitchell King, who, once upon receiving a judgeship, had used his salary to support the family of his predecessor; Henry Middleton, former ambassador to Russia, and many others.

Though Legaré was the more intellectual, Petigru was probably one of the most colorful personalities who ever practiced at the South Carolina bar. He had learned his forensic speaking in the old pine-board courtroom at Coosawhatchie, where the climate was reported to be so bad that any prisoner left a month in jail sometimes died before his lawyer could save him.

Petigru well needed all the ruggedness of his training, all of

[13] Legaré to Mary Swinton Legaré, December 15, 1828. Legaré Papers.
[14] Charleston *Courier*, December 20, 1828; Pendleton (S.C.) *Messenger* December 19, 1828.

his wit, together with his subtle leadership when nullification was set in motion by Calhoun's lieutenant, George McDuffie. At a dinner given in his honor in Charleston on May 19, the fiery politician declared: "The responsibility will not rest upon [South Carolina] . . . but upon her oppressors." [15] By the wave of his hand which ended his speech McDuffie forced Calhoun to justify his "remedy" openly.[16]

Prior to the South Carolina convention to nullify, the Unionists made two efforts to head off what they considered an impending disaster. The first of these was the Unionist Party celebration of the fifty-fifth Independence Day. On that day a "vast multitude" assembled in the Charleston market to the firing of cannon, the ringing of bells, and a parade of the militia. A procession moved out from the marketplace consisting of twenty-four stewards, two Revolutionary War veterans carrying the flag, sixty youths, seventy ship-masters and seamen, and the party members, altogether "exceeding 1200 souls." Then came the committee of arrangements, the distinguished guests, a "goodly number of Fathers of the Revolution, the clergy, the twenty-four vice-presidents, the intendent of the City, James R. Pringle, and finally the Orator of the Day, William Drayton, escorted by the Secretary of the Committee of Arrangements."

All proceeded to the First Presbyterian Church, where, after the reading of Odes and Washington's Farewell Address, Drayton delivered "an able, patriotic and exceedingly beautiful oration." [17] His words served as a sober warning: ". . . we should

---

[15] Charleston *Courier*, May 20, 1831.

[16] Charles M. Wiltse, *John C. Calhoun, Nullifier, 1829–1839* (Indianapolis, New York, 1949), 110; see Calhoun's Fort Hill letter in the Pendleton (S.C.) *Messenger*, July 26, 1831; see also David Duncan Wallace, *The History of South Carolina* (4 vols.; New York, 1934), II, 439.

[17] Henry D. Capers, *The Life and Times of C. G. Memminger* (Rich-

bear in mind, that we became a voluntary party to the Union—
. . . that no government, however guarded by definitions . . . ,
can be exempt from occasional abuse—that any other substi-
tuted for it would not be perfect—that it could not secure
us against party spirit—against the real or supposed oppression of majorities, and the jealousy and discontent of minori-
ties." [18]

Drayton discussed the calumny of the Nullifiers which had
been directed against many men of talent throughout the
state, merely because they upheld the Union. He did not mention that he again and again had been reviled for his opposition to nullification in the United States Senate.[19] Before closing, he warned his listeners against "frightful despotism":

The alternate domination of one party over another, sharpened by
the spirit of revenge . . . is itself a frightful despotism. The dis-
orders and miseries which result, gradually, incline the minds of
men to seek security and repose in the absolute power of an individual; and sooner or later, the chief of some prevailing faction,
more able and more fortunate than his competitors, turns this disposition to his own elevation on the ruins of public liberty.[20]

No one in the audience doubted whom Drayton had in mind.

After the ceremonies the entire assemblage moved in parade
to "The Bower," a huge building erected especially for the
dining and speaking of that day. The tables filled quickly with
men eager to take part in the festivities which followed for six
hours. No one thought of leaving—not even the thousand or

---

mond, 1893), 37–42. At this meeting William Gilmore Simms made his first
public address which he read in the church preceding Drayton's speech.
See William Drayton, *An Oration* delivered in the First Presbyterian Church,
July 4, 1831, (Charleston, 1831) 74–79.

[18] Drayton, *Oration delivered in the First Presbyterian Church,* 30.

[19] Benjamin F. Perry, *Reminiscences of Public Men* (Philadelphia, 1883),
271.

[20] Drayton, *Oration,* 30.

more who stood outside, straining toward windows and doors. Speakers gave toasts and read letters, including one to Andrew Jackson expressing faith in the Union and another extolling the justice of the national councils.[21]

Congressman Thomas R. Mitchell spoke on state rights and criticized the course of Calhoun. Then Legaré followed with the longest speech of the day. The overflow audience, the barnlike structure, as well as the growing intensity of party struggle, presented a speech situation unique for a Fourth of July celebration. A few blocks away the Nullifiers held forth at a similar meeting. In both gatherings, instead of eulogies or testimonials to departed heroes, the speakers advanced statements of principles for future actions.

The theme of Legaré's speech was that South Carolina must be bound by the same strictures she placed upon others: " 'We have a right to judge for ourselves' [the Nullifiers say]. Granted. But what of the other twenty-three [states]? Shall they not think for themselves, because we say an act which they have all declared to be within the meaning of the treaty and binding upon us, is not so? *If* our opinion is just, we are not bound. Admit it. But *if* theirs is just, we are bound." Having laid a long fuse, he applied the match: "The whole fallacy of the Nullifiers consists in coolly taking for granted the very matter in dispute, in blotting out this 'if,' in denying to others the very right of judging, which we claim for ourselves, and in expecting them . . . to act upon our convictions instead of their own." Then, in a powerful peroration, Legaré predicted the coming struggle: "The exertions of this day will call forth events which will make a different spirit necessary for our salvation. Look to the *end*. Whoever supposes that shouts and hosannas will terminate the trials of this day entertains a childish fancy. . . . Let us weigh and consider before we advance

21 Camden (S.C.) *Journal*, July 23, 1831; Drayton, *Oration*, 55.

to those measures which must bring on the most trying and terrible struggle this country ever saw.[22]

On this occasion Legaré spoke for the last time to the Unionists as a party, for, with the exception of repeating his warnings at the next Washington's birthday celebration, he devoted his energies in the following years in the service of the national government. Like Drayton, he was driven from South Carolina by "the Rule of Calhoun."

Petigru spoke next. He was as popular as any man in the party, and, indeed, in the entire state. On this day he argued that, though the tariff "ought never to have been passed," and though it was "contrary to the spirit of . . . mutual concession" in which the Constitution was conceived, and though it was "injurious to the South," nevertheless it was constitutional. Petigru argued the theme then and for the rest of his life. The Union, "formed by the wisdom and cemented by the blood" of our Fathers, and the liberty it gives to men "must [not] be torn asunder." [23]

A short time later Calhoun published the Fort Hill letter[24] and avowed nullification. Though Calhoun was the author of the doctrine, Governor James Hamilton presented it throughout the state. Hamilton organized the political clubs to draw votes for the coming convention of the Nullifiers. With membership open to anyone upon payment of one dollar, the association meetings became popular social events where the poorest farmer and the richest planter met together to curse the Northerners.[25] And the Nullifiers surged in strength in the spring of 1832 until they were strong enough to carry the

22 Hugh S. Legaré, *Writings of Hugh Swinton Legaré* (2 vols.; Philadelphia, New York, Boston, 1846), I, 275.
23 Capers, *Life and Times of C. G. Memminger*, 62.
24 Pendleton (S.C.) *Messenger*, July 26, 1831.
25 William W. Freehling, *Prelude to Civil War: The Nullification Controversy in South Carolina, 1816–1836* (New York, 1966), 228.

fall elections. The call for convention would occur shortly after.

Seeing before them not only nullification but secession, the Anti-Nullifiers took their final stand as they met in Columbia on September 10, 1832. Petigru charted their course. The few words with which he presented a set of resolutions to the party became momentous in the South, for out of that little speech grew an action which helped stifle nullification, and, in so doing, postponed the Civil War thirty years.

Knowing that his audience had heard the arguments many times, Petigru made his points simply. They had come together, he said, to determine "the best mode of providing for the public safety," for the Nullifiers shouting opposition to the tariff had disturbed the peace of the South. If nullification were peaceful, a "mere law suit" could dismiss it as "feeble" and "inefficient." But nullification, he argued, called for revolution, as it would deny to the central government "the power to execute its own laws." Revolution, he emphatically declared, was inconceivable to the Unionists.

He deplored the "rage and passion" of the Nullifiers, which would "sweep away the inestimable institution of freedom." Against such a catastrophe any plan, short of revolution, which would remove the burden of the tariff, would be preferred. He suggested the calling of a convention of the states of the South, a meeting at which they could deliberate upon the issue.

Before offering the resolutions he stirred the patriotism of the delegates by his final remarks: "We cherish a sacred attachment to the Constitution," to liberty fought for and won. It is an obligation "to repay in some degree the debt of gratitude, by transmitting the same inheritance to [our] posterity."

Petigru then offered four resolutions. First, the Unionists would unite with the Nullifiers in any constitutional means of redress for the unjust tariff laws. Second, a general meeting of representatives of the southern states was desirable. Third,

Unionists should abide by the results of such a convention.

The fourth resolution, one to have greater importance than the others, was the appointment of a committee of carefully chosen men to journey to the other southern states to urge support for such a convention. The Anti-Nullifiers voted with Petigru on the resolutions 112 to 1.[26]

Within the odysseys of these committeemen (certainly of those who fulfilled their missions) emerged an interesting part of the southern decision to reject a confrontation with the federal government by nullification. For, although the travellers ostensibly sought a southern convention to gain the consensus of the South, they, in their turns, strongly influenced the antinullification sentiments in those other states.

That committee included Mitchell King, Judge Daniel Huger, Joel R. Poinsett, Judge David Johnson, and Senator William Smith.[27] The first committeeman, Judge Mitchell King, a sincere Unionist, set forth to Tennessee. Fully aware of the direness of the time, he wrote to Legaré, in Brussels: "Language cannot describe . . . the feelings, the anxieties . . . which . . . filled our bosoms. War—in the most horrid of its forms—War Civil—seemed inevitable."[28]

Although he was an exceedingly able lawyer and had been trained in public speaking, he possessed greater ability in persuasive conversation in small groups. He had, indeed, originated the then famous Conversation Club of Charleston and had long been its president.[29] He had a quality of agreeableness before the bar, and in private conversation, an oral sweetness.[30]

As a conversationalist King attained his objectives during

[26] *Niles Weekly Register*, XLIII (October 6, 1832), 87–88.
[27] *Ibid.*, 89.
[28] Mitchell King to Legaré, May 5, 1833, with a postscript on May 8, 1833.
[29] John Belton O'Neill, *Biographical Sketches of the Bench and Bar of South Carolina*, (2 vols.; Charleston, 1859), II, 365–66.
[30] Ravenel, *Charleston: The Place and the People*, 474.

his month-long stay in Nashville. He represented a minority faction of South Carolina. The legislature of Tennessee usually followed a precedent of not recognizing any "self-constituted body or party of men, unknown to and unrecognized by, the existing laws of a sister state." Yet King communicated the message from the South Carolina Unionists. In September it was read to the senate and the house of representatives of Tennessee, along with a set of resolutions on nullification by Richard S. Dunlap, senator from Knox and Anderson counties. On September 24 both documents were laid on the table and ordered to be printed.[31]

David W. Dickenson brought forth the fact that the legislature had been so excited in electing a United States Senator that it had delayed considering the words of "a most respectable gentleman" [Mr. King] deputed by "one of the most respectable conventions of the kind ever assembled, to communicate to her Sister States around, the true state of public sentiment in South Carolina, and the imminent perils ... which are threatening the existence of the Union." [32] The necessity for Tennessee and the other southern states to support the Anti-Nullifiers of South Carolina was the emphatic theme of his speech: "Sir, The Union—the Constitutions of these States are in jeopardy. Whether South Carolina will nullify or not, depends upon the support she is likely [to] receive in the West or Southwest. A mighty effort is making to carry Georgia in support to the doctrine; Alabama is strongly infected." South Carolina, Dickenson continued, "waits [Tennessee's] declaration with anxious interest. Will she be for or against nullification?" [33]

---

[31] Nashville *National Banner and Nashville Whig*, October 24, 1832.

[32] David W. Dickenson was congressman from Tennessee, 1833–35, and later a Whig in Congress, 1843–45.

[33] Nashville *National Banner and Nashville Whig*, October 24, 1832.

So persuasive was Dickenson that the Select Committee from both houses of the legislature to which the communication had been referred made its report four days later. Though the committee did not favor the proposed southern convention, it, nevertheless, in no way sought to "prevent [its] constituents from selecting [delegates] on the further development of events." It categorically declared nullification to be a dangerous and unconstitutional doctrine. Finally, the report "most heartily concur[red] with [the Unionists of South Carolina] in the end and purpose of this mission—the preservation of our hitherto happy and glorious union." [34]

The resolution was accepted and adopted by the Assembly "by a nearly unanimous vote." Before the legislature adjourned, it placed on the records further evidence of the first anti-nullification victory with the words: "It becomes the duty of this assembly to denounce nullification as a heresy." [35]

The first state had been won. A chain of events was set in motion. Certainly one cannot say that Mitchell King and the South Carolina Anti-Nullifiers had caused Tennessee to declare itself as they wished. But the mission had brought out the Tennessee sentiments at the proper moment to have the greatest effect upon the Nullifiers of South Carolina!

Yet Petigru, not at all optimistic, wrote to Legaré, "We are compelled to rely on the doubtful allegiance of Georgia." [36] Even as he wrote, the second chosen man was riding to that critical state. He was Judge David Johnson, a man "with no pretensions to eloquence" in public speech, but, like King, a fine conversationalist. Time and again in ordinary talk he proved his great personal power. It is reported that he had

[34] *Niles' Weekly Register*, XLIII (November 17, 1832), 177.
[35] *Ibid.*, (December 1, 1832), 220.
[36] Petigru to Legaré, October 29, 1832, in Petigru Papers, South Caroliniana Library.

once been elected to the state legislature because of this talent. On election day, riding to the polls he fell in with a company of some two hundred voters riding in military formation. The captain told him their ticket was already made up and that they were not going to vote for him. Their number was sufficient to decide the election. But he bore up calmly and continued the conversation. The leader became so impressed that he proposed to the company that they change their decision. This they did, striking off the name of their chosen candidate and putting Johnson's name in his place. Johnson won the election.[37]

In Georgia, Johnson teamed with two great debaters, Colonel William Cumming and John Forsyth, soon to become Jackson's secretary of state. The peculiar nature of the verbal battle which took place in the Milledgeville legislative chambers demanded persuasive behind-the-scenes conversation and successful parliamentary debate.

Johnson circulated among the Union men, telling them the Carolina story. He was well received. He "was so amiable, so free from all malevolence, and so frank and respectful towards his opponents and his friends, that none could dislike him." [38] That gift helped Forsyth solidly weld sufficient strength among the antinullification men to meet the test of them demanded by this convention.

Forsyth planned the strategy. Long a champion of Jackson and his policies he was "acute, witty, full of resources . . . adroit . . . when flanked and outnumbered," as was the instance here.[39] His chief opponent was John McPherson Berrien, an open and avowed enemy of President Jackson. Berrien was regarded by his contemporaries as the "best off hand

[37] Perry, *Reminiscences of Public Men*, 148–49.
[38] *Ibid.*, 151.
[39] Stephen F. Miller, *The Bench and Bar of Georgia: Memoirs and Sketches*, (2 vols.; Philadelphia, 1858), II, 51.

debater in the world." [40] The two of them locked horns in Milledgeville for three days.

On the afternoon of Monday, November 12, one hundred thirty-four delegates from sixty-one Georgia counties gathered in the chamber of the house of representatives. [41] The Anti-Nullifiers had only fifty-one votes, a minority which, in this instance, could not be augmented by normal persuasion.

The second day of the convention, after a conference with Johnson and William Cumming, Forsyth rose to speak. At ease in public, he was free from any trace of a studied manner. "He opened the discussion calmly . . . and gave specimens of eloquence never heard before in the Representative Chambers." He argued that action was "here to be taken by the Convention and it was binding or not binding." If it were to be binding, the delegates, he declared, "should produce their authority, showing that they were selected in good faith."

At this statement the Nullifiers looked at one another. They had brought with them no stated authority from a Georgia electorate, nor had they thought to secure any such authority. Forsyth pressed his advantage. He would not, he said, "deliberate with men, however respectable, on issues so grave, unless they exhibited their authority to speak in the name of the people." [42]

One reporter states that "Mr. Berrien was evidently surprised by this side-blow at the Convention, for his reply to Mr. Forsyth . . . lacked his usual cogency." Berrien, says this historian, "always preferred time to reflect, to arrange his views." On the other hand, Forsyth, "with look and gesture, inflection and voice" was at his best that day. There was no

---

[40] *Dictionary of American Biography*, VI, 533.

[41] Perry, *Reminiscences of Public Men*, 151. There are fifty-one signatures on the Protest. *Niles' Weekly Register*, XLIII (December 1, 1832), states that there were 134 delegates and lists fifty-three names on the document.

[42] Miller, *The Bench and Bar of Georgia*, II, 31.

hurry, no discord, or accidents, in "his constant stream of vocalization." He "had no fear of failure" as he met the thrusts of the Nullifiers.[43]

The next day Berrien offered a counterresolution which was opposed by Colonel Cumming, a delegate from Richmond County, the same county that had sent Forsyth. Cumming was reported to be able, dominating, an excellent speaker, yet not as overpowering as either Forsyth or Berrien. Then came the vote. Forsyth's resolutions calling for proper authorization of the members of the convention were rejected, 63–56, a surprisingly good vote for the Anti-Nullifiers. Several Nullifiers had evidently been persuaded to change their votes, and some had abstained.[44]

At the moment for the next parliamentary move Forsyth strolled to the front of the chamber and, according to the recorders of the scene, said that "in compliance with a promise he had made to the Convention when he proposed the inquiry which had just been denied, he would no longer remain. . . . After some remarks disclaiming all personal unkindness, he advanced to the clerk's table, deposited a paper on it, and then retired from the hall, followed by fifty-two other delegates." [45] The paper which Forsyth left with the clerk was a protest that the convention had adopted a course "inconsistent not only with the rights of our constituents, but with justice to the whole people." [46] As the delegates left the convention, Judge Johnson rose and followed them out. Of his action the Augusta *Chronicle* wrote: "Such a rear guard was an honor to the cause." [47] Full galleries witnessed the exit. Everything was conducted in order by the withdrawing

[43] *Ibid.* See also Lawton B. Evans, "John Forsyth," in *Men of Mark in Georgia*, ed., William J. Northen, (6 vols.; Atlanta, 1910), II, 292.

[44] Miller, *The Bench and Bar of Georgia*, I, 37.

[45] *Ibid.*, II, 32; *Niles' Weekly Register*, XLIII (December 1, 1832), 221.

[46] Miller, *The Bench and Bar of Georgia*, II, 33.

[47] Augusta (Ga.) *Chronicle*, November 18, 1832.

party, and the utmost decorum was observed by those who remained in the convention.

But what had been a convention was now only a rump meeting with forty counties wholly unrepresented. Those who remained, adjourned. Before they left, however, Berrien scored a minor victory. As someone moved that the paper be taken up and read, "Mr. Berrien objected, remarking that it might not be prudent to do so. The paper was not read." Thus he prevented many persons for the moment learning the nature of Forsyth's protest. But it soon appeared, in the next issue of the *Federal Union* and in other papers of the same politics.[48] The Georgia *Telegraph* sardonically remarked of the Nullifiers: "Their actings and doings and all their mighty works will doubtless be found in the books of the Chronicles. . . . Well may it be said a mountain was in labor, and brought forth a mouse." [49]

Shortly after, in his message to the Georgia legislature, Governor Wilson Lumpkin declared nullification unsound and dangerous.[50] By a vote of 102–51 the legislature voted a resolution saying, "We abhor the doctrine." [51]

A second state thus agreed with the South Carolina Unionists. The extent of the influence of Johnson in producing the final results of the "Rump Convention" cannot be determined. But he gave support to a strong minority at the right time, a move to keep Georgia in support of the Union position.

Insofar as the Nullifiers were concerned, South Carolina was isolated politically. To the southwest, Georgia condemned the doctrine; to the northwest, Tennessee agreed. North

[48] *Ibid.*

[49] Macon *Georgia Telegraph*, n.d., quoted in *Southern Recorder*, November 22, 1832.

[50] *Niles' Weekly Register*, XLIII (December 22, 1832), 279; Wilson Lumpkin, *The Removal of the Cherokee Indians from Georgia, 1827–1841*, (2 vols.; New York, 1907), I, 125; *Southern Recorder*, November 29, 1832.

[51] Milledgeville (Ga.) *Federal Union*, June 4, 1833; *Niles' Weekly Register*, XLIII (December 22, 1832), 280.

Carolina had felt no threat in the tariff. Late in 1831 that state's governor, Montfort Stokes, said: "It is to me a source of much gratification to have observed . . . that the excitement which seems to pervade a Sister State, upon the subject of the tariff, has effected little change in the opinions of the Citizens of North Carolina." [52] Since then the Piedmont continued a drive "for improved transportation, and in return for Federal aid would yield some scruples on state sovereignty." [53] Voicing the opinion of many, Senator Willie P. Mangum said that nullification was "a rank absurdity which had made no favorable impression upon the people of North Carolina.[54]

Committee member Judge William Smith went to Alabama where he was received with such cordiality that he never returned to South Carolina. He spoke for the Anti-Nullifiers at Huntsville, sponsored by Governor John Gayle, Senator Rufus King, and Clement C. Clay. Smith congratulated the citizens of Alabama for "taking time by the forelock and resisting the most dangerous and alarming doctrine." [55] Shortly thereafter, the Alabama legislature voted against any affiliation with the Nullifiers.[56]

Mississippi followed suit. Robert J. Walker spoke at a great Union meeting in Natchez. He summarized what had happened in the states to the east: "Georgia has already expressed her firm response to remain with the Union. Tennessee has made the same response." He then asked a solemn question: "Will Mississippi receive the bribe thus offered to dissolve the Union?" He gave his answer: "Carolina's remedy is death—it is suicide. . . . let us then abjure the people of South Carolina

[52] Governor Montfort Stokes to the General Assembly, November 22, 1831. In Governor's Letter Books, Montfort Stokes, 1830–32, p. 85, North Carolina Department of Archives and History, Raleigh.
[53] Archibald Henderson, North Carolina, The Old North State and the New (5 vols.; Chicago, 1941), II, 69.
[54] Fayetteville North-Carolina Journal, July 25, 1832.
[55] Huntsville (Ala.) Democrat, November 1, 1832.
[56] Niles' Weekly Register, XLIII (December 1, 1832), 220.

to repeal her ordinance. . . . The Union shall be preserved." [57]

As the western states expressed their disapproval, within the state of South Carolina the battle of nullification became a local skirmish. As the Anti-Nullifiers gathered in December, 1832, the outlook was civil war. The legislature had prepared itself for war; it "had passed acts to enforce the Nullification Ordinance; it had drawn up the Test Oath; . . . it had appropriated $200,000 for the purchase of arms." [58] Opposing the action of the state government were the strong stand taken by President Jackson, the isolation of South Carolina by the other southern states, and the continuing opposition of the Anti-Nullifiers within the state.

When the Unionists met in Columbia, they sensed the beginnings of victory. Earnest determination was still with them. It was in Petigru's voice as he spoke: "Nullification is not the State. Nor have I ever believed that my country was the swamps of the lower, nor the rocks of the upper, nor the pines of the middle portion of the State, but I have been taught to believe that my country was a wise and rational system of liberty." [59]

Judge Daniel Huger continued the thought, "refusing allegiance to a state that no longer gave its citizens liberty. . . . He would lay down his life for South Carolina, but not for tyrants who ruled her." On the following day, in the midst of a great speech, he demanded: "Can I be called a freeman when I am tried by a *perjured Judge* and a *packed jury?*" He condemned the test oath, for it voiced treason against the federal government.[60]

[57] Natchez *Mississippi Journal,* January 3, 1833.

[58] Lillian A. Kibler, *Benjamin F. Perry, South Carolina Unionist* (Durham, 1946), 146. The purpose of the oath was to disqualify Unionist Party members from holding military or civil office in the state.

[59] Quoted in *ibid.;* Benjamin F. Perry, "Autobiography," 1849. MS in possession of Mrs. Hugh C. Haynsworth, Sumter, S.C., 87.

[60] Perry, *Reminiscences of Public Men,* 220.

Following the suggestion of C. G. Memminger, the Unionists organized a "Washington Society" in each district, accepting Joel R. Poinsett as commander-in-chief and depending upon arms to be supplied by the federal government. If the situation worsened, they felt that they could offer successful opposition to the already armed Nullifiers.[61]

On the fourteenth a "Remonstrance and Protest of the Union and State Rights Party" against the nullification ordinance, the test oath, and the tyranny and oppression of the legislature was brought before the convention. It consisted of ten remonstrances, formulated by Petigru, followed by a formal protest produced jointly by Poinsett and Memminger. After one hundred eighty members signed their names, the meeting was adjourned.[62]

The atmosphere was tense, ripe for conflict, but the Nullifiers recognized that they were isolated and widely condemned for their stand. When a compromise, reducing the tariff gradually, passed in Congress (especially since Calhoun approved the measure and George McDuffie called it "an olive branch to the South"), Nullifiers were only too glad to concede that they had won even as they accepted the compromise.

Now that the conflict had been confined to South Carolina, Jackson sought from Congress a bill to give him power to put down the recalcitrants by means of federal marshals.[63] Not too much in accord with this idea, the Anti-Nullifiers would have preferred that the President call out the militia. Of greater threat to the Nullifiers than that of federal in-

[61] James Petigru Carson, *Life, Letters, and Speeches of James Louis Petigru: The Union Man of South Carolina* (Washington, 1920), 108–11; Kibler, *Benjamin F. Perry*, 147.

[62] Carson, *James Louis Petigru*, 108–10; Kibler, *Benjamin F. Perry*, 147–48; Perry, *Reminiscences of Public Men*, 152–53; Chauncey Samuel Boucher, *The Nullification Controversy in South Carolina* (Chicago, 1916), 287–95.

[63] Boucher, *The Nullification Controversy*, 305–307; David Franklin Houston, *A Critical Study of Nullification in South Carolina* (New York, 1896), 128; Petigru to Legaré, February 5, 1833, Petigru Papers.

tervention, however, was the material fact that they were unable to gather sufficient arms to be impressive even to themselves. More and more the Nullifiers realized that it was not the time to act. On January 21, 1833, at a meeting in Charleston they agreed on the desirability of avoiding a clash with the federal government.[64]

In a March convention, attended by Calhoun, the legislature repealed the nullification ordinance. Defiantly, however, the Nullifiers retained the test oath, which placed allegiance to the state above that to the national government, a condition obnoxious to the Anti-Nullifiers. Until the oath could be rescinded, the battle was not over for them.[65]

The Anti-Nullifiers objected to the oath not only because it was a rejection of federal authority, but because it was actually a restatement of nullification itself. The strongest resentment flared out in the northwestern part of the state. Petigru wrote to William Drayton that "the mountain region is aflame," and added that "unless the Court of Appeals declares the law unconstitutional or Hayne gives way, there will be a border war." [66]

Before the state supreme court made a final decision, events moved closer to civil conflict. Union meetings were held daily, with the strongest antinullification sentiment in and around Greenville. Protest after protest came into print as resolutions were voted in Spartanburg, Darlington, Pickens, and in the parishes near Charleston.

In Charleston three voices spoke the strongest—those of Petigru, Poinsett, and Thomas S. Grimké. Poinsett, at a dinner in his honor in Georgetown, uttered the feelings of many Unionists:

[64] Charleston *Mercury*, January 23, 1833.
[65] Boucher, *The Nullification Controversy*, 295; Perry, *Reminiscences of Public Men*, 152–53.
[66] Petigru to Drayton, March 26, 1834; Carson, *James Louis Petigru*, 130; see also Freehling, *Prelude to Civil War*, 314–18.

To obtain power our opponents have trampled on all the rights of our fellow citizens and plunged their native state into the most appalling difficulties. To preserve their power at this time . . . they seek to agitate the country. . . . They have presumed to present an Oath of Allegiance to South Carolina, to us! To us who have showed our deep devotion . . . to our native state by breasting the storm in her defense.[67]

At Seyle's Hall in Charleston all three leaders spoke. The Anti-Nullifiers gathered there to elect delegates to the Unionist convention at Greenville in March. Grimké presided. Poinsett offered the resolutions which suggested the final strategy against the Nullifiers. As he spoke, there came a cry, "Fire!" For a moment the audience thought it was simply the enemy trying to break up the meeting. Although he knew the fire to be real, Poinsett spoke out, "It's a false alarm. The real fire is in the mountains—a fire that makes tyrants tremble." And, as the fire in the rear of the hall was extinguished, he continued, "It is not strange that the reading of such an Ordinance should create a disturbance." Petigru seconded the resolutions "in a spirited address, equally distinguished for potent argument and brilliant wit." He condemned the ambiguity of the test oath, saying that "if those who passed it were brought up in court, and subjected to a cross examination, they would stumble more than a witness with a short memory." When he had finished, the resolutions were unanimously adopted.[68] The delegates went to Greenville, met with the other representatives and agreed as to what they must do. On their return to Charleston, Poinsett reported what their stand must be.

Speaking again in Seyle's, he declared that it had been the grimly determined agreement of all the convention members to continue a stout opposition to the Nullifiers until the oath was finally defeated. He told them "to stand fast—that they

---

[67] Charleston *Courier*, February 4, 1834.   [68] *Ibid.*, March 17, 1834.

had a right to the soil . . . on which they stood." With deep emotion showing in his face and in his words, he assured them that "for his part, here he was, and here he was resolved to die, and no persecution should drive him from the soil of Carolina." He concluded with the words his federalist ancestors could have used had they been present: "Here the Star Spangled Banner should be his shroud—pure and spotless, he hoped—but even if stained with blood, still it would be his shroud." [69]

Grimké and Petigru, as lawyers, fought the oath before the Court of Appeals, in front of a packed courtroom. Grimké spoke for seven hours and "enchained a large and gratified audience." The speaker had refused a Doctor of Laws degree from Yale because he did not believe that a man should use a title. He had made a lifelong study of extempore speaking, and, since his admission to the bar, he and three of his professional friends had carried on a practice of speaking on subjects chosen beforehand. For the previous several years they had discussed the important acts of the state legislature.

When he finished the first five hours of his speech, a reporter hurried out to write: "This effort of Mr. Grimké . . . we do not hesitate to pronounce the most masterly exposition of our political system that we have ever heard. It was profound in argument, adorned with eloquence, and enriched with legal and historical lore." [70] The next day, speaking softly, almost casually, as if his words were an understatement, Grimké concluded: "If there be any among us who would wish to dissolve this Union, or change our Republican form of government let them stand undisturbed monuments of the safety with which error of opinion may be tolerated, where reason is left free to combat it." [71] Throughout the speech he challenged the constitutionality of the test oath, by the state Constitu-

[69] *Ibid.*, April 1, 1834.   [70] *Ibid.*, April 3, 1834.
[71] *Ibid.*, April 4, 1834.

tion, by the federal constitution, and finally by legal precedent.

After the state attorney had finished, Petigru spoke. In contrast to Grimké, who had dealt with constitutionality, Petigru considered the meaning of allegiance itself. His manner of speaking in court—and indeed, in all of his speeches—was peculiarly his own. Frequently he would pause at a thought, as if to look upon it. He would even change a word, search for the right one to better express the idea. Yet he always held the interest of his listeners through his logical power, by the variety of his voice, and by his vigorous gestures.

Observers thought his voice was unusual. At times it was shrill and discordant, demanding attention. Again it was mellow. In passion it would "crash like the blast of a bugle." A contemporary explained Petigru's power: "His learning is great, but it is not that; his reasoning faculty is great, but it is not that; his industry is untiring, but it is not that; it is his quaint, original, magnetic eloquence. When his feelings are enlisted, he is the greatest speaker I have ever heard, and I have heard them all." [72]

The test oath case called upon all the passionate feelings that had burgeoned in Petigru during the six-year controversy. He centered his analysis around two great issues—the meaning of the allegiance demanded by the oath and the ambiguity of the oath itself: "It is not wonderful [he said to the court] that a new Oath, speaking a language unknown to our constitution, should excite inquiry. Men are not to be blamed for asking what it is they are required to swear to. But where shall they search for the meaning of *allegiance* as used in this Oath?" [73]

[72] Joseph Daniel Pope, "James Louis Petigru," in William Draper Louis (ed.), *Great American Lawyers* (8 vols.; Philadelphia, 1908), IV, 60.

[73] *The Book of Allegiance; or a Report of the Arguments of Counsel, and Opinions of the Court of Appeals of South Carolina, on the Oath of Allegiance, Determined on the 24th Day of May, 1834* (Columbia, 1834), 117.

Because the Nullifiers had often used the word "allegiance" carelessly, in whatever way to serve their purposes at any given moment, Petigru had felt a great fear of an impending civil strife in South Carolina which might spread throughout the nation. Expressing this dread he said to the court: "The end of these things is DEATH! A free Constitution cannot co-exist with this dangerous and paracidal power, in the hands of the ordinary Legislature." [74]

On the twenty-fourth of May the judges decided in favor of the Anti-Nullifiers, and held "that the Convention [of the Nullifiers] had gone beyond its powers in its attempt to pass the Oath as an ordinary enactment." [75] On June 12 Governor Robert Y. Hayne issued a proclamation accepting the decision.[76] The crisis of nullification neared its end. The state supreme court had given the Anti-Nullifiers a weapon powerful enough to end the conflict. But the last battle must still be won, for, in the fall elections, the Nullifiers again won a two-thirds majority in the legislature, a number sufficient, if they desired, to formulate another test oath.

Petigru, however, felt that enough of the Nullifiers would be amenable to a compromise satisfactory to both sides. After a conference with Charleston Anti-Nullifiers, he went to Columbia to a Union convention for the purpose of protecting the gains the party had made. He was called upon "to make them a long speech," arguing that the oath was unlawful "so long as it offended the conscience of any lover of the Union," and that for such people to swear to the oath would break down the moral sense and feeling both of party and of country. There would, in his judgment, always be three ways to resist: by the judiciary, by arms, and by political agitation. The first was inapplicable, because the court had ruled that the oath was contrary to the Constitution. The second recourse, he

[74] *Ibid.*, 123.   [75] *Ibid.*, 280–282.
[76] Charleston *Mercury*, June 13, 1834.

101

thought, was "repugnant" both to "patriotism" and to "Christian feeling." The third means of action Petigru considered to be the best.

He declared that the Unionists should send to the Nullifiers the simple communication that they would never "take the Oath"; that they must be admitted to their seats "without any Oath," or else "a third of the State would be unrepresented." Even Nullifiers, he said, must know that "an attempt to carry on government without representation is absurd." This they knew; this they understood; and this they would respond to.

Persuaded, the assembled Unionists agreed to this course of action, and Petigru became their messenger to the new governor, George McDuffie, to former Governor Hamilton, and to the other nullification leaders. He "excited [himself] to the utmost to render [his] views agreeable and give them strength." [77] That the time was ripe and the agent persuasive was evident, for the Nullifiers accepted his proposals and sent them on to the legislature, where they were received, surprisingly enough, with great courtesy.

Hamilton made a conciliatory speech to the legislature and, by vote, the Nullifiers modified their demands. They proceeded to remove the ambiguity which had surrounded the term "allegiance." Now, the oath, clearly worded for the first time, stated that the allegiance demanded would be only that "which every citizen owes the State *consistently with* the Constitution of the United States." [78]

Petigru wrote to Legaré in Belgium: "All hail to the dawn of a brighter day. The spell of party is broken and nullification in Carolina is no more than a recollection." [79] At almost the same time Legaré wrote to Forsyth, then President Jack-

[77] Petigru to Legaré, December 15, 1834, Petigru Papers.
[78] Greenville (S.C.) *Mountaineer*, December 20, 27, 1834; Carson, *James Louis Petigru*, 171; Kibler, *Benjamin F. Perry*, 169.
[79] Petigru to Legaré, December 15, 1834.

son's secretary of state in Washington: "From the tenor of one of my last letters from Charleston [from Petigru, November 29, 1843] I am led to think my presence there may be necessary." [80] But when Petigru's second letter arrived, Legaré was reassured and remained in Belgium. The Anti-Nullifiers, having won their battle, could well say, "The spell of party is broken."

The long struggle had been a battle with words spoken in courage, by men well trained to speak in whatever situation made its demand. When they were in a majority in South Carolina, from 1824 to 1830, the Unionists had found it sufficient to voice their opinions in the legislative halls and then place their confidence in the vote.

After 1828, when they disagreed with the Nullifiers as to the meaning of nullification and of allegiance, the two groups separated. By 1830, although a minority, the Unionists still had a strong enough voice to thwart attempts to call a convention to nullify. But with each passing day they saw the opposition augmented. In 1832 they had lost.

The Anti-Nullifiers, however, never succumbed. They sent men with great conversational powers to the states surrounding South Carolina and thus allied themselves with the Anti-Nullifiers in the neighboring states. One state after another proclaimed itself sympathetic to the South Carolina Unionists and condemned nullification. When the actions of those states had isolated South Carolina, the Unionists made their oratory sufficient to carry their cause. They remained firm in Columbia until the Nullifiers offered and accepted compromise. When the struggle was over and the debate was ended, each side once again accepted the other as friends.

---

[80] Legaré to John Forsyth, April 24, 1835.

III

The Southern Whigs

ROBERT G. GUNDERSON

From its beginning in 1834 the Whig Party included a heterogeneous conglomeration of conflicting sectional, economic, and
ideological elements. It contained Masons and Anti-Masons,
proslavery planters and abolitionists, advocates and opponents
of a National Bank, a protective tariff, and internal improvements. Members were united only by a dedicated antipathy
to President Andrew Jackson and his Democratic "Spoilers."
Jacksonians described a "piebald" Whig Party of many diver-
gent hues, "a ruffled shirt party" of "city dandlings" and "silk-
stocking Southern gentry," and "a discordant combination of
the odds and ends of all parties." Predicted Democrat Thomas
Ritchie hopefully, "Like the image of Nebuchadnezzer, which
was made of clay and brass and various materials, a single
stone must shiver it to pieces." [1]

South of the Potomac, Whiggery was further complicated
by personal antipathies and ideological enthusiasms engendered by the nullification and bank controversies. John M. Berrien, "master spirit of the Opposition in Georgia," resigned
from Jackson's cabinet during the Peggy Eaton affair; Hugh
Lawson White of Tennessee rebelled against the succession of

[1] Richmond *Enquirer*, n.d., quoted in *Niles' Weekly Register* LIX (November 28, 1840).

Martin Van Buren; John Tyler and Thomas Gilmer of Virginia, and William C. Preston and George McDuffie of South Carolina broke with Jackson during the nullification controversy; Willie P. Mangum of North Carolina deserted him on the bank issue.[2] Uniting the dissidents required masterful political strategy. "Now," wrote one fearful North Carolina Whig in 1835, "if some plan is not fixed upon to unite all these interests defeat is certain."[3]

Dedicated in their support of the slave system, southern Whigs appealed to old-line aristocrats and to the most wealthy planters, particularly to those with subsidiary interests in commerce or banking. James Graham, in a letter to his brother, William, described the party in North Carolina as a coalition of "the friends of good order."[4] In Florida, Whigs held more land, more slaves, and more bank deposits than Democrats.[5] The Richmond *Whig* asserted that two-thirds of the slaves of Virginia were held by Whigs, and the Montgomery, Alabama, *Journal* concluded that between three-fourths and seven-eighths of all the slaves in the South belonged to Whigs.[6] Whiggery was usually strong in the more prosperous agri-

2 Robert G. Gunderson, *The Log-Cabin Campaign* (Lexington, 1957), 36–38; William S. Hoffmann, *Andrew Jackson and North Carolina Politics* (Chapel Hill, 1958), 70–72.

3 James S. Smith to William A. Graham, December 2, 1835, in J. G. de R. Hamilton (ed.), *The Papers of William A. Graham* (4 vols.; Raleigh, 1957–), I, 401. (Hereinafter cited as Hamilton (ed.), *Graham Papers*.)

4 James Graham to William A. Graham, October 26, 1835, *ibid.*, I, 395. James Graham (1793–1851), a brother of William, served in the U.S. House of Representatives, 1833–43, 1845–47.

5 Herbert J. Doherty, Jr., *The Whigs of Florida, 1845–1854* (Gainesville, 1959), 63–72.

6 Arthur C. Cole, *The Whig Party in the South* (Washington, 1913), 69. Grady McWhiney argues that "the correlation between the Whig vote and slaveholding in Alabama is slight. Some of the largest Whig majorities were received in counties where there were few slaves." He nevertheless admits that "in the state as a whole it may have indeed been true that more large planters were Whigs than Democrats." McWhiney, "Were the Whigs a Class Party in Alabama?" in *Journal of Southern History*, XXIII (November, 1957), 521–22.

cultural areas: the tidewater region in Virginia, the Black Belt across central Georgia and Alabama, the rich plantation country along the Lower Mississippi, and the bluegrass regions of Kentucky and Middle Tennessee.[7]

Whiggery flourished also in those sections with developing industries such as the Kanawha region in Virginia and the Georgia Piedmont, and in isolated communities hoping for internal improvements.[8] The Savannah *Republican* reminded its readers that the Whig Party "has shown itself publicly, openly, as a matter of political faith, the true friend of the manufacturing industry." Campaigns to industrialize Georgia were "especially energetic in such centers as Athens, Augusta, and Savannah, cities in which the Whig party was particularly strong." [9] Salt, iron, cotton, and woolen manufacturers, hemp growers, and sugar planters, indeed all those looking for a tariff, found Whiggery congenial, as did mercantile and banking interests.[10]

Throughout the South Whigs were prominent railroad builders. Thomas Butler King of Georgia was active at the Macon railroad convention in 1836 and later became president of the Brunswick Railroad and Canal Company. James C. "Lean Jimmy" Jones of Tennessee was president of the Memphis and Charleston. Thomas A. R. Nelson devoted a good portion of his life to the fight for better transportation for

---

[7] Ulrich B. Phillips, "The Southern Whigs, 1834–1854," in *Essays in American History Dedicated to Frederick Jackson Turner* (New York, 1910), 207; Cole, *The Whig Party in the South*, 58 ff.; Paul Murray, "Economic Sectionalism in Georgia Politics, 1825–1855," *Journal of Southern History*, X (August, 1944), 293–307.

[8] Henry H. Simms, *The Rise of the Whigs in Virginia* (Richmond, 1929), 165; Cole, *The Whig Party in the South*, 78.

[9] Horace Montgomery, *Cracker Parties* (Baton Rouge, 1950), 4.

[10] Roger W. Shugg, *Origins of Class Struggle in Louisiana* (Baton Rouge, 1939), 148; J. Carlyle Sitterson, *Sugar Country, The Cane Sugar Industry in the South, 1753–1950* (Lexington, 1953), 88; Charles G. Sellers, Jr., "Who Were the Southern Whigs?" *American Historical Review*, LIX (January, 1954), 340–41; Phillips, "The Southern Whigs," 207.

East Tennessee.[11] As governor of North Carolina, John Motley Morehead favored improvement of navigation, the building of highways, and state aid for railroad construction. Morehead promoted several railroad companies and served as president of the North Carolina Railroad. A fellow Whig, William A. Graham, promoted the Central Railroad of North Carolina. In a farewell speech in 1849, after completing a term as governor, Graham gave a toast summarizing his goals: "The improvement of the mind, the improvement of the soil, and, above all, improvement in the means of transporting the fruits of the soil to the best markets." Graham's dedication to improvement led him to support the first geological survey of North Carolina, the public school system, and schools for the deaf, dumb, and blind. "Seconding the efforts of that Christian philanthropist, Miss Dix of Massachusetts," Graham also secured legislation to erect "a Lunatic's Hospital." [12]

Enlightened Whigs, particularly in the Upper South, spoke in behalf of educational progress. Thomas Nelson was "an outstanding supporter of public education" in Tennessee where even the Whig demagogue, Governor "Lean Jimmy" Jones, established the first schools for the blind and deaf. Charles S. Morehead and John J. Crittenden championed public education in Kentucky. In his last annual message to the Kentucky legislature, Governor Crittenden made "an eloquent plea" for public schools which would unite "the high and the low, the rich and the poor." He argued, "Educated poverty will repay a thousand fold . . . its portion of the debt." In Virginia, Henry A. Wise urged his constituents to tax them-

11 Edward M. Steel, Jr., *T. Butler King of Georgia* (Athens, 1964), 9–17 and *Dictionary of American Biography*, X, 403; *Dictionary of American Biography*, X, 177; Thomas B. Alexander, "Thomas A. R. Nelson as an Example of Whig Conservatism in Tennessee," *Tennessee Historical Quarterly*, XV (March, 1956), 27.

12 *Dictionary of American Biography*, XIII, 159; Hamilton (ed.), *Graham Papers*, III, 271 fn.; *Ibid.*, III, 45, 146, 270.

selves to educate their children. Knowledge, he said, "is the power which overcomes all *social* obstacles; it is the power which prostrates *political* inequalities; it is the power which overcomes all *physical* obstructions in the way of man." Wise hoped to see free common schools "with their delightful uproar." [13] In looking back upon southern educational accomplishments, one Whig eulogist argued that the aristocrat was the true progressive. The "reactionaries," he concluded, "were the neighborhood political bosses, whose principal stock in trade was an attack upon the kid-gloved [Whig] aristocracy." [14]

Paradoxically enough, however, an ultra-state-rights group within the party rejected many measures which a majority of Whigs held dear: the national bank, a protective tariff, and internal improvements. In South Carolina William Preston championed free trade and nullification. Francis Lieber of South Carolina College established himself with local Whig aristocrats by "his unquestioned devotion" to free trade and laissez faire.[15] Rebelling against Jackson's "executive usurpation," state rights advocates joined Whig ranks in spite of an uncongenial relationship with tariff and bank supporters. The bitter controversy which developed during Tyler's "accidency" resulted from the serious ideological differences within the southern Whig Party. Motives were thus complex, if not contradictory and elusive.

Compounding Whig ideological confusion was a romantic hallucination of aristocracy. Fastidious Whigs feared and distrusted "that scene of wild impulse, and tyrannical misrule—

[13] Alexander, "T. A. R. Nelson," 23; *Dictionary of American Biography,* X, 177; *Dictionary of American Biography,* XIII, 157–58; Albert D. Kirwan, *John J. Crittenden: The Struggle for the Union* (Lexington, Ky., 1962), 243–44; *Niles' Weekly Register,* XVI (March 9, 1844).

[14] Hamilton (ed.), *Graham Papers,* I, 79–80.

[15] Frank Freidel, *Francis Lieber: Nineteenth-Century Liberal* (Baton Rouge, 1947), 132.

a pure democracy." [16] John Tyler voted against the franchise for poor men even in local and county elections. Many opposed "equal manhood suffrage" as a "mischievous suggestion." Hugh Legaré of South Carolina called unlimited democracy "the most dreadful form of 'state sovereignty.' " Seargent Prentiss of Mississippi confessed, "I have lost confidence in the people—not so much in their honesty as in their capacity." Noting that Whigs were invariably "honest, high-toned, and patriotic," Ulrich B. Phillips concludes that the party constituted "a company of gentlemen, politically inclined." One observer even suggested that they could identify one another by "the instinct of gentlemen." [17]

But Whig aristocrats found it difficult to popularize progressive positions on internal improvements and education, to say nothing of their legalistic abstractions about state rights. Consequently, they sometimes found it expedient to resort to demagoguery. Representing wealth, they felt compelled to solicit votes with the means at hand—stump oratory, a calliope for enticing literate, semiliterate, and unthinking masses.[18] Oratory was, said W. J. Cash, "the *sine qua non*" of southern leadership, "a gorgeous, primitive art, addressed to the autonomic system and not to the encephalon." [19] In the somewhat different imagery of a contemporary North Carolinian, oratory provided "the steam power of society." [20]

[16] Hugh S. Legaré quoted in Parrington, *The Romantic Revolution in America* (New York, 1927), 119.

[17] Oliver P. Chitwood, *John Tyler: Champion of the Old South* (New York, 1939), 185; Hamilton (ed.), *Graham Papers*, III, 235; Hugh S. Legaré, *Writings of Hugh Swinton Legaré* (2 vols.; Charleston, 1846), I, 210; Dallas C. Dickey, *Seargent S. Prentiss, Whig Orator of the Old South* (Baton Rouge, 1945), 171; Phillips, "The Southern Whigs," 228; Cole, *The Whig Party in the South*, 69.

[18] Montgomery, *Cracker Parties*, 9.

[19] W. J. Cash, *The Mind of the South* (NewYork, 1956), 63–64.

[20] Hamilton (ed.), *Graham Papers*, IV, 364. In his *Southern Diary*, Bishop Henry B. Whipple noted that "backwoods people are easily gulled and made the dupes of for the benefit of designing men. . . . " He concluded,

Despite romantic stereotypes of its pillared mansions with high ceilings and booklined walls, the Old South remained a blighted area where, according to Phillips, "Caesar and Cicero were more often the names of Negroes in the yard than of authors on the shelves." There was a ready audience for demagogues. Southern audiences suffered from an intellectual as well as a regional provincialism. In 1840, 40,000 white Kentuckians admitted to being illiterate.[21] In contrast to New England where the illiteracy rate for persons over twenty was less than $\frac{1}{2}$ of 1 percent in 1850 and to Mid-Atlantic states with a rate of 3 percent, the rate in the South was 20.3 percent and the deplorable situation was not improving. There were, for example, more illiterates in Virginia in 1850 than there were in 1840.[22]

A Whig orator did not need to consult an almanac to know that his listeners were predominantly rural and provincial. Isolated by an inadequate system of transportation, as well as by the inability to read, many Southerners remained culturally impoverished. "Everything is arid here," complained Francis Lieber at South Carolina College; "arid soil, arid life, arid society; nor a breath of scientific air, nor a spark of intellectual electricity." After seven years at Silver Bluff on the Savannah River, James H. Hammond called his neighbors "the most ignorant, vulgar & I may add most narrow minded set of people in the world. There is not a soul to whom I can converse of anything save neighborhood news & crops." [23]

"This gives Georgia elections the character of drama." Quoted in Clement Eaton, *Freedom of Thought in the Old South* (Durham, 1940), 83.

[21] Ulrich Bonnell Phillips, *Life and Labor in the Old South* (reprint ed.; New York, 1929), 110; United States Census Office, *Compendium of the . . . Sixth Census of the United States: 1840* (Washington, 1841), 75.

[22] John Hope Franklin, *The Militant South, 1800–1861* (Cambridge, Mass., 1956), 131.

[23] Freidel, *Francis Lieber*, 129; James H. Hammond diary, July 3, 1841, quoted in Clement Eaton, *The Growth of Southern Civilization* (New York, 1963), 297.

Of 235,532 North Carolinians employed in 1840, 217,095 or more than 92 percent were engaged in agriculture. Small farmers and poor whites made up the great majority. In 1850, 69 percent of the farms of North Carolina had less than 100 acres; more than 72 percent of the families held no slaves.[24] A large propertyless class of poor whites formed the base of the economic pyramid: farm hands, tenants, squatters, and ne'er-do-wells. It was this class that appalled northern soldiers during the Civil War. "I tell you," wrote one invading Yankee, "people of the North have very little idea of the ignorance and degradation of the citizens of the South." [25] Enervated by hookworm, malaria, and alcoholism, the poor whites were, according to Fanny Kemble, "the most degraded race of human beings claiming an Anglo-Saxon origin that can be found on the face of the earth." [26]

The downtrodden could take comfort in religion. If North Carolina was typical, about half of the people belonged to a church, and of those belonging about 80 percent were either Methodists or Baptists. Aristocratic Whigs were more likely to be Episcopalians or Presbyterians.[27] A restraining orthodoxy had replaced the religious skepticism which prevailed among the eighteenth century gentry. The Mississippi Constitution of 1830 barred from public office those who denied the existence "of God or a future state of rewards and punishments." [28] The unrestrained exhortations of Methodist and Baptist preachers readied listeners for high-pitched political harangues. Great revivals at Red River and Cane Ridge, Kentucky, were duplicated throughout the South, leaving an undisciplined heritage of emotionalism. Participants joined in shouting their

[24] Guion Griffis Johnson, *Ante-Bellum North Carolina: A Social History* (Chapel Hill, 1937), 53, 54, 56, 65.
[25] Eaton, *The Growth of Southern Civilization*, 171.
[26] Phillips, *Life and Labor*, 347.
[27] Johnson, *Ante-Bellum North Carolina*, 353, 369.
[28] Eaton, *The Growth of Southern Civilization*, 314.

praise to God or in praying and crying "most earnestly for mercy." Those more deeply stirred were known to shake, bark, or succumb to catalepsy.[29] Consciously or unconsciously, politicians adopted revivalist techniques, including the use of rousing songs to enhance the suggestibility of oratory.

Alternately frightened and elevated by religion, isolated by geography and illiteracy, cursed by poverty and a semicolonial status, threatened by abolitionists, degraded by the slave system, fearful of slave uprising, repelled yet fascinated by thoughts of miscegenation, the antebellum Southerner provides a convenient target for Freudian analysis. Although such fears, phobias, and insecurities provided themes for impassioned oratory, Whig demagogues were not motivated by Freudian but by economic impulses—an unsophisticated hankering for office and the financial advantages which accompany political success.

In presidential elections from 1836 to 1852 Whigs won only in 1840 and 1848 when leaders resorted to demagoguery, abandoning the defense of party principles, rejecting attempts to formulate a party platform, and nominating military heroes with ambiguous political convictions. In the "log-cabin and hard-cider" campaign of 1840 they cynically took the position that "passion and prejudice, properly aroused and directed, would do about as well as reason." Again in 1848 they refused to acknowledge responsibility "for any of the old whig measures," and as one Georgia Democrat complained, they "won't tell what they are for, and go it blind for Taylor as a slaveholder and a hero." Representatives of the aristocracy assumed plebeian manners and campaigned in coonskin caps and linsey-woolsey. "I have always accomodated [sic] my *habits* and Dress when electioneering," said one North Carolina Whig. "I have always dressed *chiefly in Home spun* when go-

29 Johnson, *Ante-Bellum North Carolina*, 394–95, 405–406. See also Bernard Weisberger, *They Gathered at the River* (Boston, 1958), 24 ff.

ing among the people. . . . Wit, Pleasantry, & Anecdote are the weapons for execution. Arguments like cannon will not do for every day fighting."[30]

Characteristic of Whig dissimulation was the stumping expedition which took the fastidious Hugh Legaré into five states during the campaign of 1840. This former congressman from South Carolina, onetime editor of the *Southern Review*, and erudite student of Greek mythology and Roman law donned coonskin for raucous appearances at cabin raisings and barbecues. Stimulated by hard cider and hope of victory, the classical orator whose chaste speeches were once compared to "the flights of an eagle, or the murmuring of a dove" abused the "small-beer statesmen" of the Van Buren administration in the idiom of a backcountry redneck.[31] "The classical Mr. Legaré, so famous for his *learned* allusions to the Romans, the Spartans, the Macedonians, the Persians, the Medes, the Parthians, the Cappadocians, &c. has lately tried his hand at another style," observed the Washington *Globe*. "Instead of expatiating upon Sparta and Lycurgus and Dorian polity . . . 'the eloquent H.S. Legaré' discourses right sturdily about 'gammon,' and 'scare crow,' and 'scape goat,' &c. Although in a different line, the learned gentlemen's phraseology is, as usual, extremely picturesque."[32]

Their linsey-woolsey notwithstanding, aristocrats were not at home on the hustings. Whigs needed authentic frontier spokesmen like Jackson to convince voters that they represented the newly enfranchised masses. One such spokesman soon presented himself with ghostwritten hyperbole caricaturing the

[30] Richard Smith Elliott, *Notes Taken in Sixty Years* (St. Louis, 1883), 120–21; W. H. Hull to Howell Cobb, July 22, 1848, quoted in Cole, *The Whig Party in the South*, 132; James Graham to W. A. Graham, May 20, 1840, in Hamilton (ed.), *Graham Papers*, II, 92.

[31] Linda Rhea, *Hugh Swinton Legaré, A Charleston Intellectual* (Chapel Hill, 1934), 183, 191–93; Gunderson, *Log-Cabin Campaign*, 199–200.

[32] Washington *Globe*, August 13, 1840.

untamed West: "I'm . . . David Crockett, fresh from the back-woods, half-horse, half-alligator, a little touched with the snapping-turtle; can wade the Mississippi, leap the Ohio, ride upon a streak of lightning, and slip without a scratch down a honey locust." [33] The irrepressible Tennessean hardly needed to add, "I'll wear no man's collar." An intrepid scout who once served under Old Hickory in the Creek War, Davy boasted of his lack of education. Correct spelling, he insisted, was "contrary to nature," and grammar was "nothing at all." Although he flourished in the romantic role of bear hunter and Indian fighter, he failed miserably in the realistic drudgery of farming. Capturing the fancy of his compatriots, he was sent to Congress as a Jacksonian, but he broke with his former chief and marshaled his frontier wit in behalf of Whiggery.[34]

Though refusing to wear Jackson's collar, Davy was duped into becoming a dancing bear for the Bank of the United States. Indebted to Nicholas Biddle who magnanimously wrote off at least one of his notes "as a loss," Crockett fulsomely assured him that "for Your friend-Ship to me You Shall never be forgotten by your friend & obt Servt." Thus committed, the "Coonskin Congressman" relied thereafter upon Whig ghost-writers for his congressional speeches. Intensifying his denunciations, he called Jackson "a greater tyrant than Cromwell, Caesar or Bonaparte" and predicted that "the will of Andrew, the first king, is to be the law of the land." He even suggested that government money "might be in his royal Majesty's pock-

---

[33] *Sketches and Eccentricities of Col. David Crockett* quoted in Parrington, *The Romantic Revolution in America*, 176.

[34] Even at the time of his first election to Congress, Crockett's Jacksonianism was under suspicion, particularly since he voted against Old Hickory for the Senate during a term in the Tennessee legislature. He nevertheless claimed that "during my first sessions in Congress . . . I worked along with what was called the Jackson party pretty well." [David Crockett], *Life of David Crockett, The Original Humorist and Irrepressible Backwoodsman* . . . (New York, n. d.), 138, 166; *Dictionary of American Biography*, IV, 555–56.

et, or in the pocket of that imp of famine, his fourth auditor [Amos Kendall]."[35] Democratic social reforms were like shearing a pig, with a "big squeal and little wool." Congress was "a better place to manufacture orators than to dispatch business." He complained, "No one can imagine what dreadful hard work it is to keep awake and listen to what's said. Splitting gum logs in August is nothing beside it."[36]

Annoyed by Crockett's demagoguery, Jacksonian congressmen testified that "he was the last man in the house that a stranger would have pitched upon as a wit and humourist." Congressman William J. Grayson of South Carolina described him as "a dull, heavy, almost stupid man, in appearance. I never heard him utter a word that savoured of wit or sense."[37]

In spite of his ghostwritten humor and lack of sense, Crockett aroused a great pseudoequalitarian outcry for Whiggery during his celebrated tour of the North in April and May of 1834. Deserting his post in Congress for almost three weeks, the peripatetic backwoodsman made appearances in Baltimore, Philadelphia, New York, Jersey City, Newport, Boston, Lowell, Providence, and Camden. Although prominent eastern Whigs had planned, financed, and rigged the tour right down to the last rustic peroration, gawking crowds nevertheless trampled one another, as Davy rightly supposed, "to see the wild man" from the canebrakes.[38] Apologizing because he was "a plain, unlearned man . . . hardly . . . fitted to address the people

[35] Joseph Gales and William W. Seaton of the Washington *National Intelligencer* apparently wrote "many of his speeches." James Atkins Shackford, *David Crockett: The Man and the Legend* (Chapel Hill, 1956), 124, 152, 167, 171, 287.

[36] Charles S. Sydnor, *The Development of Southern Sectionalism, 1819–1848* (Baton Rouge, 1948), 290; Shackford, *David Crockett*, 191.

[37] Kenneth S. Lynn, *Mark Twain and Southwestern Humor* (Boston, 1959), 36–37.

[38] David Crockett, *An Account of Colonel Crockett's Tour to the North and Down East . . .* (Philadelphia, 1835); Crockett, *Life*, 175; Shackford, *David Crockett*, 156–62. Shackford identifies William Clark as author of *Crockett's Tour to the North*, 163.

of Boston," he had sufficient self-assurance to denounce Democrats: "I had rather be a *nigger's* man or a rackoon dog than to belong to such a party." [39] He accepted a handsome rifle from the Whigs of Philadelphia and a broadcloth suit from Abbott Lawrence of Massachusetts; he worried for fear Harvard might grant him an honorary degree, as it had to President Jackson. In Lowell he admired the "ladies of the loom," observing that after work they "looked as if they were coming from a quilting frolic." More significantly, he changed his views on the tariff and "wished that some of the leading politicians of the southern states, would visit the new England manufactures." The fanfare resounded southward, and a Mississippi Whig convention proposed Crockett for the presidency. [40]

Voters of West Tennessee, however, showed greater discrimination. Throughout the summer of 1835 Crockett "bushwhacked" his district "in the most approved style," regaling listeners with anecdotes and striking metaphors, but on election day in August he was "completely rascalled out" of Congress by the "villainy" of his Jacksonian opponents. [41] Failure to secure passage of his "squatter relief" bill contributed to his defeat, but his support of Biddle and the tariff cannot be discounted. In a pique the former congressman abandoned his wife and family and set out for a hero's death in Texas, faithful to his well-publicized motto: "Be allways [*sic*] sure you are right, then Go, ahead." [42] His last political legacy, a scurrilous *Life of Martin Van Buren* ghostwritten by a more literate accomplice, characterized its subject as an effeminate dandy who forgot "all his old companions and friends in humbler walks of life."Concluded Davy in a narrative calculated to end Matty's

[39] *Niles' Weekly Register*, XLVI (June 7, 1834).

[40] Crockett, *Life*, 214, 216, 223–24; *Niles' Weekly Register*, XLVI (June 7, 1834).

[41] Crockett, *Life*, 247–48.

[42] *Niles' Weekly Register*, XLIX (December 5, 1835); Shackford, *David Crockett*, 136.

political career, "He struts and swaggers like a crow in a gutter. It would be difficult to say from his personal appearance, whether he was a man or woman, but for his large *red* and *gray* whiskers." Whig orators declaimed these slanders for several campaigns to come. Davy's demagoguery has been called "a hoked-up synthetic mixture," but it served as a deadly venom to Van Buren in 1840, four years after the Alamo.[43]

Although most southern Whigs supported Henry Clay for the presidential nomination at the Harrisburg Convention in 1839, they willingly switched to the nominee, William Henry Harrison, a somewhat tarnished military hero, because as one southern editor explained, "for the first time" they had "a popular candidate with no political sins upon his head." During the summer and fall, cider-drinking strategists kept Old Tip's name on every lip. In Louisiana, politics "all but excluded the more prosaic pursuits." [44] In Raleigh, North Carolina, Whigs raised a log cabin called "Harrison Hall," where after three-hour "oratorical feasts," prominent local women, "appropriately gowned in calico," served "barbecue and brandy." In Virginia seventeen communities raised log cabin Whig headquarters, and each cabin-raising served as an occasion for oratory.[45] Whig presidential electors served as "Slangwhanging Missionaries" with assignments to "traverse their districts, mount the stumps, abuse the Administration, puff the military chieftain, and gull the People." Never had Thomas Ritchie, editor of the Richmond *Enquirer*, seen Whigs "so fanatical, so desperate in their purposes or so reckless in their means." Great

[43] David Crockett, *The Life of Martin Van Buren* (Philadelphia, 1835), 80–81. Shackford identifies Augustin Smith Clayton, congressman from Georgia, as the likely author. Shackford, *David Crockett*, 188–89; Lynn, *Mark Twain*, 68.

[44] Lexington *Observer & Reporter*, August 29, 1840; Leslie M. Norton, "A History of the Whig Party in Louisiana" (Ph.D. dissertation, Louisiana State University, 1940), 162.

[45] Simms, *The Rise of the Whigs in Virginia*, 148; Johnson, *Ante-Bellum North Carolina*, 150.

117

Whig conventions were staged in Wheeling, Richmond, Alexandria, Baltimore, Little Rock, and Nashville. "Since the world began," exclaimed Senator John J. Crittenden of Kentucky, "there was never before ... such a glorious excitement & uproar among the people." [46] George D. Prentice, editor of the Louisville *Journal,* published anti-Van Buren epigrams which provided Whig stump speakers with a convenient source of humor. Even Whig women were mobilized. "This way of making politicians of their women is something new under the sun," observed a Georgia Democrat, "but so it is they go to the strife." [47]

Nathan Sargent, a Whig congressional observer, claimed that five thousand or more Whig speakers were "on the stump." Former Congressman Seargent S. Prentiss of Mississippi, "one of the greatest of the great guns of the Whigs," cannonaded from his home in Vicksburg to his birthplace in Maine and back, appearing in nine states before audiences varying from two to six thousand. Reporters exclaimed about the "fertility of his illustration," his "power of ridicule," and his "infinite copiousness of nervous language," but often failed to mention the substance of his speeches. Among other things, Prentiss stalwartly defended "the fair flower of womanhood" from "the pestilential effluvia" of Democratic Locofocos. "The man who does not appreciate the Log Cabin," he concluded, "can feel no sympathy with the associations of our national flag." [48]

[46] Richmond *Enquirer,* February 20 and 27, 1840; John J. Crittenden to Daniel Webster, October 27, 1840, quoted in Frederick Jackson Turner, *The United States, 1830–1850, the Nation and Its Sections* (New York, 1935), 482.

[47] William H. Venable, *Beginnings of Literary Culture in the Ohio Valley* (Cincinnati, 1891), 398; A. P. Powers to Howell Cobb, October, n. d., 1840, quoted in Cole, *The Whig Party in the South,* 60–61.

[48] Nathan Sargent, *Public Men and Events* . . . (2 vols.; Philadelphia, 1875), II, 108; Dickey, *Seargent S. Prentiss,* 174–75, 178, 192–93; Cleveland *Herald,* July 27, 1840; Washington *National Intelligencer,* July 8 and August 3, 1840; Norton, "Whig Party in Louisiana," 159.

Senator William Preston of South Carolina campaigned in six states, describing the contest as one between the people and a "trained corps of Janissaries" led by Martin Van Buren, "the Chief Spoiler at Washington." Elaborating on the slanders of Davy Crockett, Preston described the President as "that prince of modern Democrats" with "his superb English coach, four blood horses, and liveried outriders." In "torrents of withering invective," the South Carolina senator denounced the "long black catalogue of crime which lies at the door of the Administration." If Van Buren could not be removed by ballot, he declared, "I, for one, am ready to resort to such means as GOD and NATURE have put in my reach, to FORCE a change." [49]

Although quite ill at ease in the hard cider fanfaronade of 1840, the austere vice-presidential candidate, John Tyler, was prevailed upon to campaign in Ohio and Pennsylvania, as well as in his home state of Virginia. Concealing his differences with Whig sentiment on the bank and the tariff, Tyler engaged in long flights of patriotic fancy, doing obeisance to his revolutionary ancestors, and talking hopefully of "deliverance" from "the oppression of domestic tyranny." [50]

Tyler's fellow Virginians, the excitable Henry A. Wise and the diminutive William C. Rives, were more at home on the stump than was the genteel squire from Williamsburg. "A model partisan speaker," Wise was so annoyed over the "reckless course of the Administration," that he sometimes labored under an "excitement evidently too deep for words." In one outburst, he proclaimed that he favored "any decent *white* man in the nation" in preference to Van Buren.[51] After leaving the Democratic Party in 1838 Rives, leader of the Virginia Conser-

---

[49] Washington *National Intelligencer*, July 17, 1840; *Niles' Weekly Register*, LVIII (May 9, 1840); Washington *Globe*, August 1, 1840.

[50] Washington *National Intelligencer*, September 21 and 26, 1840; Gunderson, *The Log-Cabin Campaign*, 195–98.

[51] *Niles' Weekly Register*, LVIII (April 18, 1840); Washington *National Intelligencer*, July 11, 1840.

vatives, turned on his former associates with a fury that astonished Thomas Ritchie, who could hardly believe "that such a volcano could have been compressed into any little man's bosom." Said the editor of the *Enquirer*, "The burning lava is poured out in torrents." In florid, verbose speeches of four hours' duration Rives predicted that although "the ark of liberty has been wafted about by the tide of misrule . . . , seven months hence it shall rest upon some Ararat, and there shall be restored to us the olive branch of peace—the emblem of returning health and prosperity to the nation." [52]

The successful demagoguery of 1840 provided a model for the Whig canvass of 1848. At the Philadelphia convention southern Whigs abandoned their longtime favorite, Henry Clay, in favor of a military hero who had never voted in his life. Even a majority of the Kentucky delegation voted for Taylor, a Louisiana slaveholder. Horace Greeley called the convention "a slaughterhouse of Whig principles." [53] As in 1840, delegates failed to adopt a platform. None was needed, said the New Orleans *Bulletin*, save "the broad platform of the Constitution." Astute party managers fully appreciated the advantages of political ambivalence, particularly on the slavery issue now intensified by squabbles over territorial expansion. "One great advantage the Whigs have in argument is that they have no common platform . . . ," grumbled one Georgia Democrat; they "take the most ultra Southern ground and abuse us as traitors to the South for not going as far as they do." [54]

As hero of Palo Alto and Buena Vista, Old Rough and Ready commanded popular attention. Whigs heralded him as "a second Washington," a fiction Old Zack encouraged by maintain-

[52] Richmond *Enquirer*, April 21, 1840; Washington *National Intelligencer*, April 18, 1840.
[53] Holman Hamilton, *Zachary Taylor: Soldier in the White House* (Indianapolis, 1951), 20, 87–97.
[54] New Orleans *Bulletin*, n.d., quoted in *Niles' Weekly Register*, LXXIV (July 19, 1848); Phillips, "*The Southern Whigs*," 220.

ing a perverse political impartiality, even going to the point of saying that he also would have accepted the Democratic nomination "had it been tendered on the same terms." [55] While such Olympian nonpartisanship annoyed zealots, realistic Whigs knew that "if the great mass of the people" were "to be rallied to the support of one man,—it must be some man whose name has not been for years the watchword of party divisions." [56] In a series of letters, some ghostwritten, Taylor confused voters by outlining his enigmatic positions on major issues: the Wilmot Proviso was "a mere bugbare [sic]"; the tariff was the responsibility of Congress; the national bank was a dead issue; internal improvements would continue regardless of the party in power; the South should protect slavery where it existed by force of arms if necessary. He had no sympathy for extremists. "I AM A WHIG," he concluded, "but not an ultra-Whig." [57]

Clay's southern supporters were of course dismayed, complaining that Taylor was "an *Ultra* Slaveholder & no particular Whig." [58] But, like Harrison, Old Rough and Ready roused support in areas not normally Whig. Orators emphasized his southern birth, his slaveholding, his distinguished forty-year military career, and his lack of partisanship. According to W. H. Hull, a Georgia Democrat, Whig speeches consisted "of three parts—miscellaneous abuse of Cass and the Democrats, comments on the danger to slavery, and the impossibility of trusting any Northern man . . . and lasting glorification of Old Taylor's battles. I have never heard one of them advance a principle." Governor Crittenden of Kentucky, one of Taylor's

[55] Joseph Rayback, "Who Wrote the Allison Letters: A Study in Historical Detection," *Mississippi Valley Historical Review*, XXXVI (1949), 54.
[56] New York *Courier* & *Enquirer*, September 6, 1847, in *Niles' Weekly Register*, LXXIII (September 11, 1847).
[57] *Dictionary of American Biography*, XVIII, 349-55; Rayback, "Allison Letters," 51-72; *Niles' Weekly Register*, LXXIV (July 8, 1848); Hamilton, *Zachary Taylor*, 79-81, 121-24.
[58] Kirwan, *John J. Crittenden*, 222-23.

most influential supporters, directed the last stages of the campaign, sending Kentuckians Charles S. Todd, Leslie Combs, Robert P. Letcher, and Thomas Metcalfe to exhort voters in critical districts of both the North and the South. In Tennessee, John Bell lauded Taylor as a candidate on whom "the honest and patriotic of all parties could unite." [59] In Louisiana, Balie Peyton, Judah P. Benjamin, and Seargent Prentiss "exposed the shuffling and unsoundness" of the Democratic candidate, Lewis Cass, "on the subject of slavery," and made the Bayou State "ring with one loud acclaim for noble old Zack." Cass was, cried Prentiss, an apostate "among the mongrel host of free-soilers, abolitionists, amalgamationists, and vote-yourself-a-farm men." Throughout the country, Whig crowds encouraged their orators by repeating the General's order at Buena Vista: "A little more grape, Mr. Bragg." [60]

In Washington congressmen organized a Whig "Executive Committee" to supply "every section of the country" with political pamphlets and to assist with party organization. The Committee promoted a "Rough and Ready" campaign paper, *The Battery*, and maintained a busy "document room." A former Kentuckian, Abraham Lincoln, remained after the close of Congress to assist in these operations. Among the speeches for distribution was his burlesque of Cass, "a General of splendidly successful *charges*—charges, to be sure not upon the public enemy, but upon the public Treasury." Another popular document was the speech of Alexander H. Stephens of Georgia denouncing the Democratic administration for precipitating the Mexican War. "My old, withered, dry eyes are full of tears yet," Lincoln wrote his law partner, William H. Herndon, after

---

[59] W. H. Hull to Howell Cobb, July 22, 1848, quoted in Cole, *The Whig Party in the South*, 132; Kirwan, *John J. Crittenden*, 232 ff; Charles S. Todd scrapbook, The Filson Club, Lexington, Kentucky; Joseph Howard Parks, *John Bell of Tennessee* (Baton Rouge, 1950), 232.

[60] Dickey, *Seargent S. Prentiss*, 327, 328, 330; Dorothy Burne Goebel and Julius Goebel, Jr., *Generals in the White House* (Garden City, 1952), 132.

hearing it delivered. In establishing Rough and Ready Clubs he
suggested that each member "play the part he can play best—
some speak, some sing, and all hallow." The club in Raleigh,
North Carolina, met every week for "very enthusiastic meetings." Those of Georgia fed "the wool-hat boys of Cherokee
and the pine barrens . . . a steady diet of barbecue and
eighteenth-century natural-rights political philosophy." [61]

Following accepted protocol for presidential aspirants, Old
Zack modestly avoided the semblance of electioneering. Although he occasionally turned up at Rough and Ready barbecues in Louisiana and Mississippi, he confined himself to a discussion of his military exploits. He even refused an opportunity
to appear in Indiana for an anniversary celebration of his defense of Fort Harrison during the Indian wars. His silence on
political matters was interpreted, in the idiom of the day, as
"a mash for anti-slavery opinions." Silence was the better part
of Whig political strategy, if not of valor; Taylor could rely
upon his noisy partisans who cheered him into the presidency
that November:

> Then go it, boys, strong and steady
> And raise the shout for Rough and Ready. [62]

At his inaugural on March 5, 1849, President-elect Taylor
was escorted to the Capitol from Willard's Hotel by a procession which included the Rough and Ready Clubs of Washington, Georgetown, Alexandria, and Baltimore "with banners,
badges and music," a bodyguard of a hundred Whigs "mounted
on spirited horses," and the students of Georgetown College.
An observer of many such pageants described Old Zack as
"not imposing," with short legs and a "portly" figure; thin,

[61] Roy P. Basler (ed.), *The Collected Works of Abraham Lincoln* (9
vols.; New Brunswick, 1953), I, 491, 498, 512, 517; II, 1; Lincoln to W. H.
Herndon, February 2, 1848, and June 22, 1848, *ibid.*, I, 448, 491; Hamilton
(ed.), *Graham Papers*, III, 244; Montgomery, *Cracker Parties*, 9.
[62] Hamilton, *Zachary Taylor*, 103, 119, 127, 128.

gray unbrushed hair; "weather-bronzed and care-furrowed" features; and whiskers of the prescribed "military cut." At the East Portico of the Capitol the President-elect read his address "almost inaudibly," [63] and "very badly as to his pronunciation and manner," [64] but the crowd of some twenty thousand nevertheless greeted his conclusion with "vociferous cheering." [65] Democrats complained of his noncommittal platitudes and ultra-Whig federalism; Whigs applauded his simple, direct, Republican style and his strict adherence to constitutional principles.[66]

Although the only southern Whig to become President, Taylor can hardly be classified as a representative southern Whig speaker. His brief, platitudinous inaugural, one of the shortest in history, was undistinguished by felicitous phrase or invigorating idea. Senator William H. Seward of New York called it "negative and general." [67] The new President proclaimed his "fixed determination to maintain . . . the Government in its original purity and to adopt the basis of . . . public policy those great republican doctrines which constitute the strength of our national existence." He repeated Jefferson's warning against "entangling alliances"; promised to make "honesty, capacity, and fidelity indispensable prerequisites to the bestowal of office"; and urged "prudence and moderation," hoping to "assuage the bitterness which too often marks unavoidable differences of opinion." [68]

In his plea for moderation Taylor might well have alluded to the closing hours of the Thirtieth Congress which featured a fistfight in the Senate and blood-spilling on the floor of the

[63] Poore, Benjamin Perley, *Perley's Reminiscences of Sixty Years in the National Metropolis* (2 vols.; Philadelphia, 1886), I, 353–54.

[64] James K. Polk quoted in Hamilton, *Zachary Taylor*, 159.

[65] Poore, *Perley's Reminiscences*, I, 353–54.

[66] *Dictionary of American Biography*, XVIII, 352.

[67] Hamilton, *Zachary Taylor*, 158.

[68] James D. Richardson (ed.), *A Compilation of the Messages and Papers of the Presidents, 1789–1897* (9 vols.; n. p., 1898), V, 4–6.

House.[69] The flamboyant demagoguery of 1840 and 1848 had aroused passions and intensified existing tensions over critical economic issues, but perhaps it diverted attention somewhat from the engrossing moral question of slavery. With all the cheering for Tip and Zack, Whigs attracted a new nationwide audience, an audience content to find party unity in identification with past military victories and a mindless reiteration of catchy shibboleths. Inevitably, however, demagoguery provoked violence, particularly in the South where a frontier heritage of self-assertive individualism and chip-on-the-shoulder pride conspired to demand catharsis.[70] Log cabin headquarters and Rough and Ready Clubs stood as targets for stonings, if not arson. Orators sometimes spoke with pistols at full cock. "You ought to have side Arms with you [while campaigning]," advised a correspondent of Governor Graham of North Carolina, "to be ready for any contingency." "Little Alec" Stephens was knifed by a Democratic orator in Georgia, a mishap which Whigs exploited to their advantage. After calling his opponent "a liar a scoundrel and a Coward," Whig Thomas A. R. Nelson of Tennessee willingly offered to place his life on the field of honor.[71] When sallying forth to champion Whiggery, Cassius Marcellus Clay of Kentucky, a belligerent distant cousin of the more moderate Henry, carried a bowie knife and a brace of pistols. During oratorical festivities at Russell's Cave, Kentucky, a notorious brawler fired at him with a "six-barrelled" pistol almost at arm's reach. Although struck by the shot,

---

[69] Hamilton, *Zachary Taylor*, 153.

[70] Cash, *The Mind of the South*, 55–56; Franklin, *The Militant South*, 131–32. It is wrong to conclude, of course, that the South had a monopoly on violence during this period. Philip Hone complained that in New York "riot and violence stalk unchecked through the streets." Allan Nevins (ed.), *The Diary of Philip Hone* (2 vols.; New York, 1927), entry for November 3, 1840, I, 506.

[71] James Graham to W. A. Graham, April 7, 1846, in Hamilton (ed.), *Graham Papers*, III, 115; Hamilton, *Zachary Taylor*, 108; Alexander, "Thomas A. R. Nelson," 24.

Clay unsheathed his bowie knife, cleaved his antagonist's skull, gouged out an eye, cut off an ear, and tossed his mangled body over a nearby cliff. Surprisingly, both lived to testify to the hazards of political speaking in the prewar South.[72]

Whig demagoguery in 1840 and 1848 can be contrasted with a Whig tradition of responsible conservatism and moderation. Epitomizing this spirit, Henry Clay spent a lifetime in an attempt to build a federal unity based upon economic nationalism and negotiated adjustment of the controversy over slavery. Unlike his contentious cousin, Clay found the role of compromiser congenial both to his political situation and his personal taste. Representing a border state with close economic ties north and south of the Ohio, he designed his American System to promote national unity, with a tariff to encourage industry, a bank to stimulate commerce, and internal improvements to develop better markets for agriculture, a program identified with him for almost three decades. Before the founding of the Whig Party, he championed the Missouri Compromise as a means of settling the slavery controversy. Continuing in his role as "The Great Pacificator," he negotiated the Compromise Tariff of 1833. Although greeting news of his defeat for the Whig nomination in 1840 with understandable rage, he nevertheless magnanimously campaigned for the ticket, thus demonstrating a disposition to compromise even in the face of humiliating sacrifice. "Let him who elevates himself above humanity, above its weaknesses, its infirmities, its wants, its necessities, say, if he pleases, I never will compromise," he concluded, "but let no one who is not above the frailties of our common nature disdain compromises." [73]

[72] William H. Townsend, *Hundred Proof: Salt River Sketches & Memoirs of the Bluegrass* (Lexington, 1964), 122–23; see also David Smiley, *Lion of White Hall: The Life of Cassius M. Clay* (Madison, 1962).

[73] Ernest J. Wrage, "Henry Clay," in William Norwood Brigance (ed.), *A History and Criticism of American Public Address* (2 vols.; New York, 1943), II, 623–24.

Contemporaries applauded Clay's common sense, his effective use of the vernacular, and above all his warm, if not to say impassioned, oratory. His many devoted friends joined George D. Prentice, editor of the Louisville *Journal*, in proclaiming him "the first orator, the greatest statesman, and the most distinguished benefactor of his country":

We have listened to all our great public men. If we wanted a grammarian in the ancient sense of the word, we would take Mr. Calhoun, whose mind seems to have no fixed views of truth; if we wanted the clearest demonstration of a given proposition, we would have none but Webster, the greatest logician that lives; if we desired the aid of all that is rich, full, and overwhelming in true eloquence, Preston is the man; if we needed the clearest, purest and most beautiful advocacy of all right and noble things, Crittenden is the living model; but if we desire to know the truth, to be taught the right, to be kept from delusion, to be set in the way in which we ought to walk for our country's good, and to be supported in the noble race, then Henry Clay is the true guide.[74]

An early biographer, Carl Schurz, thought that the "rare brightness" of Clay's intellect made listeners forget "his lack of accurate knowledge and studious thought." In print, his speeches have what Schurz described as a "heavy tameness." [75] Yet he could say commonplace things so as to arouse enthusiastic conviction. A Capitol correspondent declared that he was "formed by nature for a popular orator." His "spirit stirring" appeals were the result of his dramatically effective delivery.[76] "Much of Mr. Clay's oratorical power," said Nathan Sargent, "consisted in that 'action' recommended by Demosthenes." Although sometimes careless in his choice of words and epithets,

[74] Louisville *Journal*, n. d., quoted in *Niles' Weekly Register*, LXXIII (August 10 and September 11, 1847).

[75] Carl Schurz, *Life of Henry Clay* (2 vols.; Boston, 1895), II, 408–409.

[76] Poore, *Perley's Reminiscences*, I, 33–35, 143–45; clipping from Diary of Fayette B. Tower, February 27, 1841, in William H. Harrison MSS, New York Public Library.

Clay often escaped criticism because of his basic good humor and friendly personality. While practicing emotionalism, he opposed it in principle: "I lament the necessity, real or imaginary . . . of appealing to the feelings and passions of our Countrymen, rather than to their reasons and their judgments." [77]

Clay painstakingly rebuilt the Whig organization after the congressional caucus in effect read Tyler out of the party in 1841. Rallying all except a "corporal's guard," Clay outlined a positive economic program of conservatism designed to give the party a national coherence. Increased commerce and manufacturing in the South made an increased tariff and a national bank more palatable to southern Whigs, and the Great Compromiser demonstrated moderation in promoting the upward tariff revision of 1842, an act which brought new enthusiasm for Whiggery in northern industrial areas and subsequent presidential support for Clay.[78] Indeed, so cheering were prospects, Clay saw "scarcely a speck in the whole political horizon." [79] On a trip through the South in the spring of 1844, "immense concourses" greeted "The Farmer of Ashland" at Milledgeville, Savannah, Charleston, and Raleigh.[80] Northern and southern Whigs at last had resolved their differences on the issues of the Jacksonian era.

But a new era was at hand, an era of controversy over territorial expansion intensified by the combustible problem of slavery. In a futile attempt to remove the disagreeable issue from politics, both Clay and Van Buren, the leading presidential contenders, in 1844 claimed no immediate necessity for the annexation of Texas, a decision which cost Van Buren the nom-

[77] Sargent, *Public Men and Events*, II, 34; Clay to John J. Crittenden, July 31, 1840, quoted in Glyndon Van Deusen, *The Life of Henry Clay* (Boston, 1937), 334.

[78] Cole, *The Whig Party in the South*, 64 ff., 100, 102.

[79] Clay to William A. Graham, February 6, 1844, in Hamilton (ed.), *Graham Papers*, II, 473.

[80] *Niles' Weekly Register*, LXVI (April 13 and 20, May 11, and July 6, 1844).

ination and Clay the election.[81] When it became apparent that many Southerners favored annexation, Clay retreated from his initial position, claiming in the Alabama letters that he "should be glad to see" annexation "without dishonor, without war, with the common consent of the Union, and upon just and fair terms." [82] Equivocation of this sort jeopardized his ethical appeal. The Great Compromiser was, according to his enemies, "abashed by no inconsistency, disturbed by no contradiction . . . and void of both moral and intellectual conscience." [83] The straightforward jingoism of the Democrats won the Presidency, defeating Clay even with an unredeemed mediocrity in the person of James K. Polk, twice defeated candidate for governor of Tennessee. Whigs everywhere were stunned by what to many was a very personal loss. "Yesterday we had the solemn ceremony of the Electoral College," mourned one Tar Heel partisan, "and I felt as though I were at the obsequies of a departed friend." [84]

In opposing the annexation of Texas, Clay had the support of both northern and southern Whigs in Congress. Every southern Whig senator except John Henderson of Mississippi voted against Tyler's annexation treaty.[85] But northern and southern motivations differed. Fearful of competition with Texas cotton, wealthy Whig planters opposed opening Texas lands which might depress the market; northern industrialists opposed any expansion which might reduce the labor supply. The perilous motivation, however, was northern Whig opposition to extension of slavery, a matter which threatened to disrupt the party. When Polk's policies precipitated the anticipated war with

[81] Washington *National Intelligencer,* April 27, 1844.
[82] *Niles' Weekly Register,* LXVI (August 31, 1844).
[83] *Brownson's Quarterly,* n. d., in *Niles' Weekly Register,* LXVI (July 13, 1844).
[84] Hugh Waddell to W. A. Graham, December 5, 1844, in Hamilton (ed.), *Graham Papers,* II, 530.
[85] Cole, *The Whig Party in the South,* 111.

Mexico, Whigs were torn between patriotism and party principle. Clay eloquently opposed acquiring "any foreign territory whatever, for the purpose of propagating slavery." Senator John M. Berrien of Georgia introduced a resolution that the war with Mexico "ought not to be prosecuted ... with any view to the dismemberment of that republic, or to the acquisition, by conquest, of any portion of her territory," a declaration supported by Whigs William S. Archer of Virginia, George E. Badger and Willie P. Mangum of North Carolina, Thomas Clayton and John M. Clayton of Delaware, John J. Crittenden and James T. Morehead of Kentucky, Reverdy Johnson and James A. Pearce of Maryland.[86] Perhaps Robert Toombs of Georgia was most eloquent of all: "It matters not," he said, "that Mexico is weak, that the acquisition is easy. The question is just the same: Is it right, is it just, is it the policy of this country to enlarge its territory by conquest? The principle is condemned by the spirit of the age, by reason, and by revelation. A people who love justice and hate wrong and oppression cannot approve it." [87]

Yet an empire was up for grabs and venal men both north and south sought not only political but economic advantage from the new territory. Enticed by possibilities of trade and commerce, as well as by a heady romanticism, some imaginative Southerners dreamed of a great slave empire. In an early reflection of this spirit, Preston had forecast manifest destiny as early as 1836 with the toast: "To the western and *Pacific* progress of our language and our liberty." [88] Accompanying this dream was the kind of chauvinism which prompted Reverdy Johnson to boast that "no nation exists endowed with greater military power" and that our victories over Mexico

[86] *Niles' Weekly Register*, LXXIII (November 20, 1847, and October 23, 1847).

[87] Pleasant A. Stovall, *Robert Toombs: Statesman, Speaker, Soldier, Sage* . . . (New York, 1892), 53.

[88] *Niles' Weekly Register*, L (July 23, 1836).

furnish "ample indemnity for all the wrongs and obloquy we have heretofore suffered and ample security against their recurrence." [89] Impatient to exploit the victories, a host of land grabbers and speculators schemed to acquire a stake in the disputed territory. Others, less bold or perhaps more hungry for office, worried for fear that opposition to the war and territorial expansion would *"ruin* the Whig party." [90]

An even greater threat to Whig unity, and a continuing challenge to southern Whig equanimity and moderation, was the Wilmot Proviso, a northern effort to prohibit slavery in territory that might be thereafter annexed. Waddy Thompson of South Carolina preferred secession to acceptance of the obnoxious measure. "I yield to no man," he said, "... in a sincere attachment to this Union. In speaking of it, I shall not talk of 'its cement of the blood of our glorious ancestors—of broken pillars and shattered fragments,' nor use any of the stereotyped phrases on that subject of a *falsetto* rhetoric. My attachment to the Union is not that of a school girl or a love sick swain, but the more rational and stronger attachment of interest, of reason, and reflection. I love and cherish that Union ... because it gives us peace at home and security abroad; advances the interest and prosperity of the people, and effectually secures public liberty." Thompson's plea was: "Take no more Mexican territory," thereby avoiding the disruptive controversies over slavery and the threat of disunion.[91]

With the Wilmot Proviso promoting talk of secession, southern Whigs remained amazingly loyal to Clay's course of moderation. Tutored in a nationalistic school of politics, they declaimed against "Mr. Calhoun's desperate remedies," including the radical southern movement and the Nashville Convention.

[89] *Niles' Weekly Register*, LXXIII (January 22, 1848).
[90] James Graham to W. A. Graham, January 10, 1847, in *Graham Papers*, III, 171.
[91] *Niles' Weekly Register*, LXXIII (October 30, 1847).

Not a single Whig paper in Mississippi supported this secessionist gathering of Democratic Hotspurs, and Whig members of
southern state legislatures spoke effectively against sending delegates. Even South Carolina Whigs, including Preston, opposed secession in 1850, but clearly some dramatic proposal
was needed to end sectional animosity over the problems raised
by territorial expansion.[92]

Once again assuming his role as compromiser on January 29,
1850, Clay proposed an omnibus bill with eight sections designed to resolve the prevailing questions at issue. Holding a
"precious relic" from the coffin of President Washington, the
Kentucky Senator projected the macabre fiction that "the ven-
erated Father of his Country" was urging senators to "pause"
before destroying the Union.[93] A week later, on February 5
and 6, Clay dramatically defended his proposals with a point-
by-point exegesis. Alternately addressing his friends north and
south of the Ohio, he objectively outlined antagonistic positions
and then fervently begged his listeners to take heed of history
and human nature so as to avoid a dissolution of the Union. In
an emotional peroration, he implored his colleagues to prevent
"the extinction of this last and glorious light which is leading
all mankind":

Can you yield yourself to the tyranny of passion, amid dangers
which I have depicted in colors too tame of what the result would
be if that direful event to which I have referred should ever occur?
Sir, I implore gentlemen, I adjure them, whether from the South
or the North, by all that they hold dear in this world—by all their
love of liberty—by all their veneration for their ancestors—by all
their regard for posterity—by all their gratitude to Him who has
bestowed on them such unnumbered and countless blessings—by
all the duties which they owe to mankind—and by all the duties

92 Cole, *The Whig Party in the South*, viii, 136, 158 ff.
93 Holman Hamilton, *Prologue to Conflict: The Crisis and Compromise of
1850* (Lexington, 1964), 54.

which they owe to themselves, to pause, solemnly to pause at the edge of the precipice, before the fearful and dangerous leap be taken into the yawning abyss below, from which none who ever take it shall return in safety.

Finally, Mr. President, and in conclusion, I implore as the best blessing which Heaven can bestow upon me, upon earth, that if the direful event of the dissolution of this Union is to happen, I shall not survive to behold the sad and heart-rending spectacle.[94]

Ernest J. Wrage has rightly called Clay's compromise speech "a masterful case for his cause, replete in legal historical arguments, revealing the heart of the patriot and hand of the artist."[95]

Yet despite his eloquence Clay failed to change enough votes in the Senate. His omnibus bill was defeated on July 31. "And so the Omnibus is smashed—wheels, axles and body—nothing left but a single plank termed Utah," concluded Horace Greeley. "I even saw the gallant driver abandoning the wreck between six and seven this evening, after having done all that man could do to retrieve, or rather to avert the disaster." As Holman Hamilton has observed, "neither Clay nor any other compromiser on the floor really controlled the situation."[96]

Clay's rhetoric of conciliation contributed to an improved emotional climate, but the Compromise of 1850 that eventually passed was not the result of his stirring appeal. As Senator Robert W. Barnwell noted at the time, the machinations of the Texas bond lobby and the "ten millions of money to be paid to the Texas creditors carried the day."[97] After defeat of his omnibus, Clay left Washington for a New England vacation, leav-

---

[94] *Congressional Globe*, 31 Cong., 1st Sess., Appendix, 115–27.

[95] Wrage, "Henry Clay," 630.

[96] New York *Tribune*, August 2, 1850, quoted in Hamilton, *Prologue to Conflict*, 111; Hamilton, *Prologue to Conflict*, 109.

[97] *Ibid.*, 129; Holman Hamilton, "Texas Bonds and Northern Profits: A Study in Compromise, Investment, and Lobby Influence," *Mississippi Valley Historical Review*, XLIII (March, 1957), 579–94.

133

ing Senator Stephen A. Douglas and his moderate Democratic colleagues to recast the terms of adjustment. Of the eleven senators who consistently favored the various provisions of the compromise, eight were northern Democrats, one was a southern Democrat, and two were Border State Whigs.[98]

Although the Compromise of 1850 provided a temporary respite in the sectional controversy, it did nothing to enhance the fortunes of the Whig party. A critical feature of the compromise, the Fugitive Slave Law, antagonized many northerners who heretofore had demonstrated little sympathy for abolitionism. Antislavery or "Conscience" Whigs found scant reason for continued cooperation with their slaveholding colleagues, who, in turn, found their awkward liaison with men like Seward and Thaddeus Stevens an increasing liability in southern politics. After threatening disunion during the congressional debates, Stephens and Toombs returned to Georgia to defend the compromise and counsel moderation; but they also initiated the Constitutional Union Party, a means of divorcing themselves from the stigma of "Sewardism" and "Conscience" Whiggery.[99] Senator John Bell returned to Tennessee with thoughts of forming a "conservative Union party." [100] Less bold partisans cautiously awaited the outcome of the 1852 convention.

To entice voters in 1852, Whigs nominated another military hero, General Winfield Scott, "Old Fuss and Feathers," a perennial candidate genuinely unpopular in the South. Although born in Virginia, Scott had long been associated with the political schemes of New York Boss Thurlow Weed and Senator Seward, who doggedly sustained him through fifty-three ballots. "I felt dis-heartened, disappointed and grieved at the result of the balloting," came a typical reaction from North Car-

[98] Hamilton, *Prologue to Conflict,* 135, 143, 149
[99] *Ibid.,* 170; Cole, *The Whig Party in the South,* 180–83.
[100] Parks, *John Bell,* 140.

olina, "for I feared we would not well rid ourselves of the idea that it was a triumph of Sewardism, and a reproach upon Southern men of a want of true chivalry, in abandoning such a standard-bearer as Mr. Fillmore." To compensate somewhat for a presidential nominee distasteful to Southerners, delegates fashioned a platform congenial to them and selected former Governor William A. Graham of North Carolina for the vice-presidency. But Scott failed to endorse the platform, and influential southern Whigs like Stephens, Toombs, Thomas L. Clingman, and William G. Brownlow failed to support the candidate. Those who did lacked enthusiasm. Graham's nomination, said one North Carolinian, "was the only way in which the bitter cup could have been made palatable." [101]

Although Secretary of the Navy in Fillmore's cabinet, a former United States senator and governor of North Carolina, Graham was not particularly well known nationally, and the Washington *Signal* took occasion to introduce him as tall, slender, and dignified with "an intellectual countenance, aquiline features, a bright, penetrating hazel eye, and manners prepossessing and graceful, but slightly reserved. He is distinguished for uprightness of character, solidity of judgment, and cool sagacity; is eminently conservative in his views and principles; and enjoys in a striking degree that sincerity of purpose, freedom from ostentation, hearty patriotism, and unaffected sobriety, which usually characterize men of the Old North State." [102] A thoroughgoing moderate, he opposed disunionist movements like the Nashville Convention. In his statement to the Alabama Southern Rights Convention, he hoped for "an end to the agitation of slavery" and predicted that "faithful adherence" to the Compromise of 1850 would bring "repose and security." Limiting his campaign to two brief speeches, he

[101] John S. Gallaher to W. A. Graham, June 22, 1852, in Hamilton (ed.), *Graham Papers*, IV, 313–15.
[102] Washington *Signal*, July 10, 1852, *ibid.*, IV, 350.

appeared in Washington after his nomination on June 21 to thank his admirers and to indicate that "the prosperity of this country, the stability of its institutions, and the perpetuity of the Union, depend upon the ascendancy of Whig measures." In an equally bland speech at his home in Hillsboro, North Carolina, on September 17, the former governor made "the very welkin ring with cheers." Speaking with "evident emotion" and "with the greatest propriety of language and sentiment," the cautious Whig champion avoided "all the contested issues between the two parties." [103]

Graham's modest exertion and moderate policy failed to enliven the Whig cause in the South, where apathy prevailed even with the "Hero of Lundy's Lane" at the head of the ticket. "Chippewa Clubs" attempted to revive the excitement of Tippecanoe days, but the pompous and choleric "Fuss and Feathers" provoked little popular enthusiasm. Whig verses reached a new low:

> Damn the locos,
> Kill 'em—slay 'em.
> Give 'em hell
> With Scott and Graham.[104]

Violating tradition, Scott engaged in a "series of stump speeches" that proved to be "a sad falling off from the Triumphal Entry into Mexico." Said George Templeton Strong, "The General electioneers as badly as Coriolanus would have done if he had condescended to try." [105] Southerners remained, as Graham reported, "lukewarm still, in respect to Gen'l Scott." [106] "We

---

[103] Hamilton (ed.), *Graham Papers*, IV, 379–80; Washington *Signal*, July 1, 1852, *ibid.* IV, 312; *Hillsboro* (N.C.) *Recorder*, September 22, 1852, *ibid.*, IV, 402.
[104] Goebel and Goebel, *Generals in the White House*, 149.
[105] Allan Nevins and Milton Halsey Thomas (eds.), *The Diary of George Templeton Strong* (4 vols.; New York, 1952), II, 106.
[106] W. A. Graham to David L. Swain, October 13, 1852, in Hamilton (ed.), *Graham Papers*, IV, 423.

need ardour and enthusiasm, and are greatly deficient in Stump Speakers," complained another southern Whig; ". . . the Whig fires are waning only for the want of Breath." [107] When the votes were counted in November, Franklin Pierce, another undistinguished Democratic obscurity, had won every state but four: Massachusetts, Vermont, Kentucky, and Tennessee. All but the most optimistic concluded that the Whig Party was dead and soon to be "decomposed into its original elements." [108]

From 1833 to 1853 Whig speaking rosters included an impressive listing of personalities, none of whom fit a common mold, unless perhaps it be that of a sturdy, or even fierce, individualism. Contrasting Southerners included orotund declaimers like Henry W. Hilliard—some said it was worth going the length of the state "to hear him pronounce the word 'Alabama' ";[109] crusty, blunt-spoken military heroes like Zack Taylor and Charles S. Todd, who spoke plain common sense in a conversational manner; fearsome duelists and Hotspurs like Cassius Clay, William J. Graves, Thomas Clingman, and Edward Stanly, "a noisy quarrelsome braggadocio" and "terror of the Lucifer party";[110] austere aristocrats like John Tyler and Benjamin Watkins Leigh; fiery and impulsive "slang-whangers" like "Parson" William G. Brownlow, who had "as strong a voice as any man in East Tennessee," and Robert Toombs with his "bold, dashing, Mirabeau style";[111] men of commanding presence like Berrien, Bell, Scott, and John M. Morehead; those of insignificant stature like Stephens, Wise, and Rives; and cripples like Legaré and Prentiss; cautious, logical conservatives like Thomas A. R. Nelson, who would "express no opinion

---

[107] James W. Osborne to W. A. Graham, July 23, 1852, *ibid.*, IV, 363–64.
[108] Nevins and Halsey (eds.), *The Diary of George Templeton Strong*, II, 109.
[109] Cole, *The Whig Party in the South*, 81.
[110] Hamilton (ed.), *Graham Papers*, II, 452; Charles Francis Adams (ed.), *Memoirs of John Quincy Adams . . .* (12 vols.; Philadelphia, 1874–77), XI, 19.
[111] Poore, *Perley's Reminiscences*, I, 149; Stovall, *Robert Toombs*, 70.

until he had examined the question carefully";[112] demagogues like "Lean Jimmy" Jones, a "stump stereotyped speaker" without "depth or substance" but with great capacity for wit, ridicule, and mimicry;[113] strict constructionalists "of the purest type" like Hugh Lawson White, "mild in all his ways" and with "little sense of humor and imagination";[114] a master of the extemporaneous style like Prentiss; brilliant legal thinkers like Judah P. Benjamin and Reverdy Johnson; scholars like Legaré, Lieber, and Preston; self-educated zealots like Brownlow; and know-nothings like Davy Crockett.

Heavy reliance was placed upon legal and constitutional precedent and appeals to authority. Little use was made of statistical proof; indeed, statistics were not readily available, a deficiency Francis Lieber hoped to remedy with a "great national statistical bureau." [115] Since Whigs often preferred to avoid a defense of conservative economic principles, there was little coherent rationalization for a bank, a tariff, or internal improvements. On occasion, of course, intellectual champions like Legaré might defend the credit system as "the natural fruit" of "all that is most precious in civilized life." [116] Prentiss coined the slogan, "Credit is the poor man's capital." [117] But slogans and shoddy analogies seemingly served better than reason in the struggle against Jacksonian "Spoilers." In meeting Democratic demagoguery and jingoism on the issues of slavery and territorial expansion, however, Unionist Whigs spoke with eloquence and great courage, risking the charge of treason against their class and region.

The prewar generation specialized in pathetic appeals or in Waddy Thompson's inspired phrase, a *"falsetto* rhetoric." There were appeals to patriotism, to a common heritage, to the

112Alexander, "Thomas A. R. Nelson," 29.   113 Parks, *John Bell,* 275.
114 *Dictionary of American Biography,* XX, 107.
115 Freidel, *Francis Lieber,* 108.
116 Quoted in Parrington, *The Romantic Revolution in America,* 123.
117 Washington *National Intelligencer,* August 6, 1840.

"associations of our national flag," and to "the fair flower of womanhood." [118] Benjamin Watkins Leigh of Virginia, for example, drew tears from his Northampton, North Carolina, listeners when he "alluded to the perils and sacrifices of our forefathers in achieving the blessings which we now enjoy." [119] It was an age of easy weeping, of unashamed sentimentality. Henry Clay delighted in reminding audiences that they met together "for the last time." He said at Raleigh: "We are about, fellow citizens, finally to separate. Never again shall I behold this assembled multitude. . . . But you will never be forgotten in this heart of mine." When the Kentucky Electoral College met in Lexington after Clay's defeat in 1844, the beloved three-time loser spoke with "deep emotion which at times, almost overpowered him, and well nigh choked his utterance," while those who had gathered to console him "all wept together." [120]

The southern Whig idiom varied with each contrasting personality, but a grandiose, if not to say inflated, style was fashionable. More worldly listeners would have found some of the impassioned passages ludicrous, perhaps even grotesque. Whig spokesmen of the Old South occasionally embellished argument with pseudopoetic fancy or with studied and not always appropriate comparisons to Greek or Roman history or mythology. If no classical allusion came to mind, an earthy frontier image might do. But much of the metaphor was stale even to nineteenth century taste. The New York *Evening Post,* for example, ridiculed Prentiss for his "true Whig veneration for antiquity." Said the *Post,* "Thus we had old arguments, old figures, old anecdotes, old phrases, old jokes, old falsehoods, and old scraps, shreds, odd ends, and what not." [121] Serving as en-

118 Dickey, *Seargent S. Prentiss,* 179–90.
119 Richmond *Whig,* n. d., in *Niles' Weekly Register,* XLIX (November 28, 1835).
120 *Niles' Weekly Register,* LXVI (July 6, 1844), and LXVII (December 21, 1844).
121 Dickey, *Seargent S. Prentiss,* 178.

tertainment as well as enlightenment, oratory required verbal excitement as well as mimicry and histrionics. Individualism flourished, and speakers were identified by distinctive attributes: the nervous eloquence of Prentiss, who spoke so rapidly he could hardly be reported; the ponderous absurdity of Tyler; the cogent but sometimes tedious logic of Crittenden; the classical erudition of Legaré; the interminable legal reasoning of Rives; the vitriolic intensity of Wise; the ingenious imagery of Preston; and the rustic analogy of Crockett.

Contemporary speech criticism applauded florid oratory in the unrestrained manner of the day. When Philip Hone visited the United States Senate on February 22, 1841, he found occasion to praise two prominent southern Whigs: "Never did human voice utter anything more beautiful than this well-merited panegyric" of John J. Crittenden by William C. Preston, who was "warm and glowing, tender and touching, by turns. . . . The Audience seemed to be rapt in mute attention until the close, when the effect was irresistible and there was a pretty general applause in the gallery. . . . But what a glorious triumph of eloquence! I would have given the world at that moment to have been Preston, but I would have given two such worlds to have been Crittenden. The latter was greatly moved; those who were near him say that he wept visibly. He is beloved by all parties." [122] Hone's ecstasy demonstrates that Yankees as well as Southerners could be florid and ephemeral. [123]

Although southern Whigs appealed to sentiment, tradition, love of Union, and a common heritage, they failed to rally a conservative national following dedicated to a peaceful adjustment, particularly after 1850 when the northern wing of the party became increasingly "abolitionized." Fire-eating Democrats in Dixie and northern Free Soilers successfully pro-

[122] Nevins (ed.), *The Diary of Philip Hone*, II, 524–25.
[123] Dallas C. Dickey, "Were They Ephemeral and Florid?" *Quarterly Journal of Speech*, XXXII (February, 1946), 16–20.

jected the concept of "irrepressible conflict" and the conviction that the nation could not coexist half slave and half free. Moderate men, especially Border State Whigs, cried out against the suicidal alternative. "We talk about not compromising a family quarrel," pleaded Crittenden the night before Lincoln's inauguration. "In the name of God, who is it that will adopt that policy? We are one people in blood; in language one; in thoughts one. . . . It is our infirmity to have . . . difficulties. Let it be our magnanimity and our wisdom to compromise and settle them." [124] But southern extremists silenced moderates by hysterical accusations of "abolitionist" or "submissionist" and prepared for a test of arms. In dedicating themselves to a compromise of the sectional controversy, southern Whigs upheld a tradition essential to functioning democracy. When the Civil War came, it represented not only failure of the Whig policy of moderation but of the democratic process itself.

[124] *Congressional Globe*, 36 Cong., 2nd Sess., 1375–76.

IV

The Moderate Democrats

1830–1860

LINDSEY S. PERKINS

A careful counting of noses during this turbulent period shows that a majority of Democrats, southern as well as northern, occupied an essentially middle-of-the-road position. Some of the leaders, quite naturally, sought a nebulous mid-path because it was the most politic place to be; others took the same position from principle and were as adamantine in defending their ideas as were any of the extremists. These men may be categorized (and so distinguished from their more rabid fellows) as moderate Democrats.

Among moderate southern Democrats were four notable men who are eminently worthy of study as orators. They differed sharply in their persons, and none more so than the two who remained in the Democratic fold throughout their lives. James McDowell of Rockbridge was a typical Virginia aristocrat and the only one of the four who approaches the stereotyped "southern orator." [1] Herschel Vespasian Johnson was a Georgia country man of wholly unimposing antecedents, distinguished from the one-gallus plowhand only by intelligence and education. The much older McDowell served in the Vir-

---

[1] Waldo W. Braden, "The Emergence of the Concept of Southern Oratory," *Southern Speech Journal*, XXVI (Spring, 1961), 176–77.

ginia legislature from 1830 to 1838, as governor from 1843 to 1846, and as representative in Congress from 1846 until his death in 1851. Johnson filled an unexpired term as United States senator, 1848 to 1849, served as Georgia's governor, 1853 to 1857, and ran as vice-presidential candidate with Stephen A. Douglas in 1860.[2]

Paired with these two are Alexander H. Stephens and Robert Toombs, the Damon and Pythias of Georgia politics, who climaxed some sixteen years in Congress by serving as vice-president and secretary of state, respectively, of the Confederacy. Although both were nominally Whigs until 1851, this was a "choice of evils." Their political principles are generally indistinguishable from those of McDowell and Johnson, but they were alienated from the Democratic Party by the personal power drive of Andrew Jackson and the nullification-secessionist fever in the South. They joined the Whig Party "to link their local units with a country-wide organization and to resist the Jacksonian surge." [3]

Both Alexander Stephens and Herschel Johnson were reared in modest circumstances, and both built fortune and position for themselves. Despite his sneering references to "the Chivalry," Robert Toombs came from a substantial family, and so, of course, did James McDowell. All four received college educations; and here, too, there was a good deal of difference. Stephens was consistently brilliant, leading his class at the University of Georgia; the equally brilliant McDowell led his class at Princeton; Johnson was a plodder, a steadily commendable student; but the nonconforming Toombs faced expulsion upon occasion.[4]

[2] The standard biography of Johnson is that of Percy S. Flippin, *Herschel V. Johnson of Georgia, State Rights Unionist* (Richmond, 1931). James G. Collier completed a thesis on "The Political Career of James McDowell" (University of North Carolina, 1963).

[3] *Dictionary of American Biography*, XVIII, 569–70.

[4] The "Toombs Oak" stood until recently on the University of Georgia

From 1830 to 1860 Southerners were basically concerned with two issues: slavery and state rights. The harmony which had characterized the Era of Good Feeling extended to all questions about slaves and slavery. The slave trade was ended without acrimony. In the first third of the century there was a strong voluntary emancipation movement throughout the South. But shortly after 1830 the violent controversy over President Jackson's seizure of power at the expense of the states came to a head; from this point onward there was constant pressure for and against centralized power theories. The Georgia electorate, heretofore united on national issues, split over the question of the Force Act and organized the state rights and the Union factions. The state rights wing later became Whigs and the Union wing became the Georgia Democrats.

The point has often been made that secession, the last of the pre-Civil War issues, stemmed from this question of the rights reserved to the states by the Constitution and not from slavery. Secessionism was extremely strong in 1832, and slavery was not the issue at all. When the national Democratic Party repudiated most of Jacksonian Democracy, the shift to a restricting constitutionality guaranteed the states their reserved rights. State rights men could return to the national party, and the open wound was partly closed.

Then came the abolitionists. In January, 1831, the first number of William Lloyd Garrison's *Liberator* appeared, and with it a set of beliefs which were symbolized finally (years later) by the editor's burning a copy of the Constitution. This essentially unnoticed beginning brought no immediate change in

---

campus near the site of the old chapel. Legend credits Toombs, resigned (dismissed?) from the college, with delivering an unscheduled address under this oak. His brilliant speech allegedly drew all of the students out of the chapel, while the scheduled speeches of the honor graduates were delivered to empty seats.

the southern emancipation movement. One year later, in 1832, James McDowell could plead for the passage of an abolition bill in the Virginia legislature and be supported in his stand by a strong minority. However, by the time William H. Seward found it politically expedient to preach the doctrine of a "higher law" than the Constitution, abolitionism was insolubly united, in the southern mind, with those who would destroy the states' sovereign power—and by whatever means necessary. No state had followed South Carolina in nullification, 1832; an enormous majority had supported the Constitutional Union Party of Stephens and Toombs in Georgia, 1851; but, by late 1860, even moderate southern Democrats had been alienated by Black Republican extremism.[5]

Toombs pinpointed the main contention of disenchanted Southerners in his "Hamilcar speech," June 15, 1850, when he demonstrated that while Southerners would vote (however unhappily to admit states which had excluded slavery in their territories, no northern radical could be persuaded to say that he would ever vote to admit a slave state. Obviously, a state had not the right to determine any of its institutions, whether or not the right to do so was reserved to it by the Constitution. "I intend to drag off the mask," said Toombs,[6] and more and more Southerners who had been lukewarm in their defense of slavery began to approach the boiling point as the unmasking revealed maneuvers by central power advocates much more subtly sinister than those of Jackson.

When the slavocracy apologists attempted to go on with their argument, they were backed into a corner by their own logical inconsistencies. States, they said, were absolutely sov-

[5] William B. Hesseltine, *The South in American History* (New York, 1943), 228; Frances Butler Simkins, *The South, Old and New* (New York, 1947), 22–23; Charles S. Sydnor, *The Development of Southern Sectionalism, 1819–1848* (Baton Rouge, 1948); Rudolph Von Abele, *Alexander H. Stephens: A Biography* (New York, 1946), 60–61.

[6] *Congressional Globe*, 31st Cong., 1st Sess., 1216.

ereign in their right to establish slavery. But let a moderate Democrat like Douglas maintain that a state could prohibit slavery, and the "True Southrons" howled with incendiary fervor matching that of the abolitionists. They demanded that the Constitution (here, the hated federal power!) be invoked to permit Southerners to use their slaves in any territory or free state.

Johnson and McDowell, lifelong Democrats, were not always politically allied with Stephens and Toombs. The latter pair founded their own Constitutional Union Party after breaking with the Whigs in 1852. However, their stand upon the issues shows the strong political kinship of all four. The touchstone upon which they relied as a standard was the preservation of a constitutional union of sovereign states. They were therefore opposed to "ultras," northern or southern. They were not willing secessionists: they did not believe that the Union was a servant to be used or discarded as self-willed self-interest dictated. They were not diehard Unionists: they did not believe a state could be forced to surrender the rights reserved to it in the Constitution. Stephens defined the line which not even Herschel Johnson, the most ardent Union supporter of the four, would cross: "When Georgia seceded in 1861, even against my judgment, I stood by her act. To her alone I owed my ultimate allegiance." [7]

The defense of slavery grew in direct proportion to the violence and bigotry of abolitionist attacks. McDowell's first noteworthy speech, that of January 21, 1832, in the Virginia legislature, advocated an emancipation bill. Persuasively, but unequivocally, he said that slavery should be abolished: (1) no act could invoke a more favorable response from "intellec-

[7] Alexander H. Stephens' preface to his *Address Delivered at Crawfordsville on the Fourth of July, 1834,* when he issued it as a pamphlet thirty years later (Augusta, Ga., 1864).

tual and moral and christian man"; (2) slavery is a "leprosy," slave property "an evil . . . [and] you will rear your posterity to the scenes of the dagger and the torch." [8] McDowell's revised thinking, when he was governor and congressman, reflected not a belief in the virtues of slavery but a defense of his state's right to determine the nature of its own legal, economic, and social institutions. In his speeches on the Wilmot Proviso at the close of his life he simply contended "that it was not only unconstitutional, and, as to the free States, an unnecessary measure . . . but that it was a harsh, offensive, and dangerous violation of the equal rights of the States." The argument that the Massachusetts man and the Virginian were to be equal in the new territory was a sophism: "The emigrant who has no slaves," and whose state does not give him the right to have any, can settle with all his property; the other emigrant "who has slaves . . . and who has always had the right to have them under the constitution and laws of his State . . . is not permitted to settle in the same way, but is first required to give up his slaves." [9] Though these closely reasoned speeches defended slaveholders against abolitionists, they in no way conflicted with McDowell's advocacy of emancipation nineteen years earlier.

As abolitionist vituperation increased, the Georgia men stepped up their defense of the rights of slaveholders—in Congress, and in their speeches at the North. But in private and in their southern speeches they wasted no time on the question save to regret that it divided the nation. On the nomination of Franklin Pierce in 1852, Johnson admonished: "It is impossible to exclude Free Soilers so long as a national organiza-

[8] *Speech of James McDowell, Jr. (of Rockbridge) in the House of Delegates of Virginia on the Slave Question* (pamphlet; Richmond, 1832), 8–9, 33.

[9] *Congressional Globe*, 31st Cong., 1st Sess., 1679–80.

tion of parties shall be maintained. They came into the Convention not as free Soilers [*sic*], but as national Democrats." [10] Although Toombs repeatedly denied it, he may well have said publicly that he would "call the roll of my slaves at the foot of Bunker Hill monument"; but in private, he admitted: "As to the cursed "slave pens" [slave market in the District of Columbia], we will try to trade them off to advantage. No honest man would regret their annihilation .... The temper of the North is good, and with kindness, and patronage skillfully adjusted, I think we can work out of present troubles, preserve the Union, and disappoint bad men and traitors." [11]

For all his fiery rejoinders to Locofoco agitation, Toombs, the most choleric of the quartet, was nonetheless a steadily logical supporter of the Union and strict justice. Without doubt, he expected to lose Kansas through a fairly elected constitutional convention. Yet a fair election is precisely what he advocated in his speech of February 28, 1856, and in the bill he offered on June 23–24, 1856: to have a federal census taken, all male residents twenty-one or over registered as voters, and these voters to elect delegates whose Constitution should be at once accepted. Kansas was then to be admitted to the Union.[12]

In upholding the rights of southern slaveholders these men were saddled with the Fugitive Slave Law, which became an increasingly embarrassing sub-issue. They supported it stolidly as did Johnson or vehemently as did Toombs. Their weakness, and a source of immeasurable strength to the abolitionists, lay in the ease with which free Negroes could be hounded or illegally forced back into slavery, and in the conscience-

[10] Manuscript of notes, probably for a speech, in Herschel Johnson Papers, Duke University Library.

[11] Robert Toombs to John J. Crittenden, Jan. 3, 1849, in John J. Crittenden Papers, Library of Congress.

[12] *Congressional Globe*, 34th Cong., 1st Sess., 1439, and Appendix, 115–118, 762 ff.

less action of some slaveowners in abusing the law.[13] Toombs gave some support to a further interpretation permitting a slaveholder to carry slaves into a free state; but Stephens spelled out the logical inconsistency of such a stand to constituents who criticized his moderate point of view: "Everybody knows that the Constitution secures and guarantees property in Georgia and in all the slave states, but that it does not secure the use of such property in New York." [14]

Undoubtedly, what the Fire-Eaters objected to primarily was the declining political strength of the once omnipotent South. But to the moderates, this was not an issue. Stephens made the point clearly: "I see the Columbus Enquirer of Georgia is advocating the policy of our starting a ticket of Southern men for Pres. and Vice President. This I am decidedly opposed to. . . . What we want is a sound national organization upon broad—national—republican principles. We want no sectional men or sectional issues." [15]

The moderates were caught between the upper millstone of Fire-Eater demands and the nether millstone of Garrisonian abolitionism. Finally, in 1858, as the Republicans used such clearly implied threats as Lincoln's "house divided" and Seward's "irrepressible conflict," there seemed little that a believer in constitutional democracy could hope to achieve.

Feeling powerless to accomplish anything positive, Stephens retired from Congress in 1859. Toombs had almost decided that since the South was being given a choice between knuckling under or fighting, the fighting might as well begin. But not quite; for even after the election of Lincoln, Toombs served on the senatorial committee which John J. Crittenden

[13] Cf. John L. Ketcham to Howell Cobb, Aug. 9, 1853, in Howell Cobb Papers, University of Georgia Library, Athens.

[14] Alexander H. Stephens, letter to the Milledgeville (Ga.) *Federal Union*, Sept. 12, 1848.

[15] Alexander H. Stephens to W. W. Burwell, June 26, 1854, in Alexander H. Stephens Papers, Library of Congress.

had called to seek a compromise. When this attempt failed, Toombs immediately sent the newspapers a statement, addressed to his constituents, that "all further looking to the North for security for your constitutional rights in the Union ought to be instantly abandoned." [16]

Johnson had not worked with McDowell, and he had not joined Toombs and Stephens on their Georgia platform, which laid down conditions under which Georgia ought to consider secession. Indeed, he had gone further than Stephens in trying to keep Georgia in the Union. But he might well have been speaking for all three of these others, summing up their stand on the major issues when he spoke in 1854 on the Kansas question: "The South does not desire to increase the slave power . . . . She rather desires to retain her power—preserve an equilibrium—to enable her to counteract aggression under the forms of legislation." [17]

A superficial examination may tend to show some inconsistency in the stands taken by these men. Actually, a great source of strength for all was the integrity with which each took a position on most of the sub-issues. Toombs might resort to rationalizations upon occasion, but not so Herschel Johnson, who was to lose both friends and lucrative influence. Johnson never deviated from the line of his beliefs in southern Democratic principles; his steadfast march, to the end of the second mile, is a marvel of logical consistency. Stephens jeopardized his own tenure in Congress after his first election to a seat by arguing that, because Georgia had refused to establish congressional districts in accordance with the Act of 1842, the election was illegal. Constitutionality was the test.[18]

The educated southern speaker had an advantage over his

[16] Ulrich B. Phillips, *The Life of Robert Toombs* (New York, 1913), 172–74, 206–208; Savannah (Ga.), *News*, Dec. 24, 1860.

[17] Flippin, *Herschel V. Johnson*, 73.

[18] *Congressional Globe*, 28th Cong., 1st Sess., 259.

northern counterpart in approaching audiences of the coastal districts. In this region quite generally, wealth, learning, and suffrage went hand in hand. Unlike those northern sections where mechanics and day laborers were enfranchised, the tide-water states had not come close to complete democratization by the close of this era. Northern politicians had, perforce, to speak the language of the common man or lose his vote; low country politicians could maintain a much higher level of vocabulary and composition. Indeed, in areas such as Richmond or Savannah, the orator who pandered to the common taste ran the risk of being considered common. It seems quite probable that the failure of many Southrons to transmit their messages to northern audiences resulted from their failure to take such sectional differences into consideration.[19]

Another significant factor grew out of the career goals of these four statesmen. They did not make a living from office holding, as do present-day professionals from county commissioner to president. McDowell, born wealthy, could afford to indulge his desire to serve, but it cost all of them money and the other three could not have relished the loss of income. Stephens withdrew from office twice. On both occasions he profited, especially in 1859 to 1861, when his net worth was increased by $22,000. Small reason therefore for the Southerner to bend his beliefs and warp his principles to appeal to the passions and prejudices of the electorate. The undeniable prestige of a senator was small recompense for any demagogy which would mean losing one's self-respect and the esteem of his friends.[20]

The sovereignty of the state was assigned special importance in the South, where immigrants from highly centralized

[19] Hesseltine, *The South in American History,* 108, 205–207, 262; Sydnor, *The Development of Southern Sectionalism,* 283–87.

[20] Von Abele, *Alexander H. Stephens,* 76, 173; Richmond *Enquirer,* Feb., 13, 1840; Herschel Johnson to William H. Winder, Oct. 16, 1852, in Herschel Johnson Papers, Duke University Library, Durham.

European governments had made no impression on politics. Hence, southern speakers were interested in the local audience and in the state audience. Most of McDowell's emancipation speech in 1832 dwelt on Virginia's regard for the reputation of the state, slavery's effect on the state's economy, and the terrors of Nat Turner's rebellion. In his Baltimore speech for Buchanan, Johnson concentrated on the Marylander; "Citizens of Maryland, I want to know if your noble State is to be an exception, isolated from the great Southern Phalanx." [21] When he was trying to gain support for the "Constitutional Union" ideal, Toombs was interested in a wider audience; but one cannot find a speech in which Toombs or the other three tried to appeal to a general national audience, except on the vague basis of Union and the commonweal.

Each of the Georgians gloried in his prowess on the hustings. In 1844, when the Whigs were bedeviled by the tariff question, Toombs wrote to John Berrien: "The 'Chivalry' don't seem to be making much out of the Tariff . . . . I fear the gentlemen have got the 'wolf by the ear' and find it hard to hold him & death to let him go. I enjoy in anticipation the sport I shall have out of them next summer on the Stump about their unredeemed pledges to repeal the odious Whig Tariff." [22] The Georgians and the Virginian show a ready recognition of the identity of their listeners. At the Georgia Volunteer Encampment, July 4, 1857, Johnson was especially gracious in adapting to the interests of the immediate audience. As he called the roll of Georgia's illustrious names, including Milledge and Jackson, one Milledge and two Jacksons were

21 *Speech of James McDowell . . . on the Slave Question*, 20; Milledgeville (Ga.) *Federal Union*, Jan. 28, 1853; Baltimore *Republican*, Sept. 15, 1856.

22 Von Abele, *Alexander H. Stephens*, 193–98; Robert Toombs to John McPherson Berrien, Jan. 28, 1844, in John McPherson Berrien Collection, University of North Carolina, Chapel Hill.

among the officers listening to him.[23] McDowell's lengthy allusion to "the fire of a future explosion" was well calculated to pass the tests of recency and intensity, for Virginia's Nat Turner rebellion was a memory only five months old.[24]

Toombs could use the common man's language and he did so at times, especially for sardonic invective. He was then inclined to approach the harsh and vicious—not always to his advantage.[25] With the occasional exception of Stephens, none of the others used the vernacular. It was said of McDowell: "A stump orator he was not. He was too much a literary man for that." [26] The composition of McDowell and Johnson, always that of the college graduate, required the listeners to rise to its level.

Nowhere in any of this speechmaking is there evidence of a sophistic concern for ideas pleasing to the audience. Stephens and Toombs were among the creators of public opinion in Georgia as they fought for the compromise measures in 1850; and when the triumph of the northern radicals in 1860 changed the moderate majority of 1850 into a weak minority, neither Toombs, Stephens, nor Johnson showed any signs of altering their original stand. Toombs continued to work for compromise, and Stephens and Johnson insisted that their constituents should wait and hope.[27]

It is likely that men like Stephens and McDowell were apt to ask the audience to adapt to them. McDowell was thought of as "strong enough also to be as proud and aristocratic as naturally belonged to him; and he was known to be so much

[23] *An Address Delivered before the Volunteer Encampment . . . by Herschel V. Johnson.* (pamphlet; Milledgeville, Ga., 1857), Duke University Library.

[24] *Speech of James McDowell . . . on the Slave Question,* 12–17.

[25] Opinion of John C. Reed, quoted by Phillips, *Robert Toombs,* 104.

[26] "Hon. James McDowell," *Washington and Lee University Historical Papers, No. 5* (1895), 130–31.

[27] Hesseltine, *The South in American History,* 318; Simkins, *The South, Old and New,* 126–27.

above the plane of the demagogue that if he had resorted to the tricks so often employed in electioneering he would have lowered his standing with even the commonest people." [28] With a clearly relished slap in the face for partisans, Stephens published this card in 1855: "Hon. Alexander H. Stephens will address his fellow citizens of Augusta, without distinction of Party, this evening at 8 o'clock in the City Hall, in response to the calls that have been made upon him to be a Candidate again for Congress. Whigs and Democrats, Union Men and Fire-Eaters, Know Nothings and Anti-Know Nothings, 'Insiders' and 'Outsiders,' Native and Adopted Citizens, Catholics and Protestants, are invited, one and all, to attend." [29] The Democrats disregarded Stephens' refusal to ask for a party endorsement and adopted him as their candidate. [30]

All four speakers were able to gain the attention, interest, and support of their hearers. However, it was not because they cut the cloth of their rhetoric to fit the audience, either in choice of ideas or in composition. The source of their strength must be sought elsewhere.

Campaign results for these four leaders and the testimony of contemporaries offer some measure of their stature as orators. They were a stubborn group, upheld by boundless confidence. Although James McDowell's first speech "at once placed him in the forefront of the talent and eloquence of Virginia," [31] its emancipation sentiment, which he refused to repudiate, added to the handicap of his hapless penchant for supporting unpopular causes. Opposing nullification and the right to secede, backing Van Buren and the Democrats after the Panic of 1837, he was defeated four times for high office.

[28] "Hon. James McDowell," 128–29.
[29] Augusta (Ga.), *Weekly Chronicle and Sentinel*, May 30, 1855.
[30] Hesseltine, *The South in American History*, 335.
[31] Richmond *Whig*, Feb. 23, 1832. This newspaper opposed McDowell's stand on abolition.

He still managed, without becoming a political weathervane, to rebound each time. He overcame the abolitionist charge, which had beaten him in 1840, to become governor in 1842 and to be elected to the national House of Representatives in 1846.[32]

Herschel Johnson's career was similar but more successful. As a beginner, thirty-two years old, he recovered from a trouncing by the distinguished Walter T. Colquitt, and won, a month later, in a stump debate with Congressman Alexander H. Stephens. The combined might of Stephens, Toombs, and Howell Cobb demolished Johnson in 1851, but he came roaring back to win the governorship in 1853 and 1856. He was unbeatable except against overwhelming odds.[33]

"Little Aleck" Stephens and "Fighting Bob" Toombs came as close to being overwhelming odds as Georgia ever knew. Fortunately for both, they campaigned together for major issues, never opposing each other, and as a team they were invincible. Singly, too, each was invincible, stumping his own district for reelection. Stephens was the more versatile. He was one of the shrewdest, sharpest debaters in the state and national legislatures, but one of his commemorative speeches moved Abraham Lincoln to say that "my old, withered, dry eyes are full of tears yet." When Stephens was incapacitated in 1848, Toombs stumped the state by himself and carried it, singlehandedly, for the Whigs. His Hamilcar speech, directed against the supposedly invulnerable California bill, caused such a sensation in the House that its proponents thought it wise to postpone consideration for six weeks.[34]

[32] Thomas W. White to William Gaston, Aug. 23, 1832, in William Gaston Papers, University of North Carolina; Richmond *Enquirer*, Feb. 13, 1840; William H. Richardson to James McDowell, Dec. 24, 1842, in McDowell Papers, University of North Carolina.

[33] An idolatrous disquisition on Johnson's oratorical ability appears in "Herschel V. Johnson," *The Plantation*, I (March, 1860), 64–70. See *also* the Columbus (Ga.) *Enquirer*, June–October, 1851.

[34] Phillips, *Robert Toombs*, 179; M. Burns to Alexander H. Stephens,

An attempt to determine the source of the speakers' power should begin with a study of their ethos—character, reputation, appearance—the sum total of their impact on persons. Again the men display a somewhat bewildering variety of traits. The usual assumption of an hereditary southern leadership, drawn from the aristocracy, is supported in this instance only by McDowell. Nothing was amiss when a cousin of McDowell's, after hearing one of his congressional speeches, rushed up to a friend, "took him by the collar & said 'by God Smith blood will show' so overpowered he could say no more." For McDowell of Rockbridge, with his "five generations of family" in Virginia and his country seat at Colalto, was an aristocrat. But one could hardly have said that blood would show of the poor teacher's son Stephens, or of the yeoman Johnson, though each could claim good middle-class ancestry. Toombs was far from being the conventional southern gentleman, for he made his considerable fortune through hard work as a lawyer.[35]

Physically, Stephens was unique. About five feet, seven inches in height, he sometimes weighed as much as ninety-five pounds. Any other man as seriously ill as he was for so much of the time might have been a lifelong invalid, but he produced a prodigious amount of work and seemingly wrote more letters than the other three put together. His auditors saw "a little, slim, pale-faced consumptive man"—"a shrunken and attenuated figure, the shoulders contracted and drawn in, the face dead and of the color of ashes." But they must also have marked the raw courage which hurled this little tatter of skin and

---

Jan. 28, 1839, in Alexander H. Stephens Papers, Duke University Library; Von Abele, *Alexander H. Stephens*, 102–103; John J. Crittenden to Alexander H. Stephens, Oct. 6, 1848, in Linton Stephens Collection, Manhattanville College, Purchase, New York.

[35] Frances McDowell to "Mary," Feb. 21 [thus misdated], 1849, in McDowell Papers; Von Abele, *Alexander H. Stephens, passim,* 5–31; Phillips, *Robert Toombs,* 12.

bones into a cane-and-knife fight with Judge Francis Cone in 1848, so seriously contested that Stephens' wounds forced him out of the canvass. They must have observed the uncommon sweetness, discernible in some of his photographs, which appeared when he dwelt upon the pathetic. And they must have been gripped by "the piercing dark eyes" and set jaw when he dragged his ailing body out onto the campaign rostrums of his district and state.[36]

McDowell, Toombs, and Johnson were all physically powerful, above the average in height, and of commanding presence. Johnson was heavy-set, overweight; Toombs kept himself in good condition; McDowell, though lean, was strongly built. All exuded power, physical power—the massive Johnson, the sinewy McDowell, the panther-like Toombs. In the heat of forensic battle they could unleash a driving, explosive outburst that overwhelmed opponents.

Toombs's favorite characterizations in the whole of literature were Falstaff and Don Quixote. This choice is an index to the traits and personality of the man. There was a strong streak of sentiment and sentimentality in the other three which would have conflicted with Toombs's equally strong sense of humor and of the ridiculous. This streak was combined, in McDowell, with a gracious reserve which complimented his belief in *noblesse oblige* and his firm commitment to Scotch Presbyterianism. Johnson approximated the Baptist, nonaristocratic equivalent of the Virginian. Neither of them possessed a real sense of humor. Both were the most loyal of friends. Stephens stood somewhere between Toombs and the others. He was a "sober and conscientious youth"; he remained sober and conscientious; and he could see the humor of a situation, although his wit tended to be waspish. But there seems to have been an almost anomalous element of beauty in his character

[36] Von Abele, *Alexander H. Stephens*, 88, 102–103, 159.

which elicited a poem from a congressional colleague, dour old John Quincy Adams, and gained the affection of Crittenden, Toombs, and Johnson.[37]

As to platform delivery, there is an interesting similarity between Johnson and McDowell upon one point, and between Stephens and McDowell upon another—though it would be hard to imagine two who differed more than the latter pair. Neither Johnson nor McDowell were at their best in delivering the first speech in a stump debate; both required vigorous opposition to jolt them out of their natural composure. But once they were sufficiently prodded, they moved into a startling reversal of form: Johnson lost his stolidity and formality and began to thunder, and McDowell shed his dignity in rejoinders which "bristled with sharp points, and abounded in wit, satire and effective anecdotes." [38] It took a thoroughly aroused Johnson to come to the following full-throated roar:

Can you point to a single Fremont man or a single Fillmore man who is friendly to the South. . . . Is there a solitary Fillmore or Fremont man there who voted for the Kansas-Nebraska Bill, and who is now in favor of it? Where is he?—Who is he? (A voice— "Can't find him.") No; and you may take a search warrant and the best constable in your midst and search till doomsday, and you cannot find him. . . . Who are they that have been stricken down in the Congress of the United States and their places filled by the vilest and most foul mouthed Abolitionists that ever disgraced the human form? The Black Republicans, and odious Abolitionists and Free Soilers occupy the seats of the noble Democrats who stood by you in the last Congress, who voted for the Kansas-Nebraska bill, who voted to sustain the compromise of 1851, and to preserve the constitutional rights of the South and of the Union.[39]

[37] "Hon. James McDowell," 128–31; Phillips, *Robert Toombs*, 12, 179; Columbus (Ga.) *Enquirer*, July 15, 1851; Von Abele, *Alexander H. Stephens*, 103.
[38] "Hon. James McDowell," 128; Robert Toombs to Thomas W. Thomas, in Robert Toombs Papers, Duke University Library.
[39] Baltimore *Republican*, Sept. 15, 1856.

158

Stephens and McDowell had in common a love of the sentimental and, which is perhaps more important, their voices had certain decidedly similar characteristics. Stephens' voice was "shrill but musical, and while not flexible, singularly pleasing"; McDowell's "was clear and melodious, with an occasional touch of pathos which was very telling." It was his voice, as well as his dramatic ability, which made Stephens' use of appeals to the pathetic so effective and brought tears to Lincoln's eyes as he called the roll of those who had died in 1846—"a Clay, with a heart as pure, stern, inflexible, and patriotic, as the great sire from whom he sprung"—because "the Administration" had caused General Taylor to be "stripped of his men and crippled in his means." [40] Assuredly McDowell's "West Augusta" conclusion, which he used in at least two of his major addresses, could hardly have been carried by any save the voice described, powered by the utmost sincerity:

It is said, sir, that at some dark hour of our revolutionary contest, when army after army had been lost, when dispirited, beaten, wretched, the heart of the boldest and faithfulest died within them, and all, for an instant, seemed conquered except the unconquerable soul of our father-chief—it is said that at that moment . . . he roused anew the sunken spirit of his associates by this confident and daring declaration: "Strip me . . . of the dejected and suffering remnant of my army—take from me all that I have left—leave me a banner, give me but the means to plant it upon the mountains of West Augusta, and I will yet draw around me the men who will lift up their bleeding country from the dust, and set her free." Give to me, who am a son and representative here of that same West Augusta, give to me as a banner the propitious measure I have endeavored to support, help me to plant *it* upon this mountain top of our national power, and the land of Washington, undivided and unbroken, will be our land, and the land of our children's children forever. So help me to do this at this hour, and generations hence,

40 Von Abele, *Alexander H. Stephens*, 88; "Hon. James McDowell," 195; *Congressional Globe*, 30th Cong., 1st Sess., Appendix, 162.

159

some future son of the South, standing where I stand, in this same honored Hall, and in the midst of our legitimate successors, will bless and praise and thank God that he, too, can say of them, as I of you, and of all around me, These, these are my brethren, *and this, this Oh! this, too, is my country.*[41]

One account of Toombs and Johnson on the platform metaphorically contrasts their delivery as well as their composition: "Give Toombs a battle-axe and set him to work upon you, and he could not, to save his life, help hitting you sometimes a light blow. Sometimes he would turn the handle around and punch you; sometimes he would even take the axe in one hand and pinch you, or twist your nose with the other. Not so with Johnson; he would strike you with the blade of the axe every time, coming down with both hands, until he finished you." [42] Johnson personified hammer-fisted force. Toombs, the most polished of the four in delivery, used alternately light and heavy strokes.

All of these speakers were strong in logic, in marshaling supporting material, and in the use of straight-line organization for argumentative reasoning. But Johnson and McDowell could not equal the artistry which Stephens and Toombs brought to argumentation.

When Meacham of Vermont, announced that he considered the Missouri Compromise a contract and that he would "wait in great hope . . . of seeing it honestly and honorably fulfilled," Stephens savagely turned the tables on his opponent. Pointing out that "the gentleman's own predecessor upon this floor" and the entire Vermont delegation had voted against the admission of Arkansas, he added: "Did he or his colleagues have any objection to it except that it was a slave state? If they regarded the line of 36° 30′ as a solemn covenant . . . why did they not give it their sanction at that time? The gentleman

---

41 *Congressional Globe*, 30th Cong., 2nd Sess., Appendix, 219.
42 "Herschel V. Johnson," *The Plantation*, 69–70.

spoke of 'honor'—'I thank thee, Jew, for teaching me that word!' " [43] The closing quotation from Shakespeare typifies the literary, biblical, and historical allusion used by all these skillful rhetoricians.

Toombs came up with an equally effective reply in his campaign for the Union and the Compromises of 1850. Before the compromises were adopted, Toombs was pessimistic about preserving state rights, and his Hamilcar speech was a harsh one in which the asperous Georgian closed by saying: "Deprive us of this right . . . and I will then, if I can, bring my children and my constituents to the altar of liberty, and like Hamilcar I would swear them to eternal hostility to your foul domination." At Lexington, Georgia, Toombs's opponent had memorized this Hamilcar speech and used it, point by point, to attack Toombs's argument for Union. Toombs told the audience that its whole duty was to determine whether the compromise was right or wrong, and not to waste time on any little personal matter like the right or wrong of what Toombs had once said. Then, in an audacious twist, he added: "If there is anything in my Hamilcar speech that cannot be reconciled with the measures which I have supported here today with reasons which my opponent confesses by his silence he cannot answer, I repudiate it. *And*: If the gentleman takes up my abandoned errors, let him defend them." For years afterward, a man in that county could not effectively attack another's inconsistency, for the inevitable answer was, "I'm like Bob Toombs: I repudiate it, and if you want to take up my abandoned errors, you've got to defend them." [44]

Sketchy or totally absent reporting of speeches magnifies the difficulty in analyzing rhetoric in the great age of Clay and Webster. What the speaker actually said is hard to determine when the primary (and often the only) source is a

[43] *Congressional Globe*, 33rd Cong., 1st Sess., 193.
[44] John C. Reed, quoted by Phillips, *Robert Toombs*, 103–104.

pamphlet published by the speaker or his allies. All of these pamphlets, and nearly all of the congressional reports, were rewritten by the speaker before publication. Shorthand reports were the rare exception, and the most effectual speaking was extempore. Johnson, who wrote most of his major addresses, believed that he was at his best in extemporizing on a prepared outline, the method used for the hustings and his courtroom efforts.[45]

The turgid, prolix rhetoric of McDowell's published speeches raises a question. How could such a literary style have been presented with such telling effect? Half the question is eliminated by the knowledge that the speech, as published, was not the one delivered. McDowell did have a problem. He felt a need to build "some defense against utter failure." He closeted himself for hours, "to appear with a closely written manuscript which he never launched . . . till it had been first submitted" to his wife. This he "faithfully transferred to memory . . . and, as a last safety measure, voluminous notes were taken." Thus McDowell prepared that "first speech [which] was apt to be disappointing to a popular audience." But there was another McDowell. "On many other occasions, he spoke without special preparation. . . . [He] claimed a half hour of quiet; then drove to the church and made a speech that brought down thunders of applause." Too, as he gained skill in the use of the written speech, "McDowell would just play with his manuscript . . . jump out of his boat, swim about at pleasure." [46]

None of the above implies that McDowell ever abandoned

[45] See Herschel Johnson's unpublished "Autobiography," in Herschel Johnson Papers; and the title page of the *Speech of James McDowell . . . on the Slave Question* appends the following: "published by gentlemen who are favorable to the views advocated by Mr. McD."

[46] Memories of McDowell's daughter, Sally, and of various friends and political acquaintances, in "Hon. James McDowell," 130–31, 190–93.

the grand style that characterizes his composition, even when he threw away the manuscript. Delivery provided the saving grace. Delivery and extemporizing on the manuscript were probably responsible for the dazzling success of his speech on the Wilmot Proviso, and for the effect of this (probably unedited) excerpt from it: "UNION, then, was the wisdom of our revolutionary day; UNION is the wisdom of our day; and UNION will continue to be the wisdom of every day that is to come, until the nations of the earth have no rapacities and no ambition to gratify, and this poor heart of ours—that world of iniquity within itself—has no foul passions to inflame, to misdirect, to defile it." [47]

An unusual opportunity to compare oral style and literary style is offered by Toombs's Tremont Temple speech. In 1856 Toombs had invaded Boston to "preach the gospel" to the enemy. Two sources for this speech, a local newspaper report (much of it verbatim) and a pamphlet version published some months later by Toombs,[48] show the difference between the speaker and the essayist:

From the newspaper: After the war, the Constitution of the United States was formed. It was the work of delegates elected by the sovereign States of this confederacy, each acting for itself; and he called special attention to the fact that these delegates were not elected by the whole of the people. By whom were these delegates who passed this great charter of public liberty elected? Was it under the idea sometimes urged from the Declaration of Independence that all men are "free and equal." If this was a fact, our fathers were singularly unconscious of it—they were singularly disregardful of it—for throughout this country a large number of persons were excluded from voting for the delegates to the convention

[47] *Congressional Globe,* 30th Cong., 2nd Sess., Appendix, 214.
[48] *A Lecture Delivered in the Tremont Temple, Boston . . . 24th January, 1856* (pamphlet; Duke University Library), compared to the Boston *Evening Traveller,* January 25, 1856.

which bound them to the national government. They excluded minors for reasons he thought sound—they excluded women, many of whom were better qualified than most men he knew (a laugh)— they excluded the African, bond and free, from any participation in the sovereignty. Massachusetts did; nor did she admit to participate in this high duty even all the white males over 21 years of age. They excluded some because they had not land enough in many of the colonies—excluded others because they had not character enough; they excluded others because they were non-freemen, and for an infinity of reasons. There were restrictions in all the different commonwealths and in our own.

From the pamphlet: The Constitution was framed by delegates elected by the State legislatures. It was an emanation from the sovereign States as independent, separate, communities. It was ratified by conventions of these separate States, each acting for itself. The members of these conventions represented the sovereignty of each State, but they were not elected by the whole people of either of the States. Minors, women, slaves, Indians, Africans, bond and free, were excluded from participating in this act of sovereignty. Neither were all the white male inhabitants, over twenty-one years old, allowed to participate in it. Some were excluded because they had no land, others for the want of good characters, others again because they were non-freemen, and a large number were excluded for a great variety of still more unimportant reasons. None exercised this high privilege except those upon whom each State, for itself, had adjudged it wise, safe, and prudent to confer it.

The word choice in the speech is more direct, concrete: "formed" instead of "framed," "work" instead of "emanation." In some cases, the speaker amplifies, extensively, the terse, clipped sentences of the essayist; in others, he chops the phrase in half. The speaker delivers a series of periods, parenthetical amplifications, even run-on sentences—for reinforcement, for auditors who cannot read or pore over the material. He presents the immediate audience an opportunity for a response— a laugh—which is missing from the essay. In an earlier pas-

164

sage, there is a fine example of the strength which can grow out of the inspiration of the moment [italics mine]:

From the newspaper: At the time of the adoption of this Declaration of Independence, we had no *common government, but were bound together by that stronger ligament, common danger.* To the government formed during the war. . . .

From the pamphlet: At the time of this declaration we had no common government; the articles of confederation were submitted to the representatives of the States eight days afterwards, and were not adopted by all of the states until 1781. These loose and imperfect articles of union sufficed to bring us successfully through the revolution. *Common danger was a stronger bond of union than these articles of confederation.*

In this instance it is the speaker who favors terseness. The essayist is verbose. Superior force is found by the extemporizer in the repetition, "common government . . . common danger," as well as in the revised metaphor.

Stephens used the extempore method even for his literary society addresses and, if he edited them, he preserved marvelously the extempore flavor of his speaking in the published pamphlets. The following example formed the peroration to an address at Emory University:

> "Fail! Fail!
> In the lexicon of youth, which fate reserves
> For a bright manhood, there is no such word
> As—*fail!*"

So say I to you in entering upon that career that lies before you. If, at any time, fears and doubts beset you as to your success. If the world grows cold. If friends forsake and enemies combine. If difficulties multiply, and even environ you. If the future assume its darkest robes without a ray of light or hope. Never despair. Never give up. Banish your apprehensions. Rely upon yourselves. And recollect that to the man who knows himself thoroughly, who governs himself properly, who stands firmly upon principle, who has a fixed purpose to do something worthy of future remembrance, and who applies himself with energy in its execution, *there is no such word as fail!* [49]

Stephens was "direct, clear, earnest and convincing, but like all purely extemporaneous speakers falls into many grammatical and rhetorical inaccuracies." Cases in point include "sprung" for "sprang" in his commemorative speech on the Mexican War and the sentence fragments in this occasional speech. But these fragments supplement the other examples of economy in composition, and they add a driving force strong enough to make deliberate design probable. For all of the technical blemishes, Stephens was as sharply emphatic, unified and coherent in sentence structure as was Toombs. They were definitely superior to the other two, who were apt to get wound up in such sentences as Johnson produced in one of his commemorative speeches: "Let me, then, my young friends, most of whom I meet here to-day for the first time, and, what is a more solemn reflection, most of whom I meet also for the last time upon earth, adjure you, and you my brothers, *alumni*, and every one within the sound of my voice, sacredly to observe and scrupulously to comply with every provision of the constitution." [50]

But Johnson did not win his following by taking this type of rhetoric to the stump. He could also produce campaign oratory:

Stand up in the face of impudent Abolitionism, and when they taunt you with advocating sectional rights, hurl the constitution in their teeth and ask them if the constitution is sectional . . . . Fel-

[49] *Address of Hon. Alexander H. Stephens . . . Emory College . . . on Commencement Day, July 21, 1852* (pamphlet; Duke University Library).

[50] *An Address Delivered before the Volunteer Encampment . . . by Herschel V. Johnson.*

low citizens, I stand upon a rock in reference to these questions; an earthquake cannot shake me from it. And I would go to the North; to Boston tomorrow, or any other day, and meet any Abolitionist in that goodly city upon this question, and would prove to any twelve honest men, sworn to render a truthful verdict, that slavery is not sectional, but as national and broad as the constitution itself.[51]

Here are strong figures of speech and rolling rhythms, giving an impression of massive strength. Johnson's physical weight seems to be repeated in the weight of his style. These are ponderous periods; but there is fiery power in them, too.

Not many examples in American oratory can so well illustrate the motive power of the emotional peroration as does that of Toombs's farewell speech to the Senate, January 6, 1861:

You will not regard your confederate obligations; you will not regard your constitutional obligations; you will not regard your oaths. What, then, am I to do? Am I a freeman? Is my state, a free state, to lie down and submit because political fossils raise the cry of the glorious Union? Too long already have we listened to this delusive song. We are freemen. We have rights; I have stated them. We have wrongs; I have recounted them . . . . We have appealed, time and time again, for these constitutional rights. You have refused them. We appeal again. Restore us these rights as we had them, as your court adjudges them to be, just as all our people have said they are; redress these flagrant wrongs, seen of all men, and it will restore fraternity, and peace, and unity, to all of us. Refuse them, and what then? We shall then ask you, "Let us depart in peace." Refuse that, and you present us war. We accept it, and inscribing upon our glorious banners the glorious words "liberty and equality," we will trust to the blood of the brave and the God of battles for security and tranquility.[52]

The effect builds on balanced sentences and antithesis—the

[51] Baltimore *Republican*, Sept. 15, 1856.
[52] *Congressional Globe*, 36th Cong., 2nd Sess., 271.

right fist, the left fist, blow after blow. The rhythm sustains the mood. This is a war beat, near to savageness. Then comes what seems like a long drum roll of a climactic sentence, a challenge sustained to the end, and he is done.

There are many sources of stylistic strength in the whole of this speechmaking. Dignity is preserved, even though the language is that of the spoken word. There is a mastery of stylistic devices, vocabulary, and technical polish. But above all, there is a subtle, hidden source of strength—the man himself, as he faces his hearers, confident of his position and his personal integrity. Such ethical persuasion was never better represented than by McDowell in a campaign where the cry of "Abolitionist" was being raised once again:

I have never appeared before the people with a more perfect willingness to meet their decision than at this moment, tho' never, perhaps, pursued by a more embittered, and I might add, vindictive opposition. I care not for it: it cannot hurt me. I never sought to conciliate by personal acts—never by the surrender or change of a political opinion. Such as I entered into public life with I now retain unmodified and unregretted. Many of them were undoubtedly unpopular in their day, those of a small minority merely, & are undoubtedly still so—I have never retracted them for office.[53]

These, then, were four southern Democrats: a Virginia gentleman, austerely "grand" in style and delivery; a brawny, beefy, college-bred yeoman; a wisp of a man, an indescribable admixture of limpid mellifluence and rasping wit; finally, the nonconforming aristocrat, whose invective and towering flights of eloquence are legendary to this day. Which was the "southern orator"? Unquestionably, each of the four. In their infinite variety, these master speakers have left a sense of individuality, worth, dignity, and integrity which has been woven into the fabric of their region's traditions.

[53] James McDowell, "Notes for Election, 1835," prepared for his campaign of that year, in McDowell Papers.

V

John C. Calhoun's Rhetorical Method in Defense of Slavery[*]

BERT E. BRADLEY AND JERRY L. TARVER

A prolific speaker, John C. Calhoun stands, as Parrington says, "commanding every highway of the Southern mind." [1] In light of Calhoun's powerful influence, his complex rhetorical efforts to defend southern interests are worthy of critical review and evaluation. Instead of attempting a complete sweep of the long Calhoun speaking career, the present essay, limited by space, concentrates upon his handling of the single issue of slavery, for it was this subject which put the South Carolinian to his severest test and demanded the most of his rhetorical ingenuity. The great man could not have involved himself in a more difficult task than the attempt to justify this institution, bitterly condemned outside the South and fervently held to within the Cotton Kingdom. Perhaps a discussion of his debates with Webster or some of his other major efforts would have provided more accessible material and greater quantities of speeches and these efforts of course would have lent themselves to more traditional rhetorical analyses. But the intent here is to assess Calhoun's method of persuasion as

[*] This project supported in part by the University of Richmond Committee on Faculty Research.

[1] Vernon Louis Parrington, *The Romantic Revolution in America*, (New York, 1927), 65.

169

he came to grips with the paramount issue that plagued the South and placed the southern rhetorician in a difficult defensive position.

Declaring on his deathbed that were he only able to make one more speech he could do more for his country than ever before, Calhoun expressed his firm belief in the efficacy of rhetoric. His extensive career as a public speaker demonstrated, too, the importance he attached to speech as a political tool, and Calhoun held his own with Clay and Webster in monumental rhetorical contests which decided vital public questions. Yet large numbers of Calhoun's speeches were singularly deficient in appeals for action. Nor did they often contain explicit calls for a change in belief on the part of his opposition. The typical thesis sentence of a Calhoun speech is represented by such lofty declarations as, "I rise simply to state my reasons" and "I propose to make a few explanatory remarks." [2] Disdaining to corrupt himself with mass appeals of the more common sort, Calhoun was perhaps most aptly characterized when pictured as a "college professor demonstrating to his class." [3]

Yet in his speeches Calhoun attempted to describe his position so convincingly that belief and action would be altered. Seeking to defend slavery by explaining it, he typically employed a form of discourse which can best be identified as expository and before his defense can be evaluated, his method must be dissected. While some theorists consider rhetoric and persuasion as practically interchangeable terms, other teachers and critics find it at least convenient to differentiate between the simple rhetorical function of transmitting information and the more complex function of altering the listener's opinion or course of action. Regardless of the theoretical

[2] Richard K. Cralle (ed.), *The Works of John C. Calhoun* (6 vols.; New York, 1859), IV, 1, 340.

[3] John Wentworth, *Congressional Reminiscences* (Chicago, 1882), 21.

difficulties in discovering where the boundary can be set, the distinction remains useful as a descriptive tool. But guidelines, practical and theoretical, become even less clear when the speaker's avowed purpose is informative but his intent is actually persuasive. Once again, however subjectively, practical usage suggests that such a schizophrenic form of discourse does exist. The Mark Antony funeral oration is a well-known specimen—as opposed, let us say, to Patrick Henry's expressly persuasive "Call to Arms"—and politicians and advertisers furnish fresh examples daily.

J. H. McBurney and G. E. Mills find the method common enough to apply the special label "explanation" to those persuasive speeches which set forth information in such a way as to produce a desired change without calling for it.[4] According to Mills, the speaker who wishes to persuade by explaining "starts with the background of the problem, narrates some relevant events, describes some conditions, explains the trend, and thereby builds up a pressure of facts and mental images which make the outcome seem inevitable."[5] The connecting link between the speaker's facts and his conclusion must be made by the listener. In describing how this link is forged, McBurney and Mills state: "The explanatory approach in argument seeks to involve the proposition in question as a necessary circumstance of the data presented. The key to this is *implication*. The proposition is implied or suggested as naturally to be inferred, often without being expressly stated."[6] McBurney and Mills rely heavily on example to delineate the bounds of expository rhetoric and expressly decline to defend explanation as differing essentially in theory "from the traditional syllogistic-enthymematic approach."[7] They go on to

---

[4] James H. McBurney and Glen E. Mills, *Argumentation and Debate, Techniques of a Free Society* (2nd ed.; New York, 1964), 155–64.

[5] Glen E. Mills, *Reason in Controversy* (Boston, 1964), 151.

[6] McBurney and Mills, *Argumentation and Debate*, 156.

[7] *Ibid.*, 157.

point out, however: "There can be no serious question that the two approaches are quite different methodologically"; and they claim quite correctly that method is the matter of their immediate concern. D. C. Bryant and K. R. Wallace also recommend exposition to the student as a potential persuasive mode of speaking,[8] and Robert T. Oliver claims: "In many instances the most influential persuasive speaking is that which is almost entirely expository." [9]

The texts cited thus far are concerned mainly with teaching rather than with criticism. In a brief analysis of a critical approach, L. Thonssen and A. C. Baird suggest that exposition is often a necessary prerequisite for argument although the authors admit "the distinction between them is not absolute." [10] Other writers, among whom John F. Genung may be cited, take the position that exposition does not concern itself at all with persuasion.[11]

Having necessarily paid some attention to the genre of expository persuasion, the focus of attention must return to the case at hand. The specific object of this essay will be two-fold: (1) to explain the characteristics of Calhoun's rhetoric which identify it as expository persuasion, and (2) to evaluate the appropriateness of this method in the defense of slavery.

In describing Calhoun's use of the expository method, three characteristics can be identified. First, even when he could be successful only if his efforts were in fact persuasive, Calhoun consistently specified that his object in speaking was merely to inform. He deliberately elevated expository speaking above ordinary argument. In one obscure controversy he stubbornly

[8] Donald C. Bryant and Karl R. Wallace, *Fundamentals of Public Speaking* (3rd ed.; New York, 1960), 388–89.
[9] Robert T. Oliver, *The Psychology of Persuasive Speech* (New York, 1957), 218.
[10] Lester Thonssen and A. Craig Baird, *Speech Criticism* (New York, 1948), 344–45.
[11] John Franklin Genung, *The Working Principles of Rhetoric* (New York, 1900), 554.

refused to engage in debate over the merits of the case. He declared that he scorned to attack the administration for its stand on the question at issue and insisted that his object in speaking "was much higher—to state facts, point out causes, and trace consequences." [12] Repeatedly he stressed that his primary objective was simply to present necessary information. In a favorite analogy explaining his method, he often compared himself to a physician dispassionately setting out to uncover the nature of an illness.

Calhoun spoke on many occasions when he realized that the vote would go against him. Faced with certain defeat he appeared fully reasonable in disavowals of intent to convince. But he habitually turned to expository persuasion. Addressing an overwhelmingly partisan audience in Charleston in 1847, for example, he offered only to set forth the danger which threatened the South and to explain the means available for repelling it. He proposed leaving it to his listeners "to determine what measures should be adopted...." [13]

In his Charleston speech Calhoun made it clear he considered his limited objective in speaking adequate for his cause. Confident that truth in the slavery controversy was on his side and certain that it only needed to be rationally explained, he told his audience, "I have never known truth, promptly advocated in the spirit of truth, fail to succeed in the end." [14] Calhoun was equally optimistic when, facing immediate defeat on the Senate floor, he insisted on the truth of his position:

I have now, Senators, said what I intended. It may be asked, why have I spoken at all? It is not from the expectation of changing a single vote on the opposite side. That is hopeless. The indications, during this discussion, show, beyond doubt, a foregone determination on the part of its advocates to vote for the bill, without the slightest amendment, be its defects or errors ever so great. They

[12] Cralle (ed.), *Works of John C. Calhoun*, III, 501.
[13] *Ibid.*, IV, 383.   [14] *Ibid.*, IV, 385.

have shut their eyes and closed their ears. The voice of an angel from heaven could not reach their understandings. Why, then have I raised mine? Because my hope is in truth. "Crushed to earth, it will rise again." [15]

Calhoun thus attempted in his speeches to portray himself as the great explainer. He wished to be heard as the knowledgeable teacher or the helpful, informed physician rather than as a political debater. This view of his function as an orator, which he so assiduously cultivated, is the first feature of his oratory which identifies his rhetorical method as expository.

Second, Calhoun relied on the rhetorical process described by McBurney and Mills as implication. He presented information not as an end in itself but in the belief that, if accepted, his data would tend to force listeners to agree with his conclusions.

Calhoun's conviction that facts generate their own persuasive conclusions, an idea which is suggested in statements quoted earlier, emerges explicitly in a statement regarding southern attitudes toward slavery. He explained to the Senate that many Southerners had at one time considered slavery evil, but with the coming of outside agitation, they were compelled "to look into the nature and character of this great institution." The result, he asserted, was that "many false impressions" were corrected.[16] Thus the South understood the problem, and understanding produced the conclusion that slavery should be defended. This specific example of "facts" having secured "results" depicts in microcosm the implicative process on which Calhoun depended in his slavery rhetoric.

Calhoun's reliance on implication as a mode of argument might be copiously illustrated. In his resolutions of 1837, for example, he sought to gain Senate approval of a series of pronouncements on slavery. "The resolutions spoke definitely

[15] *Ibid.*, IV, 200.   [16] *Ibid.*, III, 180.

174

and on all points for themselves," he said, declaring that "it was the object of these resolutions to bring forward the facts and display them in their true light." [17] The importance of implication is evident both in the resolutions themselves and in his defense of them.

The fourth resolution, which most directly concerned slavery, illustrates the way Calhoun laid down one alleged fact after another in an attempt to make his conclusion inevitable. The resolution began with the declaration that slavery was an important part of the domestic institutions of the South and then went on to point out that the institution had been inherited. Next Calhoun reminded the Senate that slavery existed at the time of the adoption of the Constitution and further that it was recognized in the distribution of powers among the states. Finally the resolution stated that any attack on slavery growing out of a change of opinion or feeling would be "a manifest breach of faith and a violation of the most solemn obligations, moral and religious." [18]

Statements in the resolution were largely descriptive and, except for the last, essentially innocuous. Once acknowledged, however, and taken as a whole, action against slavery on the part of the government would have been unjustified. If the entire package of six resolutions could be passed, Calhoun thought that he would have constructed a network of propositions within which slavery would be forever safe. Not surprisingly, then, he announced that his resolutions would serve as a test case in which a positive vote would be a holy pledge of protection.

Calhoun forced the Senate to consider his analysis of slavery, but in the process he annoyed his enemies and dismayed his friends. Neither side fully grasped his strategy. Many senators saw the resolutions as worthless abstractions which need-

[17] *Ibid.*, III, 142.   [18] *Ibid.*, III, 141.

lessly stirred up the slavery issue at a time when no imminent threat existed.

Recognizing that these objections struck at the heart of his rhetorical strategy, he reminded his listeners that abstract truth, far from being insignificant, was the basis for all important political movements from the Magna Carta to the American Revolution. Revealing his trust in implication, he maintained that abstract truths "deeply impress the understanding and the heart" and fail to control only "the ignorant and the brute creation." [19]

When the resolutions were attacked Calhoun attempted to center the argument on the issue of understanding facts which he insisted would lead to the right conclusion. In reply to objections by Crittenden, Calhoun said "he was not at all surprised that he and the Senator from Kentucky should take such very different views of the subject. We differ totally as to the facts, and it is not wonderful that we should differ as to the remedy." [20] In pressing his physician analogy Calhoun stated "he ought not, perhaps, to be surprised that Senators should differ so widely from him on this subject. They did not view the disease as he did." [21] Denying any intent to argue, he explained his views and trusted implication to convert his facts into conclusions in the minds of his listeners.

Scorning Clay's efforts at compromise, Calhoun warned against substituting expediency for principle. Although willing to alter the language of his resolutions, he bitterly opposed changes in his carefully structured ideas from which conclusions were to be inferred, in the language of McBurney and Mills, "as a necessary circumstance." Calhoun prevailed on the Senate to endorse the first four of his resolutions, but in spite of his best efforts to keep the series intact, the fifth was amended and the sixth laid on the table.

Seldom commenting on his rhetorical methods, he scattered

[19] *Ibid.*, III, 165.   [20] *Ibid.*, III, 163.   [21] *Ibid.*, III, 177.

a few remarks through his letters making it evident that he was proud of his speaking ability and that he expected the implicative method to be effective. Writing to his daughter, Anna, and again to his son, Andrew, he expressed delight in the extensive printing of his veto speech and pointed out that the speech was "but the premises from which [nullification] *irresistibly follows.*" [22]

The importance of implication to Calhoun is strikingly clear when an effort is made to outline his position on slavery. Surprisingly, nowhere in his speeches did he systematically set forth his slavery arguments. Instead he inserted fragments and subtle references throughout various addresses.

The thesis "Slavery is a positive good," Calhoun's theme from 1837 onward, was developed with scattered bits of exposition on labor systems and social structure. By juxtaposing his conclusions and a rapid succession of supporting assertions, he implied a relationship which he never actually established. Addressing himself "to the facts" with his assertions "fully borne out by history," Calhoun can be identified as an implicative arguer who "builds up a pressure of facts and mental images which make the outcome seem inevitable." [23]

Third, Calhoun chose for the development of his ideas material which complemented his expository function. Although he buttressed the explanation of his slavery defense with a variety of types of supporting material, he demonstrated a marked predilection for specific support in the form of historical narrative, analogy, and definition. These forms of support, supplemented by amplification of ideas through restatement and explanation, provided the substance of Calhoun's expository discourse.

[22] J. Franklin Jameson (ed.), *Correspondence of John C. Calhoun*, in *Annual Report of the American Historical Association, 1889* (2 vols.; Washington, 1900), 344, hereinafter cited as *Calhoun Correspondence.* Emphasis added.
[23] Mills, *Reason in Controversy*, 151.

For one of his most important forms of support he relied on historical narrative, contending that the true state of affairs could be ascertained through study of the past. Sometimes he described early in a speech the historical background necessary for the understanding of ensuing contentions, as when he opened his attack on the British seizure of slaves on the ship *Enterprise* with "a brief narrative" of previous cases.[24] From his historical account he expected his audience to see the principles needed to justify reimbursement for the slaves freed from the *Enterprise*.

In other speeches Calhoun inserted historical narrative into the body of his argument. For example, he marshaled history to show the South's increasing numerical disadvantage in protecting slavery, to show the legal status of slavery when the government was formed, to state that no colored race had developed a free government, and to expose the rising threat of abolitionism. His historical narratives supported propositions of fact: the South is in a minority, slavery was sanctioned by the founding fathers, the Negro race is unqualified to develop and maintain a free government, and abolition endangers southern security.

Propositions of fact may of course be debated and at times Calhoun offered lessons in history which were subject to dispute. Speaking for state control over slavery he used history to support his position that the government of the United States was federal rather than national in character.[25] He found in history too the blessings of slavery for the Negro race.

Calhoun clearly intended his lectures on history to affect his listeners. In debating the nature of the government of the United States with Senator Simmons, Calhoun concluded that its history needed only to be explained: "If the Senator's eye's had been properly directed, he would not have been ignorant of

24 Cralle (ed.), *Works of John C. Calhoun*, III, 463.
25 *Ibid.*, IV, 353–54.

this; and not being ignorant, would not have made the extraordinary declaration he has made." [26]

Calhoun also made frequent use of analogy. At times he used it merely as a stylistic device, as in the case in which he referred to strands of rope holding the union together. In other instances he included an analogy as a major or sometimes as the sole form of support for a point. Numerous instances may be cited, but in one passage of some two hundred words he inserted no less than four analogies to attack abolitionist petitions. He insisted immediate action was needed (1) "to meet the danger on the frontier." Penetration of abolitionist doctrines would constitute a dangerous wound in the political body since (2) "the moral is like the physical world. Nature has incrusted the exterior of all organic life, for its safety. Let that be broken through, and it is all weakness within." Defending the South against the petitions, Calhoun saw himself comparable to one of (3) "the Patriots of the Revolution" determined that the South would not be reduced by the abolitionists (4) "to the condition of the slaves they would emancipate." [27]

In making ideas clear and vivid the analogy can be of considerable value. Even more than historical narrative, it contributes to graphic explanation. But analogy is tricky and subject to abuse, and Calhoun chose to see resemblances between highly dissimilar ideas. That he was fully aware of this potential weakness in analogy is revealed when he inquired in a Senate debate: "Now, I ask the Senator, where is the analogy between this and the present petition, the reception of which he so strenuously urges? He is a lawyer of long experience and of distinguished reputation—and I put the question to him, on what possible principle can a case so perfectly dissimilar justify the vote he intends to give on the present occasion?" [28]

Calhoun favored definition as another form of support. The

[26] *Ibid.*, IV, 354–55.　　[27] *Ibid.*, III, 445–46.　　[28] *Ibid.*, II, 473.

resolutions he presented in the Senate in 1837 and 1847, for example, were in part definitions defended in numerous speeches and designed to help the Senate to understand *his* understanding of such fundamental concepts as abolitionism, the right of petition, and the form of government of the country. Concerned with the correct definition of the term "United States" Calhoun steadfastly refused to use the word "nation," a term which defined for the states a more subordinate role than he was willing to accept.

Calhoun's obsession with abstractions and principles reflects his interest in definition. He seemed to feel that if a position to be defended in debate were based on an accepted fundamental concept, then it needed only to be defined to be accepted. Definition, like analogy and historical narrative, contributed to the identification of his rhetoric as expository.

In summary, Calhoun used argument through exposition as a method of developing his slavery defense. This method was characterized by an ostensibly informative intent which depended for persuasive effect on implications drawn from supporting material essentially descriptive in nature.

In identifying Calhoun's rhetoric as expository, no suggestion is intended that his approach was unique for the time in which he spoke. With or without Calhoun, American politicians were destined to spend much of the first half of the nineteenth century engaged in expository speaking. The brilliant compromises of the founding fathers offered no clear solutions for a growing nation's increasing problems with federalism and slavery. Webster's long dissertations probed American history no less than Calhoun's, and other men of penetrating intellect joined freely in seemingly endless debates seeking to determine the nature of the American Union. But none exceeded Calhoun in his penchant for detailed explanations. Constantly aware of the relationship between a matter of policy and the assumptions regarding the nature of government on which all legislative acts rested, he relentlessly pressed forward with his abstractions, his definitions, his facts, causes, and consequences.

Many public address and persuasion texts, as pointed out earlier, discuss exposition as a method of advocacy, but they fail to explain a critical approach for analyzing and evaluating expository speaking. And as critics have stated in regard to Aristotle's *Rhetoric*, pedagogical precepts drawn from observation do not always serve automatically as tools for analysis.[29]

The theory of exposition as a persuasive device and the appropriate means for evaluating expository speeches deserve more attention than is warranted in the present study. Here, having described Calhoun's expository method, the appropriateness of the expository defense of slavery will be evaluated by standards necessarily exploratory and tentative.

It must first be pointed out that the method was appropriate for the man. In intellect and demeanor Calhoun was especially well suited to play the role of expository speaker rather than mass persuader.

Arranging a marriage or an argument with equal deliberation, Calhoun's analytical mind was his pride and his curse. In his most famous defense of his mental processes he replied to an attack by Senator Clayton of Delaware:

The Senator . . . calls this metaphysical reasoning, which he says he cannot comprehend. If by metaphysics he means that scholastic refinement which makes distinctions without difference, no one can hold it in more utter contempt than I do; but if, on the contrary, he means the power of analysis and combination—that power which reduces the most complex idea into its elements, which traces

29 Edwin Black, *Rhetorical Criticism* (New York, 1965), 2-3, 91-92; Anthony Hillbruner, *Critical Dimensions: The Art of Public Address Criticism* (New York, 1966), 113.

causes to their first principle, and, by the powers of generalization and combination, unites the whole in one harmonious system— then, so far from deserving contempt, it is the highest attribute of the human mind.[30]

Stern and aloof, Calhoun deserved the sobriquet "cast-iron man" for his unyielding adherence to the dictates of his metaphysics. Satisfied with the soundness of his conclusions and personally incapable of the warmth of Clay or the eloquence of Webster, Calhoun preferred a rhetoric which exalted the speech over the speaker or the audience. Incapable of bending, he did not desire to plead with audiences. In his informative role he was free from the necessity of direct appeals for support. While not without passion, Calhoun was moved by ideas; consequently, exposition was the most suitable form of speech for his personality.

Even though he prided himself on his own intellectual ability, Calhoun questioned the value of reason in causing other people to act. For example, in a letter to Duff Green in 1835 he discredited "the force of reason" in persuasion. But he believed opinions could be altered by explanation, for in the same paragraph he wrote, "I have never doubted that the great truths developed in our controversy would work their way in spite of all difficulties." [31] Calhoun, having arrived at the truth, was willing to share his conclusions with less fortunate individuals who could not appreciate the reasoning process by which they were produced.

Calhoun's reputation as a master logician deserves separate attention at this point. Although an occasional biographer or critic has cited minor flaws in Calhoun's reasoning,[32] few have

---

[30] Cralle (ed.), *Works of John C. Calhoun*, II, 232.

[31] *Calhoun Correspondence*, 344.

[32] See editor's comment in H. Von Holst, *John C. Calhoun* (Boston, 1899), v–vi; Richard Hofstadter, *The American Political Tradition* (New York, 1959), 75.

perceived as did Richard N. Current that "his argument reveals gaps, inconsistencies, contradictions, and downright errors once it is closely examined." [33] Most writers praise Calhoun, as did Avery O. Craven in speaking of him as having "the best disciplined mind of his generation and a logic unmatched inside or outside of Congress." [34]

Lorenzo Sears claimed that Calhoun "made great speeches, but they were great in the closeness of their reasoning. . . . Accepting his premises it was difficult to escape from the conclusions of his rigid logic." [35] John S. Jenkins thought: "He had studied the philosophy as well as the rules of logic; or, if not that, the faculty of reasoning with accuracy was natural to him. He was capable of generalizing and of drawing nice distinctions. He was shrewd in argument, and quick to observe the weak points of an antagonist. Of dialectics he was a complete master, whether synthetically or analytically considered." [36] Julian Hawthorne noted: "Calhoun devoted himself singly to defending slavery and State rights. This concentration of so powerful a mind upon one object gave him an enormous force; and the close and unrelenting logic with which he buttressed his claims could not be successfully met by his opponents." [37] Robert Fulton and Thomas Trueblood quote Daniel Webster as saying that Calhoun's "power consisted in the plainness of his propositions, in the closeness of his logic and in the earnestness and energy of his manner." [38] Margaret L. Coit quotes Webster as declaring that Calhoun

[33] Richard N. Current, *John C. Calhoun* (New York, 1966), 112.

[34] Avery O. Craven, *Civil War in the Making, 1815–1860* (Baton Rouge, 1959), 74.

[35] Lorenzo Sears, *The History of Oratory* (Chicago, 1896), 333.

[36] John S. Jenkins, *The Life of John Caldwell Calhoun* (New York, 1887), 449.

[37] Julian Hawthorne, *Orations of American Orators* (New York, 1900), 442.

[38] Robert Irving Fulton and Thomas Clarkson Trueblood, *British and American Eloquence* (New York, 1912), 245.

"could have 'demolished Newton, Calvin,' or even John Locke as a logician." [39] An analysis of his speeches, however, reveals that so many of his arguments in defense of slavery fail to meet the tests of valid logic that Calhoun's reputed skill in logical debating must be seriously questioned.

Without doubt Calhoun was intelligent, and he set forth his contentions with masterly progression. Generally his argumentation was deductive in nature and was presented in enthymematic form. Unless his major premise is isolated and its invalidity demonstrated, Calhoun's conclusions usually cannot be avoided. For example, in several speeches he argued that slavery was so interwoven into the life of the South that abolishing it would destroy southern society. This enthymematic process can be stated in the following syllogism:

Where slavery is interwoven in society, its destruction would destroy that society.
In the South slavery is interwoven in its society.
Therefore, in the South society will be destroyed if slavery is destroyed.

If the major premise is accepted then Calhoun's conclusion irresistibly follows.

Calhoun had the ability to reduce a complex problem to its constituent parts, but he cannot be said to deserve praise for his use of logic when he chose to reassemble the problem with some of the parts missing. And this is precisely what he did with respect to slavery. For example, one of his arguments about slavery was that it benefited the Negro. In developing the point Calhoun asserted slavery improved the Negro intellectually, physically, and morally, made him more civilized, and that it increased his numbers. Even granting the accuracy of this analysis, the fact that the argument is incomplete should not be overlooked, for he failed to count the cost of loss of

[39] Margaret L. Coit, *John C. Calhoun: American Portrait* (Boston, 1950), 463.

184

liberty to the human beings enslaved. An analysis which recognized the beneficial effects of civilization ought logically to give proper weight to the atrocities that occurred too frequently, the disruption of the Negro's family life, and the frustration of educational opportunities suffered by the victims of slavery.

In short, Calhoun's metaphysical reasoning, his power "of generalization and combination," was at times counterfeit. His cast of mind was rationalistic as opposed to emotional, but while the form of his discourse was logical, his arguments were in fact frequently invalid. The elusive relationship between support and conclusion in the implicative method has perhaps contributed to the difficulty in readily exposing logical flaws.

However faulty his logic, Calhoun remained supremely confident that his vision of truth was unimpaired. And intellectual confidence, helpful for any speaker, seems especially vital for one who seeks to persuade with speeches of explanation. Calhoun once declared, "I shall go prepared to speak the truth, fully and boldly, and to do my duty regardless of responsibility." [40] Nowhere did he display his confidence more than in his use of the word "truth." He regarded his various positions and the truth as equals in an unshakable equation. In presenting his resolutions of 1837, for example, he saw his object as merely displaying the facts of the argument "in their true light." [41] In his well-known analysis of his own life, he wrote, "In looking back, I see nothing to regret and little to correct." [42]

In some respects the slavery issue was an apt subject for Calhoun's expository speaking. He seems to have appreciated the advantage he had as the defender of an established insti-

[40] *Calhoun Correspondence*, 736.
[41] Cralle (ed.), *Works of John C. Calhoun*, III, 142.
[42] *Calhoun Correspondence*, 569.

tution. The conservative South Carolinian saw a presumption in his favor as protector of an established tradition in the South where "Providence had brought together two races . . . inseparably united beyond the possibility of separation." [43]

An examination of Calhoun's case for extending slavery into the territories reveals that even this aggressive position was developed with a defensive rhetoric. Instead of arguing that slavery could or would flourish in the territories, or that its existence there would be advantageous for the territories or the nation, Calhoun argued, defensively, that it was legal for Southerners to take slaves into the territories. Since he contended that the founding fathers had not granted authority over slavery to Congress, he did not desire to have slavery extended into the territories by Congress, for he thought that would be as illegal as to have Congress interfere with it within a state. Calhoun did argue, however, that Congress could not prohibit slavery in a territory. To develop this argument, he had to explain the Ordinance of 1787 and the Missouri Compromise which were based on the premise that the power to control slavery in the territories did reside with Congress. He explained that the South had accepted the Ordinance of 1787 only because the North agreed to return fugitive slaves to the South. Nevertheless, said Calhoun, the compromise did not signify a surrender of principles; the South had not admitted that Congress had the legal right to control slavery in the territories. He explained that the Missouri Compromise was simply a case of power politics; the South had been outvoted on the floor of Congress.[44]

Calhoun also argued that neither the people nor the government of a territory could exclude slaveholders with their slaves. Until a territory became a state, it must be open to all citizens.

[43] Cralle (ed.), *Works of John C. Calhoun*, III, 179.
[44] *Ibid.*, VI, 297–98, 303; IV, 481–98, 529.

To buttress this argument, Calhoun insisted that the Constitution extended to the territories.[45] Thus his legal justification for extending slavery into the territories was a defensive posture concerned wholly with establishing the right to take slaves into the territories and not with developing a need for such action nor for even citing benefits that would accrue from it.

The expository method of advocacy, although not limited to upholding the status quo, was nevertheless appropriate for such a strategy. The attitude that "outsiders don't understand the problem" is perhaps well enough known not to need an elaborate discussion in explaining the defensive posture of those who defended slavery.

The conditions under which the expository method of persuasion could function properly, however, were not present in the slavery debate, and Calhoun's use of explanation for argument must finally be judged unsound. According to McBurney and Mills, if the speaker is to succeed with the implicative method he must "make it clear that the proposition he is defending is a part of a system which the listener cannot safely or logically deny."[46] In support of this contention Bryant and Wallace also point out that, while his conclusion may be highly debatable, the expository speaker can be successful only if he "relies upon accepted truths, verifiable facts and data."[47]

Calhoun was not unchallenged either from the vantage point of the twentieth century or of the time in which he spoke. The boiling controversy over slavery was at once the cause of Calhoun's speeches and the enemy of his method.

Obviously not drawing upon generally accepted supporting material, he nevertheless tried to give his statements the gloss

---

[45] *Ibid.*, IV, 480, 498–500.
[46] McBurney and Mills, *Argumentation and Debate*, 160.
[47] Bryant and Wallace, *Fundamentals of Speaking*, 388.

of incontrovertibility. At many points Calhoun sought to place his argument "beyond controversy." [48] He employed such asides as "I cannot be mistaken," "I speak with full knowledge [and] . . . see my way clearly," and "It is useless to disguise the fact." Prefacing a bold assertion with the ringing declaration "I appeal to the facts," he seemingly realized that his conclusions would be more acceptable if he could only convince his hearers of the incontrovertibility of the evidence and the premises on which they were based.

Calhoun spoke meaningfully, however, only to those who could not "safely or logically deny" the component parts of the system he defended. He was effective only with those to whom his descriptions, definitions, narrations, and analogies were considered indisputable. His addresses were finally little more than revelations of his conclusions in a form easily adapted into a catechism for the faithful. Thus he turned his intellect inward; he constructed a rationale for partisans, an argument for those who already believed.

The distorted and single-minded view of the truth held by John C. Calhoun had tragic results. His explanation of slavery which could not carry the Senate flourished only in its one natural habitat; the South embraced his exposition and used it in vigorously protecting slavery. His analytical prowess provided bits and pieces of argument to sustain an unworthy cause for a decade after his death.

Calhoun's defense of slavery could not ultimately succeed in the larger marketplace of ideas, because the false logic on which it was based produced arguments which the nation would not accept. In his stubborn refusal to take into account the unpalatability of his speeches, he was blind to the flaws in his thinking and was thus not the master but the victim of his metaphysics. Had he been more malleable, more willing to un-

48 Cralle (ed.), *Works of John C. Calhoun*, II, 630, 633; III, 519; IV, 494.

derstand viewpoints other than his own, he could have been more successful in explaining to the country the circumstances in which the South was caught. And a more acceptable explanation would perhaps have been based on sounder reasoning; if Calhoun had been a better rhetorician he might have been a better logician.

The arguments which finally defeated Calhoun's ideas by placing the power of the presidency in the hands of an opponent of slavery came ironically from a speaker who also looked deeply into great abstractions. Studying the same facts available to Calhoun and sharing many of the same premises, Abraham Lincoln constructed a different exposition of the slavery question. Perhaps no less than Calhoun he believed the Negro inferior and mistrusted the social results of his freedom, but when Lincoln completed his analysis, the implications he drew set slavery on the road to extinction. Calhoun was right at least in his belief that truth would prevail.

VI

Speaking in the Southern Commercial Conventions
1837–1859

OWEN PETERSON

In the quarter-century preceding the outbreak of the Civil War, Southerners were afforded an opportunity to discuss the major economic and political problems confronting the region in a series of commercial conventions. In all, sixteen conventions were held and the subject matter of these meetings ranged from politics, internal improvements, and trade with Europe, to agricultural methods and education. The movement can conveniently be divided into three periods: those conventions seeking to promote direct trade with Europe; conventions primarily interested in internal improvements; and conventions which dealt with a variety of political and commercial questions. The entire list of conventions with which this paper is concerned is as follows:

Direct Trade Conventions

October 16–18, 1837..Augusta
April 2–4, 1838..Augusta
October 15–17, 1838..Augusta
April 15–18, 1839...Charleston

Internal Improvements Conventions

November 12–14, 1845.....................................Memphis
October 23–26, 1849..Memphis
January 5–9, 1852..New Orleans

Speaking in the Southern Commercial Conventions

General Conventions

December 18–21, 1852	Baltimore
June 6–9, 1853	Memphis
April 10–15, 1854	Charleston
January 9–14, 1855	New Orleans
January 30–February 3, 1856	Richmond
December 8–12, 1856	Savannah
August 10–13, 1857	Knoxville
May 10–14, 1858	Montgomery
May 9–13, 1859	Vicksburg

During the 1840's, when interest in improving transportation to the West was high, similar conventions, embracing delegates from all regions of the country, met in Chicago and St. Louis.[1] In addition, meetings to promote the commercial interests of local regions were held periodically throughout these years, including those at Richmond and Norfolk in 1838 [2] and numerous railroad conventions.

The factors giving rise to the southern commercial convention movement go back to the early nineteenth century and the industrial revolution. During this period, the growth of manufacturing, capital, and population in the North alarmed many Southerners. Harboring the suspicion that their northern competitors flourished at their expense, Southerners began to seek measures to offset the North's economic superiority.[3] Side by side with the economic competition was a growing political rivalry as the South sought additional slave states to maintain

[1] The Chicago convention met in July, 1847; the St. Louis convention was held in October, 1849. Many men who participated in southern commercial conventions also attended these meetings.

[2] John G. Van Deusen, *The Ante-Bellum Southern Commercial Conventions* (Historical Papers Published by the Trinity College Historical Society, Duke University Press; series XVI, 1926), 16.

[3] Herbert Wender, "Southern Commercial Conventions, 1837–1859," in *Johns Hopkins University Studies in Historical and Political Science,* XLVIII (Baltimore, 1930), 431.

191

its ascendancy in the Senate. Marking the political contest were such events as the Missouri Compromise, the acquisition of Texas and California, the Compromise of 1850, the Kansas-Nebraska Bill, and, finally, the election of Lincoln and disunion.[4]

Although the political rivalry was to influence later southern commercial conventions, the economic contest motivated the organization of the first meetings. Specifically, in their early conventions Southerners sought ways to establish more direct trade with Europe. In the minds of the organizers of the Augusta and Charleston meetings between 1837 and 1839, the root of the problem lay in the fact that northern ships carried on almost all American commerce with Europe. These vessels transported cotton abroad and then returned to the North laden with European goods. After paying duties, the cargo was reshipped to the South for resale. Many Southerners believed the added costs of tariff, transportation, and northern profits to be an important cause of northern prosperity and their own declining fortunes.[5] The first commercial conventions met to seek a remedy for this problem.[6]

As early as 1835 local meetings to discuss southern economic problems had been held at various places. But not until October, 1837, at Augusta, Georgia, when a number of local groups met to discuss their common difficulties was the commercial convention movement truly started. At that initial meeting only two states were represented, Georgia with sixty-five delegates and South Carolina with thirteen.[7] The second convention, held also at Augusta, in April, 1838, drew two

[4] Van Deusen, *The Ante-Bellum Southern Commercial Conventions*, 7.

[5] "Address of the Augusta Convention (1838) to the People of the South," *De Bow's Review* XXV (November, 1858), 477–93; Van Deusen, *The Ante-Bellum Southern Commercial Conventions*, 8.

[6] "Report of the first Augusta Convention," Charleston *Courier*, October 24, 1837; *De Bow's Review*, XIII (October, 1852), 483–84.

[7] Van Deusen, *The Ante-Bellum Southern Commercial Conventions*, 14; Wender, *Southern Commercial Conventions*, 11.

hundred participants from seven states, Virginia, North Carolina, Tennessee, Alabama, Florida, Georgia, and South Carolina.[8] The third convention at Augusta in October, 1838, attracted only 140 delegates from six states,[9] but the fourth and final meeting of the early period at Charleston in April, 1839, drew a record attendance of 220 members from seven states.[10] Thereafter, although the conventions consistently attracted more than two hundred delegates, precise numbers are difficult to determine because various sources report different figures. According to J. B. D. De Bow, who attended most of the meetings, the discrepancies resulted from the failure of many delegates to sign the official register.[11] Nevertheless, convention attendance apparently reached 600 to 800 at New Orleans in 1852, 710 at Montgomery in 1858, and 857 in Charleston in 1854. The largest number of states represented was sixteen at Memphis in 1845. Based on admittedly questionable data, average attendance at a typical southern commercial convention between 1845 and 1859 was almost five hundred delegates from eleven states.

The early conventions were open to almost any interested person, with no restrictions on admission. Several of the meetings in the 1850's, however, created credentials committees to determine who was to be admitted. Before 1852 the initiative for calling a convention seems to have originated with local groups who sought to solve a specific problem. For example, merchants who felt that individually they could do little to promote direct trade with Europe organized the Augusta meetings.[12] Memphis and New Orleans business leaders, hoping to

---

[8] Richmond *Enquirer*, April 10, 1838.

[9] Wender reports delegates attending from eight states.

[10] Van Deusen, *The Ante-Bellum Southern Commercial Conventions*, 17; *Journal of Proceedings, Charleston*, 1839.

[11] *De Bow's Review*, XXII (January, 1857), 82; XXIII (September, 1857), 298.

[12] *Ibid.*, IV (October, 1847), 222; XXII (January, 1857), 89.

promote each city as a terminal point for a railroad to the West, sponsored the conventions of 1845 and 1852. The convention of 1849 came about in a similar manner when citizens of Pulaski County, Arkansas, state legislators, and others organized to try to gain a route through Arkansas for the western railroad. At their request the state legislature passed a resolution calling for a convention in Memphis on July 4.[13] The mayor of Memphis then called a mass meeting which named committees of correspondence and arrangements.[14] While the earlier conventions usually were organized in this manner, after 1852 each convention set a time and place for another meeting a year later, thereby giving the proceedings greater continuity.

Once the date and site had been determined and the necessary committees appointed, circulars announcing the meeting were distributed and published in the press throughout the South. In addition, invitations were sent directly to prominent business leaders and government officials. Responding to the announcements, governors and mayors frequently designated official delegations. For example, in 1849 the governor of South Carolina appointed more than a hundred members; the governor of Florida appointed sixty; the governor of Georgia appointed one hundred; and several of the larger cities named delegations. In Arkansas a series of county mass meetings elected delegates.[15]

In spite of this procedure, most of the conventions were informally organized. For different reasons, a substantial proportion of the officially designated members failed to attend. Although railroads offered reduced fares to delegates, many still found the expense prohibitive. Others were unable to free

13 R. S. Cotterill, "Memphis Railroad Convention, 1849," *Tennesse Historical Magazine*, IV (June, 1918), 84.

14 Little Rock *Arkansas Democrat*, May 18, 1849.

15 *Ibid.*, May 21, June 13, July 13, 1849.

themselves of business or personal commitments. On the other hand, many persons who were not official delegates attended the meetings simply because they were interested in southern commercial improvements.

As a result of these factors, many conventions were locally dominated. In fact, at all of the conventions the host state was most heavily represented. Likewise, nearby states also often had large delegations, while distant states frequently sent only a few delegates. For example, to Memphis in 1845, Tennessee sent 214 delegates, followed by Mississippi with 173; but no other state had more than 35 members and North Carolina, Virginia, and Texas each had fewer than six. Similarly at New Orleans in 1855, Louisiana had 157 delegates; but the second largest state delegation totaled only fourteen.[16] Regarding the 1849 meeting, R. S. Cotterill concludes that "many of the delegates were not delegates at all, but only visitors in Memphis or transient residents." [17] Undoubtedly this observation was true of other meetings as well. In an effort to offset the disparity in size of the state delegations, some conventions adopted a rule giving each state one vote; other conventions gave each state as many votes as it had electoral votes. However, as late as 1858 in Montgomery everyone in attendance was permitted to cast a vote. Obviously, this was unfair to distant and sparsely represented states.

At most of the conventions, the vast majority of the members were business and commercial leaders. In addition, politicians, planters, editors, preachers, professors, bankers, and railroad and steamship promoters frequently attended. However, after 1856, with the introduction of political questions at Savannah, more political figures and increasingly fewer busi-

[16] *De Bow's Review*, I (January, 1846), 10–12; XVIII (March, 1855), 355–56.
[17] Cotterill, "Memphis Railroad Convention, 1849," 89.

nessmen and merchants attended the meetings. In fact, disunionist politicians largely dominated the conventions at Montgomery in 1858 and at Vicksburg in 1859.[18]

In reconstructing the convention settings, it is important to remember that many of the cities which have since become major metropolises were then communities of considerably smaller size. Of the ten sites, only Baltimore and New Orleans could boast populations exceeding one hundred thousand in 1850.[19] Charleston had sixty thousand inhabitants,[20] and Richmond slightly more than twenty-five thousand.[21] Memphis, Montgomery, and Vicksburg had fewer than ten thousand inhabitants and the official population of Knoxville was only 2,076.[22] Although small, these cities were leading commercial centers, and Baltimore and New Orleans ranked as two of the largest cities in the country. Nevertheless, the conventions must have constituted a major event for the host cities and probably aroused great interest among the local citizenry, especially in the smaller communities. One can imagine the impact of having more than seven hundred delegates in tiny Knoxville.

The conventions met in a variety of types of halls. The Augusta, Richmond, and Knoxville meetings were all held in churches. Those of 1849 and 1853 met in the City Hall Exchange Building in Memphis. The New Orleans meetings took place in the Second Municipality Hall in 1852 and in Lyceum

18 Van Deusen, *Ante-Bellum Southern Commercial Conventions*, 62.

19 In 1850 the population of Baltimore was 169,054 and New Orleans was 116,375. By 1860 Baltimore had grown to 212,418 and New Orleans had increased to 168,675. *A Report of the Seventeenth Census of the United States, Census of Population: 1950*, (Washington, 1952), 1–46; hereinafter referred to as *United States Census, 1950.*

20 Estimate in *De Bow's Review*, XXVI (May, 1859), 596.

21 *United States Census, 1950*, 1–46.

22 All figures are based on *United States Census, 1950*, 1–46, except for that for Vicksburg which is based on an estimate in *De Bow's Review*, XXVI (May, 1859), 597.

Hall in 1855. In 1854 the delegates assembled at the Meeting Street Theatre in Charleston. At Savannah in 1856 they met in the Athenaeum and St. Andrew's Hall and the 1858 meeting convened in a new warehouse owned by the Montgomery and West Point Railroad in the Alabama capital. Exactly what facilities were provided in the halls is not known, but presumably seating accommodations and some kind of platform or dais at one end of the hall were available. According to some accounts, members had difficulty hearing and it was necessary to ask speakers to mount the stage to address the audience.

Whether spectators were permitted to attend the earlier conventions is uncertain. However, accounts of the five meetings from 1853 and 1856 all contain references to the ladies in the audience. By special invitation, the governor and state legislature of Virginia also sat in attendance at the Richmond meeting.

Although the conventions dealt primarily with economic problems, the principal speakers were best known for their political activities. The list of prominent Southerners who spoke to the delegates in the course of the sixteen conventions includes John C. Calhoun, Robert Y. Hayne, Alexander Stephens, Robert Barnwell Rhett, William Lowndes Yancey, Judah P. Benjamin, John Slidell, Hugh S. Legaré, James Guthrie, John Breckinridge, General William Walker, John Bell, Lucius Q. C. Lamar, Pierre Soulé, Henry Wise, George McDuffie, and Cassius C. Clay. Others, perhaps of lesser fame but still important, were C. C. Memminger of South Carolina, A. B. Longstreet of Georgia, William Preston of South Carolina, Henry Hilliard of Alabama, Alexander Mouton of Louisiana, H. S. Foote of Mississippi, Albert Pike of Arkansas, Benjamin C. Yancey of Georgia, J. B. D. De Bow of Louisiana, Benjamin F. Perry of South Carolina, various state governors, and several United States senators and representatives. While seldom more than three or four of these leaders attended any one convention, their presence indicates the importance which many southern politicians attached to the movement.

A typical convention opened with the call to order, prayer by a local clergyman, and announcement of a temporary chairman. Next followed the selection of a permanent presiding officer, vice-presidents, and secretaries. The list of vice-presidents usually included one man from each state represented. Following these preliminary actions, the chairman appointed the standard committees on rules, business, plans, and projects. In addition, at some meetings special committees were appointed to investigate such matters as the improvement of western rivers, military and naval resources, forts and defenses, mails, levees, lakes and harbors, warehouses, and reopening the African slave trade. The main business of the convention consisted of the consideration of resolutions offered by the committees and by individual members.

Four kinds of speeches were heard at the convention: (1) opening addresses by the chairmen; (2) discourses by distinguished visitors who had been invited to address the group on a specific topic; (3) debate on the resolutions; and (4) ceremonial orations at functions such as dinners and banquets.

The two main themes with which the conventions dealt were, "What can the South do to improve its economic position?" and "How can the South best combat the growing political power of the North?" The questions were intimately related because European immigration to fill jobs created by northern prosperity was steadily expanding the population of the North and increasing its representation in Congress at the expense of the South. Furthermore, as the population grew, it began to expand westward, creating new states which challenged the South's dominance in the Senate. Thus, the threat to the South was both political and economic.

Two trends are discernible in the speaking at the sixteen conventions. The first is the gradual shift in interest from commercial problems to political questions. In the early conventions speaking was devoted almost exclusively to economic matters; but in the 1850's the political controversy began to intrude until finally it almost completely dominated the convention proceedings. A second trend is observable in the demands that the federal government aid the economy of the South: delegates to the first four conventions ignored the central government, preferring to concentrate on ways by which the states and private commercial interests could cooperate to improve economic conditions; the next three conventions took the position that the government was obligated to help the South and demanded assistance; the later conventions adopted a belligerent stance and simply denounced the government.

The first four conventions constitute a single phase of the commercial convention movement because of their continuity in personnel and deliberations and because of their almost exclusive concern with the establishment of direct trade with Europe. Meeting at six-month intervals, each convention was a continuation of the previous one, with many of the same delegates participating. Although the deliberations were extensive, these meetings stirred little debate because of their practice of appointing committees to consider and report out the measures for adoption by the entire assembly. Known at various times as the Committee of 13 or the Committee of 21, these groups met daily in closed session to draft resolutions and to prepare reports embodying the sentiments of the delegates. While the committee deliberated, the members continued to meet but they conducted little business.[23]

The reports of the special committees were presented in the form of speeches, although the entire committee actually had worked on their preparation. Of these documents, the report of the Committee of 21 at the Charleston convention in Octo-

[23] Augusta *Chronicle and Sentinel*, April 2, 3, 6, 7, 1838, October 18, 1838.

ber, 1839, is probably of greatest interest because it summarized the deliberations of the first four conventions.[24] In the address, William Harper of South Carolina recognized that the proposed goals of the convention conflicted with deep-rooted prejudices and interests and then reaffirmed the committee's conviction of the importance of southern commercial independence.

The remainder of the address was divided into a discussion of the problem and suggested remedies. "The evil complained of," Harper said, "is that the Southern and South-western States, while producing nearly three-fourths of the domestic exports of the Union, import scarcely one-tenth of the merchandise received in exchange for them." [25] The speaker developed this contention with statistics and cause-to-effect reasoning. He estimated that the South lost more than ten million dollars anually because of outside transportation of the region's exports and imports. In addition, he contended that the federal government discriminated against the South in its collection and disbursement of public revenues. He argued that the government employed duties on foreign imports to meet almost all of its financial needs. Furthermore, duties imposed to protect northern industries from foreign competition resulted in higher prices for southern consumers. Finally, Harper claimed, the vast sums raised from these duties were spent almost entirely in the North. Of nine hundred million dollars collected by customs, he estimated that nearly three-fourths "were levied on goods received in exchange for the productions of the South and South-west, and nine-tenths of it expended north of the Potomac." [26] According to Harper, still another cause of economic depression was that the South had devoted itself "too exclusively to agriculture." [27]

[24] De Bow attributes primary responsibility for the report to Robert Y. Hayne. *De Bow's Review*, IV (November, 1847), 337.
[25] *Ibid.*, 339.   [26] *Ibid.*, 340–42.   [27] *Ibid.*, 343.

Among the solutions to the problem, Harper recommended that planters invest in commercial ventures,[28] that credit be more liberally employed, that southern banks establish credit abroad, and that the South should encourage investment by foreigners. To provide a market for European imports, the speaker urged a vigorous program of railroad construction to connect the region's ports with the interior and the establishment of a regular line of packets and steamers in partnership with British firms.

Militating against all of these solutions, according to Harper, was the apathy and ignorance of the public. He urged the delegates to enlighten Southerners and gain their support for these ventures. He also proposed the publication of a journal to arouse interest.

Disclaiming any unfriendly feeling toward the North or the federal government, Harper concluded: "Our object is a free and open trade with the whole world—and all that we desire is, that in carrying on this trade, whether at home or abroad, our own ships and our own capital should be duly employed, and our merchants be allowed to participate in its advantages." [29]

The three earlier conventions had endorsed most of Harper's recommendations. In addition, the Augusta convention had passed resolutions urging merchants to use southern ports and ships whenever possible; asking legislatures to authorize "limited co-partnerships" so that merchants might combine their capital to establish direct trade; [30] recommending that states determine whether sufficient banking capital was available to finance railroad construction and, if not, to provide for

[28] One difficulty in achieving greater diversification, which Harper did not mention in his speech but which he noted in a footnote to the printed text, was the low esteem in which southern planters held mercantile pursuits. See *De Bow's Review*, IV (November, 1847), 350.

[29] *Ibid.*, 350–56.

[30] Savannah *Republican*, October 24, 1837.

it "in such a manner as may be deemed safe and most conducive to the restoration of Southern commerce." [31]

The Charleston convention in 1839 marked the end of the first period of the attempt of the South to secure economic independence. In spite of the promises and resolves, most of the convention proposals were never realized. However, the four meetings did produce some achievements. First, they focused attention on their problems in an effective manner. Their reports and proceedings occupied prominent places in newspapers, and delegates returned home to spread the word of the conventions. Second, as a result of these sessions, a few concrete changes were effected. For example, at the second Augusta meeting a delegate reported that, in compliance with a memorial of the earlier convention, the legislature of South Carolina had authorized limited partnerships.[32] Another example of concrete action was the resurrection of *The Southern Review* in response to Harper's call for a regional economics journal.[33] Perhaps most important, these early conventions set a pattern for future discussions and when in the 1840's a means was sought to promote railway expansion and internal improvements, southern leaders turned to the commercial convention as a vehicle for this endeavor.

Six years elapsed before the commercial convention was revived. The second phase of the movement consisted of conventions at Memphis in 1845 and 1849 and New Orleans in 1852. Although they had no logical connection with each other or with the earlier conventions, their unity lies in their interest in internal improvements. Ignoring direct trade almost completely, the delegates now focused attention on railroad expansion. Unlike the 1830 meetings which sought to promote

[31] Augusta *Chronicle and Sentinel,* October 18, 1838.
[32] *Ibid.,* April 7, 1838.
[33] *De Bow's Review,* IV (November, 1847), 356.

southern economy without federal assistance, the delegates in the second period demanded government aid as their due.

The first of these three conventions, held at Memphis in November, 1845, attracted 574 delegates. The outstanding features of the speaking at this convention were John C. Calhoun's defense of government internal improvements, the scope of the demands of the delegates, and the avoidance of controversy.

Addressing an audience which traditionally favored decentralized government, state rights, and private enterprise, Calhoun provided the conservative Southerners with a rationale for a massive federal program of internal improvements. Long a foe of federal-sponsored internal improvements, Calhoun reaffirmed his position. He believed, he stated, that what private interests could accomplish alone should be left to them; what states and individuals could achieve jointly should be done through their cooperative action; and only when neither of these, separately or in combination, could solve a problem should the federal government intervene. However, with regard to the development of the Mississippi River Valley, he thought the latter was the case. Calling the river a "great inland sea," Calhoun argued that the government was as much obligated to protect and improve it as it was to defend the Atlantic seaboard. Going a step further, the stanch conservative advocated granting alternate sections of unoccupied land to the railroads and allowing them to purchase iron duty free in order to promote transportation in the region.[34]

Thus, provided with a rationale, the delegates endorsed a series of resolutions proposing extensive federal improvements to connect the ports of the Atlantic and Gulf of Mexico with the Mississippi and Ohio valleys. In the name of transportation, defense, and postal service, the resolutions proposed deepening

[34] *Ibid.*, I (January, 1846), 14–15.

the mouth of the Mississippi; digging a canal from the Mississippi to the Great Lakes; establishing a national foundry and armory to be supplied with southern minerals and labor; constructing military and naval bases, lighthouses, beacons, marine hospitals, levees, and a western military highway; extending the telegraph throughout the area; and, finally, granting land for railroad construction. Although the federal government was expected to finance all of these ventures, the delegates insisted that control, direction, and profits remain in the hands of private enterprise![35]

An unusual feature of the convention was the absence of controversy. This was achieved simply by requiring unanimous approval for the introduction of anything likely to arouse partisan feelings. Thus, when delegates offered proposals which met with opposition they were forced to withdraw them. Not surprisingly, the convention gave the impression of peace and harmony.[36] However, as the delegates were later to discover, many of the questions which they had carefully sidestepped were to reappear to vex them at later conventions.

The two remaining conventions of this period, at Memphis in 1849 and New Orleans in 1852, were neither so grandiose in their schemes nor so harmonious. In the interval between 1845 and 1849 events of vast importance had taken place. Through the Mexican War the United States had gained considerable territory and extended the western boundary to the Pacific. Furthermore, the California gold rush which began in 1848 was rapidly populating this remote area. As a result, the next two commercial conventions showed greater interest in securing a route to the West than in improving transportation within the region. This was natural because establishing connections with the Pacific Coast not only would bring valuable trade to

[35] *Ibid.,* 18–20.
[36] Wender, *Southern Commercial Conventions,* 49, 59; *De Bow's Review,* I (January, 1846), 7, 17.

the South, but might also lead to southern settlement of the area with eventual political consequences.

By the opening of the 1849 convention several cities had already put forth their claims as the most advantageously located for a rail route to the West. In the North, Chicago and St. Louis sought the title; in the South, Memphis and New Orleans were the principal claimants. Other cities not so strategically located tended to support the route which would benefit them most. As a result, the conventions of 1849 and 1852 were largely contests among the various delegations to secure approval and financing for routes which would aid their areas.

The Memphis convention of 1849, which was organized for the express purpose of promoting a western rail route terminating in Memphis, met less than a week following a similar convention in St. Louis. The St. Louis body had recommended that the federal government construct a railroad to the Pacific Coast and proposed a trunk line with branches to Memphis, St. Louis, and Chicago.[37] The St. Louis convention sent a committee to Memphis to urge cooperation, but the group's suggestion was tabled and never acted upon.[38] Having rebuffed the St. Louisans' peace overtures, the Memphis convention proceeded none too subtly to urge government construction of a route "terminating at some point on the Mississippi between the mouth of the Ohio River and the mouth of the Red River." [39]

Like the Memphis meeting of 1849, the New Orleans convention of 1852 was called for the purpose of advancing that city's interest, which lay in the Tehuantepec route. The convention turned out to be highly acrimonious, largely because of a speech by Judah P. Benjamin. As one of the leading promoters of the Tehuantepec route, Benjamin argued that because of its

[37] *De Bow's Review*, VII (December, 1849), 551.
[38] Van Deusen, *The Ante-Bellum Southern Commercial Conventions*, 26; Cotterill, "Memphis Railroad Convention, 1849," 93.
[39] *De Bow's Review*, VII (December, 1849), 552.

location New Orleans was the natural and inevitable choice as the terminus for the Pacific railroad. He furthermore asserted that New Orleans could promise no assistance to local railroad development schemes at that time.[40]

Benjamin convinced some listeners that New Orleans was selfishly interested only in promoting its own interests, and several delegates objected. J. T. Trezevant of Tennessee warned that New Orleans should give more attention to its trade with the Ohio Valley and less to the Tehuantepec route for, with the penetration of the interior by railroads from the East, the city was in danger of losing its valuable inland trade. Trezevant, as might be guessed, was promoting the Memphis to Louisville railroad. Also objecting to Benjamin's speech, the Texas delegation withdrew, explaining that the Tehuantepec route ran only through South Texas and all of the Texas delegates were from the northern part of the state. C. S. Tarpley of Mississippi did not object to the Tehuantepec plan, but he argued that a railroad through his own state was more important. Faced with the prospect of a rebellious convention refusing to endorse the Tehuantepec route, James Robb saved the day for New Orleans with an able speech supporting a network of railroads throughout the South in addition to the Pacific road. To quell the dissension, Robb pointed out the political consequences of a route to the West, saying: "Penetrate this region with railroads, and in a few years those fertile plains will be filled by a numerous, busy and energetic population. There will arise new states here, and our representation in Congress will soon equal that of the North." The speaker then outlined a plan to finance the project, assuming as had the Memphis delegates that the federal government would support construction at least in part through the donation of public lands.[41]

The three meetings between 1845 and 1852 revealed two

[40] *Ibid.*, XI (December, 1851), 687; XII (May, 1852), 564.
[41] *Ibid.*, XII (May, 1852), 543–51, 562–66.

shortcomings of the commercial conventions. The first weakness was the ease with which the meetings could be transformed from a cooperative effort to aid the entire region into a vehicle for advancing the selfish claims of a particular city or state. In his speech to the New Orleans gathering, J. D. B. De Bow provided insight into another weakness:

> Gentlemen, a great reform, like that which is necessary in our position, is not to be achieved in a day. It requires organization, agitation, the dissemination of information, the frequent meeting of practical men, memorials and addresses. The day of deliberation is at last followed by the day of action. . . . It is the misfortune with us that when we have been aroused in the past, it has been by paroxysms, and never followed by sustained efforts. We have come together in convention, but when the convention adjourned there was the end of it. Nobody had power to act in the recess.[42]

To overcome this handicap, De Bow urged that each future convention be a continuation of the preceding one and meet at a different city. At the next convention this recommendation was adopted and it was adhered to for the remainder of the movement.

Because of the continuity achieved as a result of De Bow's suggestion, the last nine conventions may be regarded as a unit. The speeches at these meetings dealt primarily with four subjects: (1) continuation of the search for ways to improve the economy of the South; (2) methods of combating the growing power of the North; (3) ways to influence the southern mind; and (4) reopening the slave trade. Apparently heeding the advice of one speaker that they should not confine themselves to matters "that smell of the Custom-House or the Ledger," but should feel that "all subjects of practical interest to them are legitimate matters for our consideration and action," the dele-

---

[42] *Ibid.*, 561.

gates to the conventions between 1852 and 1859 undertook discussion of an almost infinite variety of proposals.[43]

In their search for ways to promote the economy of the South, members continued to agitate several questions introduced at earlier conventions. As had the very first meeting, delegates sought to promote direct trade. Almost every convention also endorsed establishing southern-owned steamship lines to Europe and the reduction of the tariff, especially the duty on iron which was thought to retard railroad expansion. The adoption of free trade by Great Britain gave added impetus to opposition to tariffs. Various conventions also recommended less dependence on agriculture and more diversified economy. Delegates continued to support railroad expansion throughout the region and a southern route to the West. At the Memphis convention of 1853 the Tehuantepec route was finally settled on as the South's possibility and debate on that aspect of the issue ceased.[44] The question of financing the road, however, continued to plague the delegates. It was not until 1854 that the conventions abandoned hope of federal financing for the road. In a forceful speech, Albert J. Pike denounced expectation of federal assistance. If one were built, he argued, it would be through free, not slave, territory. In the meantime, Pike claimed, while the South waited, the North was filling the West with emigrants. At his behest, the convention endorsed the creation of a corporation supported by the various states to finance and build the railroad.[45]

In addition to these stock subjects, the conventions introduced new issues and further developed others. The most prominent was how the South might combat the growing political

[43] *Ibid.*, XVII (July, 1854), 92–93.

[44] *Ibid.*, XV (September, 1853), 270–71, XVII (August, 1854), 203; Van Deusen, *The Ante-Bellum Southern Commercial Conventions*, 41–44.

[45] *De Bow's Review*, XVII (July, August, 1854), 97, 211, 636–37.

strength of the North. Although the commercial conventions had always been tinged with a hint of sectional controversy, before the middle of the century delegates, while objecting to several federal laws as unjust, claimed that the controversy was solely economic. However, between 1852 and 1859 the political aspects of the contest came more to the forefront and accusations against the North more acrimonious.

During these years, delegates moved from a position of insisting that they met for no sectional or divisive purpose, to one of demanding certain changes if the South was to remain in the Union,[46] and finally to outright defiance of the federal government and threats of disunion. Pike was one of the most outspoken critics of the federal government and the North. In 1854 he made a strong plea for southern unity to combat northern expansion. At New Orleans in 1855 he lashed out at the North for not enforcing the fugitive slave laws, accusing it of "resolute determination . . . not to comply with its constitutional obligations to the slave-holding States" and "an utter want of fraternal spirit . . . in the legislation of twenty years." [47] Later he told the delegates: "I see, sir, only two alternatives; we must strengthen ourselves within the Constitution or ultimately resort to a dissolution of the Union, which may Providence avert! . . . If we are to remain in this Union, we must preserve that proud and lofty bearing of perfect independence and equality with which we came into it." [48] At Savannah in 1856, while disavowing disunionism, Pike argued that unless certain "steps were taken to unite the South, to strengthen her and make her independent of the North, the days of this Union [are] numbered." [49] On each occasion, Pike was enthusiastically received by the convention delegates.

[46] *Ibid.*, XV (September, 1853), 257; XVIII (April, 1855), 526.
[47] *Ibid.*, XVII (August, 1854), 209–11; XVIII (April, 1855), 522.
[48] *Ibid.*, 526.   [49] *Ibid.*, XXII (February, 1856), 311.

Because of Republican successes in the 1856 elections, the speaking at the Savannah convention turned to a wider discussion of political issues than any earlier meeting. James Lyons of Virginia, the president of the convention, expressed pleasure that the Democrats had retained control of the government, but he warned that "the war is not yet ended, but only deferred, to be finished in the year 1860, when this war upon our institutions and upon our homes, and of course upon our liberties, is to be renewed . . . the day may come—we do not attempt to disguise it, for to do so were more than folly—when the South may find that she will be driven to the necessity of exerting, and will have need and occasion for, all her powers to preserve her rights and honor." [50]

Concommitant with increasing preoccupation with political questions came concern for the minds of Southerners. Beginning with the Memphis convention of 1853, the delegates regularly approved resolutions urging the education of southern youth in the South and by native teachers.[51] Motivated by the belief that "the great evils which threaten our Union are the results of vicious theories and principles propagated by books, periodicals, newspapers, literary and theological institutions," the delegates also endorsed proposals to establish southern publishing houses, to create a committee to examine and approve textbooks, and to establish teachers' colleges and other institutions of higher learning. In their antagonism toward the North, the conventions went so far as to endorse "buy southern" and even "vacation southern" themes.[52] Other schemes advanced in the name of sectional interest included proposals to acquire Cuba, to extend slavery throughout the Gulf of Mexico, to

[50] *Ibid.*, XXII (January, 1857), 86–87.

[51] *Ibid.*, XV (September, 1853), 268; XVI (June, 1854, 638–39; XVIII (April, 1855), 522; XXII (January, 1857), 100; XXIII (September, 1857), 315; XXVI (1859), 102.

[52] *Ibid.*, XX (March, 1856), 351; XXII (March, 1857), 309, 312, 315; XV (September, 1853), 268; XVII (July, 1854), 93; XVII (June, 1854), 638.

prohibit the emancipation of any slaves, and to organize a police force to suppress insurrection.[53]

The first attempt to introduce a resolution urging repeal of the laws banning the slave trade was made at Savannah in 1856. Although the resolution was not adopted, this issue became the main topic of discussion at the three remaining conventions. The Knoxville meeting of 1857 began on an acrimonious note with a lengthy debate on whether northern editors and reporters should be permitted on the floor. Although all were eventually admitted, the controversy pointed up the increased bitterness of the delegates. Following this argument, the very first resolution submitted proposed annulling the ban on the slave trade. After extensive debate on the morality of slavery and the expediency of reopening the slave trade, the convention finally settled on a resolution to appoint a committee to "collect facts bearing upon the re-opening of the African slave trade, to be presented at the next session of the convention." [54]

The call to the Montgomery convention of 1858, written by J. D. B. De Bow, virtually assured a preponderance of disunionists and a stormy meeting. De Bow baldly stated that the meeting was to assert the rights of the South "to withdraw from an association which no longer recognizes the original compact as the rule of its government," asserting that little hope existed for preservation of the Union. Warning delegates not to shrink from the cry of disunion, he proceeded to castigate Northerners as "traducers"; "assailants"; perpetrators of "unprecedented and flagitious assaults," "cupidity," "ambition," "offensive denunciations," "wanton aggressions," and "infamous approval of vicious and unconstitutional laws"; and ruled by a "corrupt and pliant judiciary." [55]

[53] *Ibid.*, XV (September, 1853, 268; XXIII (September, 1857), 312; XXIV (June, 1858), 597; XXVII (July, 1859), 95.

[54] *Ibid.*, XXII (January, 1857), 89, 91–92, 95; XXIII (September, 1857), 302–305, 317–18, 440.

[55] *Ibid.*, XXIV (May, 1858), 424–28.

The convention concerned itself almost exclusively with with the report of the special committee on the slave trade. Debate opened with the presentation of the report by L. W. Spratt of South Carolina, who urged reopening the trade because it would benefit both the Africans and the South. Arguing from the premises that the two races are unequal in character and capacity and that no difference existed between domestic and foreign trading in slaves, Spratt contended that slavery was "the common condition" in Africa. But because of the barbarism of that continent, he argued, "there is no class of negro life that is not elevated in coming to a state of slavery at the South." The benefits to the South would include an increase in population, more labor, and greater political power. He speculated that an importation of one or two hundred thousand slaves would enable the South to control every territory in the West.[56]

Roger Pryor of Virginia, a member of the committee, claimed that he had not even seen the report before its presentation, called its conclusions "utterly repugnant to grave and sensible men," and argued that the proposal was "purely and simply a proposition to dissolve the Union, because it cannot be carried out while the Union lasts." [57]

Thereafter, William Lowndes Yancey dominated the debate, speaking frequently and at great length in support of repealing the slave trade ban. Arguing that slavery was right and that the South had endured as much as it could from the North, he proposed making the issue one of union or disunion, freely admitting that the North would not accede to the demands of the South. At one point he confessed that he had a plan for some kind of secession convention in mind, but he had not proposed it because he felt it not to be the proper time. In conclusion, Yancey said, "Let us stand up and resist them like men,"

[56] *Ibid.*, XXIV (June, 1858), 472–91.   [57] *Ibid.*, 578.

and asked: "Are you ready, countrymen? Is your courage up to the highest point? Have you prepared yourselves to enter upon the great field of self-denial as your fathers did, and undergo, if necessary, another seven years' war in order that you and your posterity may enjoy the blessings of liberty? If you are, I am with you; if you are not, I am not with you." [58] The mood of the convention was reflected in the loud and prolonged ovation that greeted this challenge. However, in spite of the distinctly disunionist sentiment of the assemblage, opponents of the resolution succeeded in postponing a vote until the next convention.

The final convention at Vicksburg was characterized by continued debate on the proposal to reopen the slave trade, by eventual victory for the resolution's supporters, and by the most outspoken and eloquent attack on the measure yet made. Instead of merely urging repeal of the ban on the slave trade, Spratt proposed defiance of the laws, employing armed force if necessary. If violators were brought to trial, he assured the convention that southern juries would not convict them.[59]

From the outset, it was clear that the proslavery resolution would pass, but the convention is interesting because of the emphatic denunciation of the proposal and its supporters by Senator Foote of Mississippi. Foote attacked Spratt, saying:

The gentleman . . . proposed to invoke his countrymen to raise arms, not for the purpose of defending their rights, but for carrying out a system of aggression. I pronounced his speech treasonable last night, and I come here today to repeat it. . . . [I] say that under the constitution of the United States, armed opposition, or the levying of war against the government of the Union for the purpose of overthrowing the laws, by two men or many, is made high treason and I say that you were invited yesterday to do that very thing.[60]

58 *Ibid.*, XIV (June, 1858), 588–601.
59 *Ibid.*, XXVII (August, 1859), 205–14. 60 *Ibid.*, 215–16.

Foote continued: "He says it may be that the object may not be obtained except through a dissolution of the Union, but if so, then let the Union be dissolved. And you acclaimed it. You undertake to denounce me for calling him a disunionist after that!" Summarizing his attack on the resolution and its sponsor, he argued: "The gentleman is not satisfied to have the government set to naught, to defy the constitution and the laws of the Union, to have the appellant tribunal of the country . . . overthrown—but the trial by jury is to be dishonored. For what say the gentlemen? 'Southern juries will acquit' . . . I say if they do they perjure themselves." [61] When his efforts to halt the resolution were defeated by the vote of the convention, Foote and a few supporters resigned from the meeting. Thus, the commercial convention movement ended, perhaps aptly, with discord and secession.

Any assessment of the speaking in the commercial conventions must separate the rhetorical elements from structural factors. When this is done, it becomes clear that many of the problems which the conventions encountered were largely the result of their organization. For example, the major weakness was their lack of continuity and purpose. Until the Baltimore meeting in 1852, when delegates voted to meet annually and to regard each gathering as a continuation of its predecessor, each convention was a separate entity with its own set of rules, procedures, committees, and, most important, delegates with little or no knowledge of earlier meetings. Even after 1852, convention personnel included only a few members who had previously attended. Furthermore, since the delegates were responsible to no one and had no authority of any kind, committee projects and studies often went uncompleted. In fact, at some conventions several committees failed even to present reports.[62]

61 *Ibid.*, 215, 217–18.
62 *Ibid.*, XVIII (April, 1855), 357, 524. At the New Orleans convention

A second structural weakness of the conventions was their failure to provide some method for determining who was entitled to membership. As pointed out earlier, at all of the meetings the bulk of the delegates came from the host state. Often all delegates were entitled to vote, with no effort being made to guarantee equal or fair representation of all of the southern states. This practice led to local domination with local interests being placed ahead of those of the entire region. This weakness also was the main reason why disunionists were able to capture the conventions of the late 1850's.

These structural deficiencies created doubts about the usefulness of the conventions. In 1853 the New Orleans *Weekly Picayune*, for example, commented that "a declaration of purposes and wishes will do little to accomplish their objects without something more than resolutions and speeches. . . . Speeches and reports, however able and convincing, produce no immediate influence on the public affairs unless accompanied by active organization and strengthened by cordial cooperation and followed by continuous effort." [63] Another New Orleans newspaper in 1855 discussed local indifference and apathy to the conventions, attributing it to the fact that earlier meetings had been antagonistic to the interests of the city.[64] Even De Bow, one of the conventions' most ardent supporters, admitted in his speech at Knoxville that the meetings had fallen short of expectations.[65]

In addition to organizational deficiencies, the speaking itself probably occasioned some distrust and apathy. The two main shortcomings of the rhetoric were the introduction of many irrelevant, or at least inappropriate, issues and the political and

---

in 1855 the committees on internal improvements, agriculture, education, and manufactures and mining all failed to report.

[63] New Orleans *Weekly Picayune*, June 13, 1853.

[64] New Orleans *Commercial Bulletin*, January 4, 1855.

[65] *De Bow's Review*, XXII (February, 1857), 232.

commercial naïveté of many of the proposals. As this essay indicates, the range of subjects discussed in the course of the sixteen conventions was almost limitless. To emphasize this fact further, a few of the more bizarre proposals might be noted here. For example, the conventions actually considered resolutions concerning navigation of the Amazon River (1853 and 1854), uniform international coinage (1854), mediation of the Russo-Turkish dispute (1854), and bounties to northern fisheries (1857). And, of course, the intrusion of the slavery and disunion issues in the late 1850's should never have been permitted if the delegates truly hoped to achieve success. The introduction of such a wide assortment of unrelated issues merely tended to obscure the true purpose of the meetings.

In addition to losing sight of the conventions' goals, the members often displayed an amazing naïveté about political and commercial affairs. For instance, the myriad of internal improvements—ranging from building railroads, canals, foundries, hospitals, levees, and highways to extending the telegraph throughout the area and deepening the mouth of the Mississippi—which the conventions of the 1840's expected the federal government to finance shows a curious innocence. But then to ask the government, after constructing all of these facilities, to leave their control and profits in the hands of private individuals bordered on the absurd.

Sectionalism frequently obscured the thinking of the delegates and led them to endorse unlikely or impractical solutions to their problems. Thus, instead of seeking to cooperate with northern interests on the route of the Pacific railroad, the Memphis convention flatly rejected the overtures of the St. Louis convention. Instead of trying to get northern and foreign ships to call at southern ports, convention after convention sought some means of establishing a southern-owned and -operated shipping line. Instead of seeking northern capital to diversify their economy and to finance their ventures, the conventions either futilely sought local funds or demanded federal appropriations.

Looking back over the conventions, it is difficult to point to a single major achievement. Of the main proposals advanced, the conventions failed to establish direct trade, to develop their own steamship lines, to reduce the tariff, to obtain a railway to the Pacific, to diversify noticeably the southern economy, or to reopen the slave trade. Some progress was made in linking southern communities by rail and in fostering schools, but whether these accomplishments were in any way the result of convention action or came about merely in the course of normal development is difficult to say. The basic, underlying idea of merchants and business leaders meeting together to promote the economy seems to have been sound. But the failure of the conventions to develop a workable organization, their lack of insight in diagnosing and treating the economic ills of the South, and their inability to cope with the divisive issues which were introduced in their last years led to their demise.

Although the conventions failed in their quest to provide answers for the economic ills afflicting the South, they did perceive the problems. As early as 1837 members sensed that a southern agricultural economy could not long keep pace with the rapidly expanding industrial North. Although originally concerned only with commercial matters, delegates later recognized that the contest had political repercussions as well. They foresaw the consequences of the expansion of the country westward. The conventions, however, proved inadequate as a vehicle for dealing with these developments. Frustrated by their inability to halt the march of events, the delegates became increasingly susceptible to the appeals of radicals and demagogues. Thus, the conventions came to be dominated by disunionists. In their final stages, the meetings proved to be but a prelude to the more violent conflict to follow.

VII

The Know-Nothing Party and the Oratory of Nativism

DONALD W. ZACHARIAS

"I am not a Know-Nothing. . . . As a nation, we began by declaring that '*all men are created equal.*' We now practically read it 'all men are created equal, *except negroes.*' When the Know-Nothings get control, it will read 'all men are created equal, except negroes, *and foreigners,* and catholics.' When it comes to this I should prefer emigrating to some country where they make no pretence of loving liberty." [1] Thus wrote Abraham Lincoln in 1855 of the third-party phenomenon that began as a secret political organization, the Order of the Star Spangled Banner; appeared in local and national campaigns from 1854 to 1860 as the American Party; and was popularly called the Know-Nothing Party because its fraternally-bound members replied "I don't know" to all questions.

Though Lincoln's indictment stressed the national party's nativist and anti-Catholic orientation, southern Know-Nothings were equally concerned with affirming Unionism by seeking common ground on issues that might subordinate the

[1] Abraham Lincoln to Joshua Speed, August 24, 1855, in Roy P. Basler (ed.), *The Collected Works of Abraham Lincoln* (9 vols.; New Brunswick, 1953), II, 323. At least six times, between 1855 and 1860, Lincoln denounced the Know-Nothing Party or denied that he had ever joined it. *Ibid.*, II, 316, 373; III, 329, 333; IV, 70, 85–86.

218

divisive question of slavery. By providing spokesmen for a nationalist view-point in a period of congealing sectional sentiments, the Know-Nothing Party earned a chapter in the annals of southern oratory.

The party developed some form of organization in thirteen southern states at various times between 1854 and 1860 and attracted, at least temporarily, such political leaders as Henry W. Hilliard in Alabama, Albert Pike in Arkansas, R. K. Call in Florida, Benjamin Hill in Georgia, John J. Crittenden in Kentucky, George Eustis in Louisiana, Henry Winter Davis in Maryland, C. D. Fontaine in Mississippi, John A. Gilmer in North Carolina, John Cunningham in South Carolina, Parson William Brownlow in Tennessee, Sam Houston in Texas, and John Minor Botts in Virginia.

A story could be written about American campaigns in each of these states, but this study will focus upon attempts by representative southern orators to give symbolic value to selected issues, the role of special occasions for speechmaking in promoting the movement, and characteristics of the language employed to express Know-Nothing appeals.[2]

In 1855 the vigor of Know-Nothing speakers in state and local elections "waked up thousands." To one critic the number and intensity of orators in these campaigns resembled "Kilkenny cats, always devouring each other."[3] Most of the speakers were members of the defunct Whig Party who had renewed

[2] The Know-Nothing Party left few official records. Proceedings of the grand council were passed from one secretary to another but eventually disappeared. Moreover, private papers of James W. Barker and Erastus Brooks, former national leaders, are unavailable. Louis D. Scisco reports in *Political Nativism in the State of New York* (London, 1909), 255, that many of the records were burned. The most comprehensive accounts of the party are W. Darrell Overdyke, *The Know-Nothing Party in the South* (Baton Rouge, 1950) and Ray A. Billington, *The Protestant Crusade, 1800–1860* (New York, 1938).

[3] Constance Mary Gay, "The Campaign of 1855 in Virginia and the Fall of the Know-Nothing Party," *Richmond College Historical Papers,* I (1916), 333.

their search for ways to save the country. Without much thought or investigation they chose immigration as one issue for uniting northern and southern Know-Nothings. On the surface it seemed an excellent topic to use in releasing tensions and explaining confusing events.[4]

Rising immigration gave the North increased political power in Congress. In 1850 the South had only 378,204 of the total 2,240,581 aliens in the United States. Five years later, when these new citizens were eligible to vote, the North had 144 representatives to the South's 90. Thus a southern orator could easily charge that immigration gave abolitionists greater power in the federal government.[5] Furthermore, most Southerners wanted to keep their cities free from foreigners, for they considered them criminals, paupers, and troublemakers. They especially resented the antislavery attitude of Germans and Irishmen.[6] The Know-Nothing position on immigration, in fact, sounded so appealing that an opponent of the movement estimated that "nine men out of ten" in the South would support

[4] Maldwyn A. Jones, *American Immigration* (Chicago, 1960), 158. For the significance of this kind of issue in a nascent movement, see Hans Toch, *The Social Psychology of Social Movements* (Indianapolis, 1965), 20; Ralph Linton, "Nativistic Movements," *American Anthropologist*, XLV (1943), 231.

[5] Samuel C. Busey, *Immigration: Its Evils and Consequences* (New York, 1856), 149. A Louisville reporter called for "some measure . . . to prevent this . . . disproportionate increase . . . of abolitionism." See also the official Know-Nothing Party newspaper, the Washington *Daily American Organ*, April 6, 1855; Lawrence F. Schmeckebier, "History of the Know-Nothing Party in Maryland," *Johns Hopkins University Studies in Historical and Political Science*, XVII, (1899), 52; Arthur C. Cole, "Nativism in the Lower Mississippi Valley," *Proceedings of the Mississippi Valley Historical Association*, VI (1913), 258.

[6] Henry J. Carman and Reinhard H. Luthin, "Some Aspects of the Know-Nothing Movement Reconsidered," *South Atlantic Quarterly*, XXXIX (1940), 221–22, and Albert B. Faust, *The German Element in the United States* (2 vols.; New York, 1909), I, 446. Germans in Texas, however, believed that "the territories were open to the slaveowners and that Congress had no right to exclude slave property from the territories." Rudolph L. Biesele, *The History of the German Settlement in Texas, 1831–1861* (Austin, 1930), 204.

220

the party's demand for a revision of naturalization laws.[7] This question, capable of being interpreted as a plot by foreign governments to dump their illiterates and criminals in America, fitted neatly into the Know-Nothing orator's cafeteria of appeals. It also supported the leading party dogma that "Americans should rule America." [8] Like most Know-Nothing arguments, however, it was abused and caused rioting in several major cities, the most destructive being in Louisville, Kentucky, where twenty people were killed on election day, August 6, 1855.[9]

Another major issue exploited during the American Party's search for power was Protestantism versus Roman Catholicism. Nationally the force behind the whole movement seemed to be hatred of Catholicism.[10] Though a concentration of Catholics could be found in only a few places in the South, party spokesmen played upon the fears of their listeners and made the possibility of papal domination appear calamitous and imminent.

Kenneth Rayner of North Carolina, speaking at a ratification meeting in Baltimore's Monument Square, envisioned his party as "fighting for the Bible and the Right of Religious Liberty." He predicted that American principles of government would succeed despite "priestly aggressions" and "machinations of the

[7] "A Calm Discussion of the Know-Nothing Question," *Southern Literary Messenger*, XX (1854), 540. See speeches by A. R. Sollers of Maryland and Stephen Adams of Mississippi in the *Congressional Globe*, 33rd Cong., 2nd Sess., Appendix, 82–85 and 34th Cong., 1st Sess., 1414. *See also* the Washington *National Intelligencer*, July 15, 1856.

[8] "Secret Societies—The Know-Nothings," *Putnam's Monthly*, V (1855), 94; [E. R. Anspach], *The Sons of the Sires* (Philadelphia, 1855), 41.

[9] Louisville *Anzeiger*, August 7, 1855, gives an hour-by-hour account of the rioting.

[10] Billington, *The Protestant Crusade*, 386. "The real question," a British journalist wrote of the political skirmishes, "is this—Protestantism or Romanism in the United States?" "The Know-Nothings—American Prospects," *British Quarterly Review*, XXII (1855), 68.

Roman Catholic Church." [11] Listeners were easily persuaded by his arguments since they were already enraged by a local school bill designed to give public money to parochial schools.

Directed by clever strategists, attacks upon Catholicism won surprising support in Tennessee even though, as late as 1850, the three Catholic churches in the state could accommodate only thirteen hundred worshippers.[12] Numbers apparently made little difference to Tennessee Know-Nothings or William Brownlow, who made Catholicism the brunt of caustic outbursts. Like other nativists, Brownlow was fighting a national plot.

Brownlow, editor of the Knoxville *Whig*, frequently published his arguments in his newspaper and repeated them in speeches. From June 17 to July 22, 1855, he delivered a speech each Saturday morning on the "true character" of Catholicism. To reach all potential converts, he offered his speeches for sale at five cents a copy or four dollars a hundred.[13]

At least two states rejected anti-Catholicism as a Know-Nothing principle. In Louisiana "thousands of staunch Catholics" supported the party because of its commitment to local reform.[14] Prominent Catholics in the movement included Charles Derbigny, candidate for governor; J. V. Duralde, can-

[11] Baltimore *Sun*, June 21, 1855. John T. Scharf, *The Chronicles of Baltimore* (Baltimore, 1874), discusses several American Party activities in Maryland.

[12] Murry Bryant Measamer, "A History of the Know-Nothing Party in Tennessee" (M.S. thesis, University of Tennessee, 1931), 20. As late as 1860 North Carolina had only seven Roman Catholic congregations, with a total membership of 350. Guion G. Johnson, *Ante-Bellum North Carolina: A Social History* (Chapel Hill, 1937), 369.

[13] Sister Mary de Lourdes Gohmann, *Political Nativism in Tennessee to 1860* (Washington, 1938), 105. For an analysis of Brownlow's speaking, see Hace Tishler, "The Public Speaking of Four Representative Know-Nothings: Brownlow, Hilliard, Crittenden, and Davis, 1854–57" (M. A. thesis, University of Virginia, 1955).

[14] W. Darrell Overdyke, "History of the American Party in Louisiana," *Louisiana Historical Quarterly*, XV (1932), 270; Washington *National Intelligencer*, July 14, 1855.

didate for state treasurer; and Charles Gayarré, delegate to the party's national council.

Most Kentucky Know-Nothings tried to mollify public hostility toward the party's anti-Catholicism. Representative L. M. Cox, for example, stated his objection to making "a man's faith either a qualification for, or exclusion from, public trust." [15] Senator John J. Crittenden expressed the "fullest confidence" in native-born Catholics and claimed that his party proscribed no religion.[16] Newspaper editor George Prentice, however, supported the Know-Nothings with daily attacks upon Catholicism and caused the party much embarrassment.[17] Nevertheless, when the American Party won control of the state government, Governor Charles Morehead allayed the fears of Catholics and foreigners by promising in his inaugural address to protect their rights.[18]

As early as 1844 some Whigs had looked longingly at a native American party as a possible way of finding a new party label and new issues. Henry Clay had advised against such a maneuver by saying that Democrats would charge "that it was the same old party with a new name or with a new article added to its creed." [19] His prediction was accurate. During the early years of the fusion between Whigs and nativists, Know-Nothing spokesmen stressed Americanism and anti-Catholicism. Their political survival, in fact, depended upon their ability to perform doctrinal contortions in avoiding a discussion of slavery. They shunned all "questions affecting the existence of slavery" and insisted on leaving the issue where

[15] *Congressional Globe*, 33rd Cong., 2nd Sess., Appendix, 72.

[16] Louisville *Courier*, July 26, and August 3, 1855; Washington *National Intelligencer*, August 2, 1855; Louisville *Journal*, August 3, 1855.

[17] Louisville *Journal*, July 4, 1855.

[18] Louisville *Courier*, September 6, 1855.

[19] Henry Clay to John J. Crittenden, November 28, 1844, in Mrs. Chapman Coleman, *The Life of John J. Crittenden, With Selections from his Correspondence and Speeches* (2 vols.; Philadelphia, 1871), I, 224.

the Constitution allegedly placed it—"neither the doctrine of pro-slavery . . . nor abolition." [20] Since Democrats were not easily fooled by this dodge or other Know-Nothing disguises, the American Party had to develop a catechism on slavery for its campaigners.

Party orators showed considerable inventiveness in answering the Democratic charge that they were "abolition-hatched." [21] Sam Houston suggested that Abby Kelly, "champion of abolitionism and women's rights," and Henry Wise, spokesman "of Southern rights and disunion," should fight at the Mason-Dixon Line. He urged them to use a bodkin and distaff for weapons and a short gown and a petticoat for armor. "Whoever triumphs in the conflict," he explained, "shall be awarded a finely embroidered apron emblematic of the manufacture of the section of the country to which the victor belongs." [22] In Kentucky, A. K. Marshall, who considered servitude the Negro's "normal condition," detested hearing "preachers from the pulpit and demagogues from the stump" emphasize this issue.[23] In Missouri, where slavery was the main issue of the state campaign, Know-Nothing gubernatorial candidate Robert C. Ewing canvassed the state saying that the Union would be safe if the American Party won, but the "horrors of intestine war" would follow if it lost.[24] These approaches to resolving sectional controversy by creating a dream world were vaporous, but the party's devotion to the Union, at least one with slavery, remained firm from 1854 to 1856.

In some states, party spokesmen focused public attention on

---

[20] Washington *Daily American Organ*, March 22, 1855; *Congressional Globe*, 33rd Cong., 2nd Sess., Appendix, 83.

[21] Louisville *Courier*, July 31, 1855.

[22] Speech delivered at a Know-Nothing barbecue at Austin, Texas, November 23, 1855, quoted in Amelia Williams and Eugene C. Barker (eds.), *The Writings of Sam Houston*, VI (6 vols.; Austin, 1941), 225.

[23] *Congressional Globe*, 34th Cong., 1st Sess., Appendix, 1246.

[24] Walter H. Ryle, "Slavery and Party Realignment in Missouri in the State Election of 1856," *Missouri Historical Review*, XXXIX (1944–45), 331.

genuine issues by advocating local reform.[25] In Florida, where voters were persuaded "less by national policies . . . than by local issues and personalities," [26] Davies S. Walker, Know-Nothing candidate for governor, and R. K. Call, prominent nativist speaker, discussed the sales policy for public lands, reform of state finances, land speculation, and entrenchment.[27] John Cunningham, a Charleston newspaper editor, tried unsuccessfully to overcome Democratic monopoly in South Carolina by calling for a purging of corruption in state government.[28] Led by Kenneth Rayner and John A. Gilmer, North Carolina Know-Nothings campaigned on the issues of free suffrage, representation of western counties, internal improvements, ad valorem taxation, and distribution of federal lands.[29] Even on local questions, however, many Know-Nothing speakers gave evasive and equivocal answers. Consequently, those who realized the importance of strong state and local councils in their crusade to elect a Know-Nothing President were disappointed by the party's inability to derive new power from reform campaigns.

If converts were to be won, American Party orators had to cater to their listeners' diverse needs. Anti-immigration, anti-Catholicism, and Unionism unquestionably attracted followers; but the strategy of staging a variety of social occasions for speechmaking was equally important in making the movement a crusade to preserve all that was virtuous in the South. Party spokesmen believed that audiences were tired of "hickory poles, pokeberry-stocks, coons and log-cabins, and ready for a new way of doing business." [30] To some critics

25 Cole, "Nativism in the Lower Mississippi Valley," 258.
26 Arthur W. Thompson, "Political Nativism in Florida, 1848–1860: A Phase of Anti-Secessionism," *Journal of Southern History*, XV (1949), 42.
27 Overdyke, *The Know-Nothing Party*, 126.
28 Harold S. Schultz, *Nationalism and Sectionalism in South Carolina, 1852–1860* (Durham, N.C., 1950), 79–81.
29 Overdyke, *The Know-Nothing Party*, 100.
30 [Anspach] *The Sons of the Sires*, 155.

this meant campaigns with "an abundance of oratory, mass meetings, name-calling, and tomfoolery." [31] Leaders of the American Party, however, considered it a call for ratification conventions, all-day barbecues, political debates, flag raisings, street preachings, parades, and fireworks.

Philadelphia's Independence Square with its aura of Americanism made an ideal setting for the first major party rally, especially since delegates to the national council were already in the city. On June 16, 1855, ten to fifteen thousand followers gathered about three speakers' stands and waited in a downpour to hear the party's best orators. Local ward members waved Know-Nothing signs announcing "We go for the Union, the whole Union, and nothing but the Union," "Samuel is right," "Sam is wide awake," "The Bible and the Constitution," and "American ladies are the true friends of Sam." [32]

In their enthusiasm to support the party, southern orators nearly monopolized the rostrums. Neil S. Brown, former governor of Tennessee, used innocuous arguments and appeals to show that "Americans should rule Americans." On the question of slavery he argued that the North, though free to consider it a bad institution, should "let it alone." Speaking from another stand, William S. Pilcher of Kentucky repeated the call for Americans to rule the country and added a brief attack upon the Pope's temporal powers. John Cunningham of South Carolina told his listeners that his state's delegation joined the party because it offered an opportunity to stop antislavery agitation and return to American principles. Kentucky's E. B. Bartlett, newly elected national council president, and Georgia's F. H. Cone were among the twenty-two other speakers who attempted to allay northern fears of a party schism by speaking either in high-level patriotic abstractions or in re-

[31] Wallace B. Turner, "The Know-Nothing Movement in Kentucky," *Filson Club History Quarterly*, XXVIII (1954), 276.
[32] Philadelphia *Daily News*, June 16, 1855.

assuring party jargon. Reports of the speeches show that the orators omitted attacks upon their Democratic opponents and concentrated upon promoting the American Party's platform and principles.[33]

A few weeks later Kentucky Know-Nothings experimented with a new method for addressing large audiences. E. B. Bartlett gave a "terse, well delivered and highly argumentative" speech from one end of a flag-draped platform while George B. Hodge spoke from the other.[34] The innovation had its drawbacks. "The speaking from two sides, and the almost uninterrupted applause," one reporter wrote, "rendered it impossible for us to pay attention long enough to any one speaker to attempt a report of their remarks." [35]

Traditional formats for speechmaking were more successful. "Excitement begets debate," one observer noted, "and debate elicits thought; and all help on the cause of truth." [36] The American Party thrived on excitement, so its candidates eagerly entered political debates wherever they found cooperative opponents. During the Tennessee campaign of 1855, for example, the "Battle of Murfreesboro" featured the first of fifty-two debates between Know-Nothing candidate for governor, Meredith P. Gentry, and his Democratic opponent, Andrew Johnson.[37] "In no canvass, previous to the war," remarked a contemporary, "was there ever manifested so much bitter personal ill-will as in that of 1855." [38]

In Kentucky the major campaign debate of 1855 between Alexander and Thomas Marshall was a family affair. While campaigning for Congress, the brothers staged one of their

---

[33] *Ibid.*, June 16, 18, 1855; New York *Times*, June 18, 1855. For an account of a similar rally held in New York City, see the New York *Times*, June 19, 1855, and the Washington *National Intelligencer*, June 21, 1855.

[34] Louisville *Courier*, July 4, 1855.   [35] Louisville *Journal*, July 4, 1855.

[36] Cincinnati *Gazette*, July 24, 1855.

[37] Gohmann, *Political Nativism in Tennessee to 1860*, 104.

[38] Oliver P. Temple, *Notable Men of Tennessee* (New York, 1912), 385.

typical meetings at Versailles on county court day. Alexander, according to one reporter, was "calm and dignified, able and lucid in his defence of the American party and its principles." Tom, usually considered the better orator, spoke "eloquently, and, in a *better cause*, would have triumphed." [39]

Giles M. Hillyer, Mississippi Know-Nothing candidate for Congress, held twenty debates with John Quitman.[40] Hillyer charged that seven-tenths of all immigrants settled in the North, giving it greater legislative power.[41] In Alabama George D. Shortridge, Know-Nothing gubernatorial hopeful, advocated state aid for railroads in his debates with John A. Winston throughout the state.[42] In all these debates a candidate not only talked for an hour or two himself but also remained on the platform, heard his arguments assailed, and then frequently shared a ride with his opponent to the site of the next debate. In spite of the strenuous demands upon speakers, the debates helped the American Party to rise from political obscurity.

Among the special occasions used to generate enthusiasm for the party, none was more popular than a "grand political barbecue." Usually occupying an entire day, the festivals featured candidates for governor, aspirants for the presidential nomination, or officers of the national council. Local managers, after promising "to maintain order and decorum," invited the entire family. To accommodate the crowds, railroad companies provided special transportation "to the grove." Bands, glee clubs, and fireworks often occupied the same pro-

---

39 Louisville *Courier*, July 7, 1855. At Nicholasville on May 26, Alexander had also debated R. W. Woolley, Democratic nominee for attorney general. Lexington *Kentucky Statesman*, May 29, 1855.

40 Overdyke, *The Know-Nothing Party*, 121.   41 *Ibid.*, 200.

42 Lewy Dorman, *Party Politics in Alabama from 1850 through 1860* (Wetumpka, Ala., 1935), 109; William Garrett, *Reminiscences of Public Men in Alabama* (Atlanta, 1872), 97.

gram; but speakers evangelizing for the American Party dominated the gatherings.[43]

Whether the occasion was a congressional session, ratification meeting, joint political canvass, barbecue, or flag raising, Know-Nothing orators embellished their language with slogans; epithets; biblical, classical, and historical allusions; and humor. Such language was used to simplify a listener's system of reasoning and his concept of social causation. Popular slogans included "Americans should rule America," "Sam is wide awake," "The Bible a good school book," "Put none but Americans on guard," and "Let the watchwords be Fillmore and Donelson—The Constitution—the Union forever." [44]

Party spokesmen delighted in using emotionally charged words to describe their enemies. Irishmen were "drunken" and "red-mouthed"; Germans, "lousy"; and Negroes, "insolent." America's foreign population was "like the serpent . . . taken from abject poverty and warmed into life, [who] repays your hospitality by stinging your vitals." [45] Abolitionists were "ingenious peace men who . . . utter speeches which are slobbered all over with treason." [46] They labeled Mary "the whore of Rome," the Pope "a temporal Prince hurling thunders against heresies," and the priesthood "rotten." [47] Democrats were "village politicians" and "place-hunting demagogues." [48]

---

[43] Nashville *Republican Banner and Nashville Whig*, July 13, 1855; Louisville *Courier*, July 3, 11, 1855; Louisville *Journal*, July 13, August 1, 1855.

[44] [Anspach] *Sons of the Sires*, 41; New York *Times*, June 8, 18, 19, 1855; Louisville *Journal*, July 28, 1855; and a broadside dated March 18, 1856, in John J. Crittenden Papers, Library of Congress.

[45] Speech by Kenneth Rayner, Baltimore *Sun*, June 21, 1855.

[46] Speech by William R. Smith, *Congressional Globe*, 34th Cong., 1st Sess., 158.

[47] Speeches by Henry W. Hilliard and Vespasian Ellis reported in the Montgomery *Alabama Journal*, July 21, 1855, and Washington *National Intelligencer*, July 7, 1855, respectively.

[48] Speech by John S. Carlile, *Congressional Globe*, 34th Cong., 1st Sess., Appendix, 653.

Democrats, too, used the "slaughter house style" in many of their speeches, but, unlike Know-Nothing orators, they attacked only avowed political opponents and not large segments of American society. They, for instance, considered Know-Nothings to be members of "an oath-bound, dark-lantern, clap-trap, hypocritical, truth-stretching, abolition-hatched party." [49] The party itself was led by "broken down party hacks" and "political bankrupts." [50] Know-Nothings, of course, had an entirely different point of view. Their party was a "generous, gallant young giant . . . like Sampson in his youth." [51]

In keeping with the religious fervor of the movement and the influence of Protestantism in the South, American Party orators borrowed their figurative language from the Bible. Neil S. Brown contended that agitation on slavery was "forbidden fruit" and that Abolitionists should be "baptized in a lake of fire." [52] W. S. Pilcher proclaimed, "Glory be to God in the highest . . . and peace and good will to all native-born American citizens." [53] Even the potential apex of the movement depended upon Fillmore, whose name "shall rise till it shall stand in its majestic proportions another Ararat." [54] Among the more sophisticated speakers such as Henry W. Hilliard and Henry W. Davis, classical illustrations were highly popular because they identified the Know-Nothing movement with selected aspects of the golden cultures of Greece and Rome.[55]

American history, especially the Revolutionary War litera-

[49] Gainesville (Ala.) *Independent,* July 14, 1855, quoted in Dorman, *Party Politics in Alabama,* 113.

[50] Lexington *Kentucky Statesman,* May 22, 1855.

[51] Montgomery *Alabama Journal,* July 21, 1855.

[52] New York *Times,* June 18, 1855.　　　[53] *Ibid.,* June 19, 1855.

[54] Speech by James J. Lindley, *Congressional Globe,* 34th Cong., 1st Sess., Appendix, 676.

[55] See Hilliard's speech in the Montgomery *Alabama Journal,* July 21, 1855, or Davis' in the *Congressional Globe,* 34th Cong., 1st Sess., Appendix, 1241-45.

ture, provided unlimited allusions and catch phrases. The men in the party were "citizen soldiers" and "disciples of Washington"; the women, "fair daughters of America." [56] Audiences were told to follow the example of Washington, who "drew from his side his trusty sword, and led the sons of freedom to battle." The Union was "darling, beloved, holy" and the "poetry of patriotism." "American" was used so regularly as a modifier that it became a cliche.[57]

By 1856 "thousands of normally tolerant Americans were captivated by seductively patriotic appeals and swayed by the printed and spoken propaganda of the Know-Nothings." [58] The party achieved its greatest success in Maryland, Kentucky, Missouri, and Tennessee. Only Arkansas and South Carolina failed to elect at least one Know-Nothing congressman. This, then, was the status of the American Party when it named former President Millard Fillmore as its candidate for the White House. Fillmore conducted a bewildering campaign. He identified himself with nativism in only three of twenty-seven speeches; he used the word "Catholic" once.[59] Northern Know-Nothings either joined the Republican Party or campaigned on an antislavery platform. Southerners, many of whom later joined the Constitutional Union Party, attempted to uphold the Union but also found themselves maneuvered into a proslavery position. When the electoral votes were tallied, Fillmore received 8; Fremont, 114; and Buchanan, 174.[60] "Sam," as many had predicted, "split upon

[56] Speech by Vespasian Ellis, former editor of the *American Organ*, made in Washington, D. C., July 4, 1855, Washington National *Intelligencer*, July 7, 1855.

[57] Speeches by Kenneth Rayner and J. R. Ricaud reported in the New York *Times*, June 9, 1855, and one by John J. Crittenden in the *Congressional Globe*, 34th Cong., 1st Sess., 2167.

[58] Carman and Luthin, "Some Aspects of the Know-Nothing Movement Reconsidered," 213–34.

[59] Robert J. Rayback, *Millard Fillmore* (New York, 1959), 407–408.

[60] Overdyke, *The Know-Nothing Party*, 154.

the rock of slavery." [61] The movement immediately began a period of "masterly inactivity" [62] and officially died after its national council meeting at Louisville on June 2, 1857.

Oratory, as this study has indicated, was indigenous to the Know-Nothing movement. It is especially important to note that southern orators often attended large rallies in the North, but rarely, if ever, did their northern counterparts visit the South. Southern spokesmen were clearly dedicated to preserving the Union—with slavery. Yet, they stated in their speeches that they saw no reason for controversy. Surely in the hierarchy of national affairs, they argued, there were questions of greater significance than the status of American Negroes. Their use of nativism, Roman Catholicism, and local reforms as topics for speeches reflected a genuine effort to achieve social and political cohesiveness with the North. Selection of these issues also revealed a misinterpretation of the national temperament during the 1850's.

Many men who should have known better joined the movement because they were left political orphans by the death of the Whig Party. With the exception of Parson Brownlow, the orators cited in this study had never before engaged in such blatant personal invective, insults, and sacrilegious comments. Nevertheless, they perceived plots destined to deprive them of a way of life they considered idyllic. If they could convince enough people of dual plots by foreign governments and the Pope, they might well save their country and their political futures. They can be commended for their unselfish devotion to the South, but they must be judged harshly for the strategies they used in winning support for the movement.[63]

[61] Washington *National Intelligencer,* June 14, 1855.

[62] Thomas H. Clay to A. J. Donelson, November 26, 1856, in A. J. Donelson Papers, Library of Congress.

[63] For suggestions on determining the characteristics of southern oratory, see Waldo W. Braden, "The Emergence of the Concept of Southern Oratory," *Southern Speech Journal,* XXVI (1961), 173–83, and Kevin E. Kearney,

The Know-Nothing Party and the Oratory of Nativism

Harsh language in Know-Nothing speeches betrayed the orators' desperation. Emotive words and fallacies of every kind marred their speeches. Not even in their own national meetings could they hold a thoughtful discussion of party strategy. Certainly the reasoning in their public rallies was superficial and specious.

Perhaps the best way to summarize the oratory of the Know-Nothing Party is to consider it a ritualistic response to a national condition that no one in the party clearly understood. The similarities between the party and a religious or fraternal order are striking. The birth and early development of the Know-Nothing movement took place under a tantalizing cover of secrecy. From its inception it tried to convey the image of a holy, mystical order given birth in America's manger at Philadelphia. The few surviving samples of early speeches show no concern for carefully reasoned arguments. Rather, they depict a group of orators bent upon inviting their listeners to enjoy the comforts of unreason in a setting where the words of the speaker and the reaction of the audience are predictable.

What may have begun as a sincere response to a political void soon became a public ritual complete with music, dialogue, and divine invocation. There were myths and symbols, saints and devils. In this state of reduced consciousness speakers and audiences mutually indulged in supplying inartistic gratifications. Phrases and acts of Know-Nothings became invested with narcissism, and party orators found a conditioned response to "American," "Catholic," and "German." Ethically bound only by their secret codes, speakers were free to appeal to any passion, any prejudice, and any pseudopatriotic sentiment. In an era of national crisis they offered their listeners no reasonable alternative to sectional conflict.

"What's Southern about Southern Oratory?" *Southern Speech Journal* XXXII (1966), 19–30.

VIII

The Fire-Eaters

H. HARDY PERRITT

At dawn, on April 12, 1861, a shell from a sixty-four-pound columbiad cannon struck the "north-east angle of the parapet" of Fort Sumter, South Carolina. The war, feared by many and welcomed by a few, had begun. The man who fired that first shot was Edmund Ruffin. He was sixty-seven years of age, a skinny but straight-backed specimen of five feet, eight inches and 120 pounds, with stringy white hair that hung down over his shoulders, a kind although stern face, and deep-set, intense eyes. For this occasion he was dressed in a loose-fitting uniform of the Palmetto Guard.[1] For many years, Ruffin had been one of the leaders in the movement for southern secession—one of those few who had been so uncompromising that they had come to be unflatteringly called "Fire-Eaters."[2]

The seeds of secession had been sowed early in the South,

[1] Edmund Ruffin Diary (MS in Library of Congress; 14 vols.) Ruffin's diary is the best single source of information on his secession activities.

[2] The term "Fire-Eater" as an opprobrium for extreme secessionists appears to have become popular following an appearance of Robert Barnwell Rhett and William Lowndes Yancey at a meeting in Macon, Georgia, on August 22, 1850; see Richard Harrison Shryock, *Georgia and the Union in 1850* (Durham, 1926), 238–85, 319. The term had been used much earlier to apply to southern duelists; see Huntsville (Ala.) *Southern Advocate*, March 14, 1828.

234

especially in the South Carolina "low country," a land of blue indigo, golden rice, white cotton, and black Negroes. In the debate on tariff in the first session of Congress, Senator Pierce Butler of South Carolina was described by Senator William Maclay of Pennsylvania as flaming "like a meteor" as he "threatened dissolution of the Union with regard to his State, *as sure as God was in the firmament.*" [3]

Not until after a period of about thirty years during which the cotton culture spread over the South and industrialism developed in the rest of the country, however, did the lines of sectionalism become taut. In 1827, when Vice-President John C. Calhoun was forced to break a tie vote in the Senate to table a high tariff bill, Dr. Thomas Cooper declared that "we shall, before long, be compelled to calculate the value of our union. . . . The question . . . is fast approaching to the alternative, of submission or separation." [4] In a series of thirty-one articles entitled "The Crisis" and published in the Charleston *Mercury*, Robert J. Turnbull advocated "resistance" and said: "If this fails, let us separate." [5] The following year, after passage of the despised tariff by Congress, twenty-eight-year-old Robert Barnwell Rhett declared in his famous Colleton address at Walterborough, South Carolina: "From the rapid step of usurpation, whether we now act or not, the day of open opposition to the pretended powers of the Constitution, cannot be far off; and it is that it may not go down in blood that we now call upon you to resist." [6]

[3] William Maclay, *The Journal of William Maclay* (New York, 1927), 69–71.

[4] Quoted in Charles S. Sydnor, *The Development of Southern Sectionalism, 1819–1848* (Baton Rouge, 1948), 189. *See also*, Chauncey S. Boucher, *The Nullification Controversy in South Carolina* (Chicago, 1916), 3.

[5] Quoted in David F. Houston, *A Critical Study of Nullification in South Carolina* (New York, 1908), 51.

[6] Charleston *Daily Mercury*, June 18, 1828. For an analysis of this speech and surrounding circumstances, see Henry Hardy Perritt, "Robert Barnwell Rhett: Prophet of Resistance, 1828–1834," *Southern Speech Journal*, XXI (Winter, 1955), 103–19.

Essays on the Nullifiers and the Anti-Nullifiers in this volume summarize subsequent events surrounding nullification. Following the nullification crisis, there were continued threats of secession as each new sectional controversy arose: slave petitions; independent treasury; annexation of Texas, California, and Oregon; the Mexican War; the fugitive slave law. There were, however, only isolated attempts at open movements to organize secession sentiment before 1850.[7]

According to James M. Mason of Virginia, John C. Calhoun said shortly before his death on March 31, 1850: "The Union is doomed to dissolution, there is no mistaking the signs." [8] In June, 1850, a southern convention—which had been called in October, 1849, by a convention of the state of Mississippi with full knowledge and approval of Calhoun—met in Nashville, Tennessee. The delegates from the nine participating states adopted resolutions and an address rejecting the pending Henry Clay and Stephen A. Douglas compromise measures and recommended the extension of the Missouri Compromise line to the Pacific Coast.[9] Almost immediately after the convention adjourned, the Fire-Eaters declared themselves in favor of secession if the compromise measures should be adopted. Although their efforts to lead the South out of the Union failed so completely that they were largely discredited and repudiated throughout the South, the agitation continued from the public platform and in the press.

Many prominent in the politics of the region joined the

[7] For attempts at secession between 1828 and 1850, see Sydnor, *The Development of Southern Sectionalism* or Henry Hardy Perritt, "Robert Barnwell Rhett: South Carolina Secession Spokesman" (Ph.D. dissertation, University of Florida, 1954).

[8] Virginia Mason, *The Public Life and Diplomatic Correspondence of James M. Mason* (New York, 1906), 72–73.

[9] The states represented were Virginia, South Carolina, Georgia, Florida, Alabama, Mississippi, Tennessee, Arkansas, and Texas. Dallas Tabor Herndon, "The Nashville Convention of 1850," *Transactions of the Alabama Historical Society*, V, (1904), 203–37.

ranks before 1860, including such names as: Jefferson Davis, Robert Toombs, James Mason, J. F. H. Claiborne, Robert M. T. Hunter, Roger Pryor, David Yulee, Langdon Cheves, Clement C. Clay, James H. Hammond, Louis T. Wigfall. None of these, however, took the prominent and unswerving position for secession—in any way it might be obtained—of the four leading Fire-Eaters: Edmund Ruffin of Virginia, John A. Quitman of Mississippi, Robert Barnwell Rhett of South Carolina, and William Lowndes Yancey of Alabama.[10]

Edmund Ruffin, the old man who had the honor of firing the first shot at Fort Sumter, was born in Prince George County, Virginia, in 1794. He was tutored at home until he was sixteen, when he entered the College of William and Mary from which he was soon expelled for neglect of his studies. At nineteen he married and took charge of Coggins Point, a plantation which had been left him by his father a short time before.

He began immediately to experiment with marl as a commercial fertilizer. Within five years he presented his theories to the Prince George Agricultural Society and in 1821 printed them in the *American Farmer*. At the same time, he had begun to fuse political questions with agricultural interests, writing in 1820 a petition to United Agricultural Societies and to Congress condemning the tariff as a "monstrous anomaly in free government." He served in the Virginia Senate from 1823 to 1826 as a Whig, but resigned in disgust because of his unwillingness to compromise his convictions for the selfish interests of his constituents and friends, and because of his

---

[10] For details of this decade of development, see Avery O. Craven, *The Growth of Southern Nationalism, 1848–1861* (Baton Rouge, 1953); Perritt, "Robert Barnwell Rhett: South Carolina Secession Spokesman," 241–308; Henry Hardy Perritt, "Robert Barnwell Rhett: Disunionist Heir of Calhoun, 1850–1862," *Southern Speech Journal*, XXIV (Fall, 1958).

ineptness in public speaking. In 1832 he published his famous *Essay on Calcareous Manures,* which went through five editions and was expanded to a volume of 500 pages; and in 1833 he established the journal, *Farmer's Register,* which was published for ten years before it failed, according to Ruffin's biographer, because of its agitation for banking reforms.[11]

After 1842, when he made an agricultural survey of South Carolina, Ruffin was closely identified with South Carolina leaders, becoming a particularly close friend of James H. Hammond. Following the secession flare-up in 1850, Ruffin wrote voluminously on the South and slavery for *De Bow's Review,* the *Southern Planter,* and the Rhett-owned secession newspaper, the Charleston *Mercury,*[12] as well as publishing privately in 1858 the pamphlet, *Political Economy of Slavery.*[13] Following the John Brown raid, Ruffin organized the League of United Southerners and collected pikes used by Brown's band, presenting one to each of the governors of fifteen states.[14]

Although Craven says that in spite of Ruffin's lack of self-confidence as a speaker he never refused an invitation to speak, Ruffin repeatedly referred in the latter part of his fourteen-volume diary to his speech on November 7, 1860, in Columbia, South Carolina, as his maiden speech.[15] At any rate, the only speech texts extant are the Columbia speech and several others that he made at various places in South Carolina during and following the session of the legislature that called the secession convention in the state. The following account from the Charleston *Mercury* of the opening of one of those speeches is typical of Ruffin's style: "Fellow citizens: I have thought

---

[11] Avery O. Craven, *Edmund Ruffin, Southerner: A Study in Secession* (New York, 1932), 66–70.

[12] *Ibid.,* 129–30, 155–57.

[13] *The Political Economy of Slavery; or the Institution Considered in Regard to its Influence on Public Wealth and the General Welfare* (Printed by Lemuel Towers, 1858). A copy is in the Library of Congress.

[14] Ruffin Diary, 533–51.   [15] Ruffin Diary, 684–700.

and studied on this question for years. It has been literally the great one idea of my life, the independence of the South, which I verily believe can only be accomplished through the action of South Carolina. [Prolonged applause] And if there is danger, gentlemen, old as I am, I have come here to join you in that danger. [Immense applause] I wish my state was as ready to move as South Carolina." [16] All accounts of these "off-hand" remarks of Ruffin's including his own, credit him with tremendous effectiveness—despite his plain style and awkward and nervous manner. As a matter of fact, his unusual ethos seems to have been reinforced by these qualities.[17]

In his diary in November, 1857, Ruffin confided that he would have liked political power, but "I felt sure that I had no talent for oratory, or to influence popular assemblies and I was too proud to be willing to be deemed below any station in which I might be placed." [18] In 1913 Lyon G. Tyler, president of the College of William and Mary, described Ruffin's character as "impetuous and severely critical of others. . . ." but with "high personal and moral courage, an invincible honesty, and great intellectual power and resources. He was a fanatic, but not one of the John Brown type—a coarse outlaw and murderer." [19] Declaring in his diary his "unmitigated hatred . . . to the Yankee race . . ." for their "outrages on noncombatant residents . . . and . . . on aged men and helpless women," Ruffin shot himself to death at 10:00 A.M., June 18, 1865.[20]

[16] Ruffin Diary, 685 ff.; Charleston *Mercury*, Nov. 8–20, 1860; Charleston *Courier*, Nov. 8–20, 1860.

[17] Ruffin Diary contains clippings from several newspapers with accounts of several appearances he made in South Carolina.

[18] *Ibid.*, 223.

[19] Lyon G. Tyler, *Edmund Ruffin—An Address Delivered at the Virginia Polytechnic Institute, Blacksburg, Virginia, April 25, 1913*, Library of Congress, 15.

[20] Ruffin Diary, 816 ff.

John Anthony Quitman was born at Rhinebeck, New York, in 1798, the third son of a German Lutheran minister. Educated by his father and at Hartwick Academy, he became a professor of English at Mount Airy College, Germantown, Pennsylvania, but after one year went west to Chillicothe and then to Delaware, Ohio, where he studied law and clerked in a government land office.

In 1821 he was admitted to the bar and moved to Natchez, Mississippi; in 1824 he married Elizabeth Turner, daughter of one of the leading Natchez citizens. From 1826 to 1838 and again in 1840 and 1845 he was Grand Master of Mississippi Masons. In 1827 he was elected to the Mississippi house of representatives and in the same year became chancellor of Mississippi, serving until 1835. In 1832 he was chairman of the judiciary committee of the Mississippi constitutional convention. Although nullification had few adherents in Mississippi, Quitman prepared the address adopted by a convention of nullifiers in Jackson in 1834. The next year he was elected to the state senate and immediately afterwards president of the body, in which capacity he was acting governor for a month.

After being defeated for Congress in 1836, he went to Texas as commander of a volunteer company but he saw no fighting. Upon his return, however, he was made brigadier general of the Mississippi militia. As brigadier under General Taylor, he commanded the first forces to enter Monterey, Mexico, in 1846, and was made governor of the city. Upon returning from Mexico, he proposed to President Polk a plan for permanent occupation.

He was an unsuccessful candidate for the Democratic nomination for Vice-President in 1848. The following year he was elected governor of Mississippi. Having been indicted by a New Orleans federal grand jury in May, 1850, for his interest in the Cuban rebellion,[21] he resigned in January, 1851, before

21 The John A. Quitman Papers, Mississippi Department of Archives and

submitting to arrest to be taken to New Orleans. Subsequently the case was nol-prossed. He was again an anticompromise candidate for governor in 1851 but withdrew in favor of Jefferson Davis, who was defeated by Senator Henry S. Foote. In constant correspondence with Rhett and other South Carolina secessionists, Quitman went to the United States House of Representatives in 1855, where he served until his death July 17, 1858.[22]

Although reams of his letters are preserved, few of Quitman's speeches, except a few relatively innocuous ones made in Congress, are available. His inaugural address, January 10, 1850, was typical: "The halls of Congress, where northern and southern men should meet as brethren, have become the theatre of this war upon slavery. . . . These measures, not only threatened, but actually introduced in Congress, too plainly speak the deliberate intention of their instigators to wage a war of extermination against our most valued rights. Whether they originate in fanaticism, affected philanthropy, or calculations of political power, they can have no other object than the ultimate destruction of our domestic institutions, or the dissolution of the union. . . . The South has long submitted to grievous wrongs. Dishonor, degradation, and ruin await her if she submits farther." [23]

In his eulogistic two-volume biography of Quitman, J. F. H. Claiborne commented: "He was never a brilliant man. He was no rhetorician. His strength lay in his earnestness, his con-

---

History, contain, among numerous letters and documents, a copy of the indictment. The J. F. H. Claiborne Papers, Mississippi Department of Archives and History, also include many valuable Quitman papers. J. F. H. Claiborne, *Life and Correspondence of John A. Quitman, Major-General, U.S.A., and Governor of the State of Mississippi*, (2 vols.; New York, 1860), contains copies of most of the materials in both the Quitman and Claiborne papers.

[22] Natchez *Courier*, July 22, 1858, carried an account of the funeral, with numerous resolutions of eulogy.

[23] Claiborne, *John A. Quitman*, II, 21–24.

stancy, and integrity, and the boldness of his views. . . . His temper, though ardent, was much under his control. The working of his mind was laborious, but it seldom failed of accurate results. He expressed himself sometimes with difficulty; he often stammered and hesitated, and was given to repetition, but he never said a foolish thing." Considering him "personally, the most popular man in America at the period of his death," Claiborne continued: "A more ambitious man never lived. He desired office for its power and distinction. He was greedy of military fame. His nature was essentially military, and he was fond of the pomp and clash of arms." [24]

Robert Barnwell Rhett, who came to be known as the "father of secession," [25] was born in Beaufort, South Carolina, in 1800, the eighth child of James Smith, an unsuccessful rice planter, who had studied law in England. He changed his name to Rhett in 1836 in memory of a famous maternal ancestor. Having been tutored at home and having studied several years at Beaufort College, Rhett had law instruction from Thomas S. Grimké of Charleston. Admitted to the bar at twenty-one, he practiced law in Coosawhatchie, Charleston, and Walterboro. At twenty-six he was elected to the South Carolina house of representatives.

With his Colleton address in 1828, he vaulted to the leadership of the most extreme faction of nullifiers. In this capacity he talked more of revolution than he did of nullification. In

---

[24] *Ibid.* 290–98.
[25] Laura White, *Robert Barnwell Rhett: Father of Secession* (New York, 1931). The title seems to have been first bestowed in an obituary in the Charleston *Daily News and Courier*, Sept. 18, 1876. Almost complete files of the Charleston *Mercury*, held by the Charleston Library Society, comprise the most valuable single source. Fragmentary Rhett personal papers, including attempts at an autobiography, are owned by I'On Rhett, Charleston, S.C. The University of North Carolina has a file of Rhett letters written during his years in Congress, 1837–50. Some useful documents and records are in the South Carolina Historical Commission.

1834, having been chosen attorney general of the state, he declared in opposition to repeal of the ordinance of nullification: "The star-spangled banner no longer waves in triumph and glory for me. . . . I fear that there is no longer hope or liberty for the South, under a Union, by which all self-government is taken away." [26]

In Congress, from 1837 to 1849 as chief lieutenant of Calhoun, he attempted to moderate his tone but frequently lapsed into threats of secession and war. Not until 1850, however, upon his return from the Nashville Convention, did he declare openly: "To maintain the Union is to acquiesce in the destruction of the Constitution; and to maintain the Constitution, we must dissolve the Union. . . . But let it be that I am a traitor; the word has no terrors for me: I was born of traitors." [27] Elected to the United States Senate in Calhoun's place in 1850, Rhett resigned after two stormy sessions because South Carolina refused to secede.

He made no public speeches from then until he opened the campaign for 1860 secession with his Grahamville address, July 4, 1859.[28] During these seven years of "profound political retirement" he continued to agitate privately and through the pages of the Charleston *Mercury*, which he owned and his son edited. With the coming of secession Rhett enjoyed a brief surge of popularity. But his austere and arrogant manner and his reputation as an uncompromising extremist made him unacceptable as president of the Confederacy or senator from his state. A member of the provisional Confederate congress, he was chairman of the committee that wrote the Confederate

[26] Perritt, "Robert Barnwell Rhett: Prophet of Resistance," 115–19.

[27] Charleston *Daily Mercury*, July 22, 1850; Washington *National Intelligencer*, July 25, 1850; Perritt, "Robert Barnwell Rhett: Disunionist Heir of Calhoun."

[28] H. Hardy Perritt, "Robert Barnwell Rhett's Speech, July 4, 1859," in J. J. Auer (ed.), *Antislavery and Disunion, 1858–1861: Studies in the Rhetoric of Compromise and Conflict* (New York, 1963), 98–107.

constitution. Unable to support the policies of Davis, he was defeated for the permanent Congress from his home district where he had never before lost an election. He died, disillusioned and bitter, in 1876 in New Orleans, where his son was editor of the *Daily Picayune*.[29]

Although many of his speeches were models of carefully reasoned exposition of the state rights position, he was generally regarded as an untrustworthy doctrinaire. Ulrich B. Phillips thought Rhett "had no camaraderie with which to give . . . charm" to his earnestness and was "devoid of personal magnetism," as his "appeal was to reason, amid a people who loved emotion." [30] Yet, he made a striking appearance—with over six feet of height, hair that curled over his ears, a well-trimmed pointed goatee, and cold blue eyes—as he screamed in his rapid-fire manner of "fanaticism, avarice, and ambition" and of "robbery," "ruin and dishonor," and "fires of insurrection."

William Lowndes Yancey, who has been called the "orator of secession," was born at Ogeechee Shoals, Georgia, in 1814. His father died in 1817; his mother married a Presbyterian preacher, Nathan Beman, in 1822 and the family moved to New York. There the stepfather was an active abolitionist. Yancey attended Williams College for two years and in 1833 began the study of law with Benjamin Perry, a leading Unionist, in Greenville, South Carolina. Yancey's first political speech was in 1834 in opposition to nullification, while he was Perry's law partner and editor of a Union newspaper, the Greenville *Mountaineer*.[31]

29 Perritt, "Robert Barnwell Rhett: South Carolina Secession Spokesman," 281–355; Charleston *Daily News and Courier*, Sept. 18, 1876.

30 Ulrich B. Phillips, "The Central Theme of Southern History," in *The Course of the South to Secession: An Interpretation by Ulrich Bonnell Phillips* (ed.), E. Merton Coulter (New York, 1939), 132.

31 B. J. Perry, "William L. Yancey," in Greenville (S. C.) *Enterprise*, Dec. 6, 1871.

In 1835 Yancey married a wealthy girl, moved to Alabama, and operated a plantation for five years until he was ruined by an accidental poisoning of his slaves. During this period he became a state rights Democrat. In 1838 he was convicted, in South Carolina, of manslaughter for the shooting of his wife's uncle, Dr. Robinson Earle, but was pardoned by the governor.[32] He was elected to the Alabama house of representatives in 1841, the senate in 1843, and Congress the following year. After two years in Congress, during which he became a follower of Rhett and fought a harmless duel with Thomas Clingman of North Carolina, Yancey was reelected, but he resigned. Although a delegate to the Democratic convention of 1848 and spokesman for the anti-Douglas Southerners in the convention of 1860, he held no public office from 1846 to 1861.[33] Following 1850, however, he was actively engaged with Ruffin and Rhett in agitating for secession. After a secession meeting at Macon, Georgia, August 22, 1850, James A. Meriwether wrote Howell Cobb: "There were not eight hundred of the fire-eaters on the ground . . . [but] the godlike Rhett and his adjutant Yancey preached most eloquently in behalf of treason." [34] He campaigned for Breckinridge in 1860 from Alabama to New York, making more than fifty speeches. He was Confederate commissioner to England in 1861–62 and senator from Alabama until his death July 27, 1863. It was rumored that he died as the result of a blow struck him by

[32] Greenville (S.C.) *Mountaineer*, Nov. 9, 1838.

[33] John Witherspoon DuBose, *The Life and Times of William Lowndes Yancey*, (2 vols.; New York, 1892), is a highly favorable, but valuable, secondary source. Austin L. Venable, *The Role of William L. Yancey in the Secession Movement* (Nashville, 1945), is somewhat more objective. The W. L. Yancey Collection in the Alabama State Archives, Montgomery, contains numerous speeches, letters, and other valuable primary and secondary sources.

[34] Ulrich B. Phillips (ed.), *The Correspondence of Robert Toombs, Alexander H. Stephens, and Howell Cobb, Annual Report of the American Historical Association for 1911* (2 vols.; Washington, 1913), II, 210.

Senator Hill of Georgia in an argument in a secret session of the Confederate senate.[35] Describing Yancey as a "handsome young man with a bright cheerful face . . . rather under average height and well proportioned," Benjamin Perry credited him with having done more than anyone else to bring about secession: "There may have been others who labored longer and more effectually to prepare the public's mind for this terrible result, but to William L. Yancey is due the awful responsibility of having applied the match which produced this bloody explosion." [36]

Joel Bartlett wrote in recollection that Colonel John W. A. Sanford considered "Yancey . . . the greatest natural orator whom the United States had ever produced." Bartlett said he heard his elders characterize Yancey as the "Demosthenes of fiery and impetuous speech, and Mr. Hilliard as the polished and faultless Cicero." [37] Yet, Representative Graham of Texas said in the Confederate house of representatives that Yancey "established his conclusions deduced from stated premises, with the clearness of mathematical demonstration. . . . [and] used nothing for ornament merely." [38] His biographer, John W. DuBose, said Yancey seldom occupied more than a square yard of space when he spoke.[39] Furthermore, when he spoke at Cooper Institute in his campaign for Breckinridge in 1860, the editor of the New York *World* considered him more moderate than was expected of the "representative fire-eater." [40]

[35] Quoted from Alabama *State Journal*, May 8, 1869, in a manuscript in the Yancey Papers, Alabama Department of Archives and History, Montgomery.

[36] Greenville *Enterprise*, Dec. 6, 1871.

[37] Montgomery *Advertiser*, July 18, 1914. For an account of Yancey-Hilliard debates on the Union, see James L. Golden, "Hilliard vs. Yancey: Prelude to the Civil War," *Quarterly Journal of Speech*, XLII (Febr., 1956), 35–44.

[38] Manuscript copy in Yancey Papers, Alabama Department of Archives and History.

[39] Dubose, *William L. Yancey*, 190.

[40] The New York *World*, Oct. 11, 1860.

As a matter of fact, his style and delivery were much more moderate and calm than one might expect from an extremist who was said to cast a spell over his listeners. Quite typical of his style was his advice to Democrats in the 1860 Charleston Convention: "Stand firmly on a constitutional basis. Go before your northern people and appeal to their loyalty to the Union and their loyalty to the constitution. . . . To my countrymen of the South, I have a few words to say. Be true to your constitutional duties and rights. Be true to your sense of right. . . . Yield nothing of principle for mere party success— else you will die by the hands of your associates as surely as by the hand of your avowed enemy." [41]

For almost forty years the voices of the Fire-Eaters fell upon the ears of the people of the South and, somewhat less regularly, the people of the entire United States. Theirs were always pleas of protest; they seldom spoke for a majority. Like Edmund Burke, Charles James Fox, Patrick Henry, John C. Calhoun, and many other better known and, perhaps, more effective orators before them, they spoke in defense of what they thought were the rights of a minority. Unlike most other political orators, they were persistently consistent in pleas for the unpopular. Their thousands and thousands of words to legislatures, at state conventions, in the United States Congress, at public political meetings, and in the provisional congress of the Confederacy were always, with only slight variations, on the same theme: the South must resist unconstitutional exploitation or suffer the loss of her way of life. They stated their proposition in general terms in 1828, translated it into nullification in 1832, threatened disunion in 1844,

[41] Copy in Yancey Papers, Alabama Department of Archives and History; also quoted in DuBose, *William L. Yancey*. For an account of Yancey's part in the 1860 convention, see Owen M. Peterson, "A Description and Analysis of the Speaking in the Democratic National Convention of 1860" (Ph.D. dissertation, University of Iowa, 1952).

and avowed secession in 1850. They began a campaign in 1859 which culminated in secession a little more than a year later. Thus, the South did what the Fire-Eaters urged them to do— not exactly when told or quite as decisively as wished, but following the general program. Furthermore, the Confederacy adopted most of the Fire-Eater platform for a new constitution. Yet, because of new fears of centralization of government, the Confederacy heard the Fire-Eaters continue the same old warnings the country had been listening to for so many years. Faced with disaster, the South did not listen.

The Fire-Eaters were peculiar products of an irrepressible conflict between an expanding industrial democracy and a growing agrarian aristocracy. A simple analysis can isolate the concept of self-interest on both sides of the core of the conflict. But the conflict was not a simple one. There were common elements in both economies. Locke's respect for property combined with Rousseau's love of liberty to affect attitudes in all sections of the country. Furthermore, there was a strong tradition of Jeffersonian democracy in the southern slavocracy and an element of Hamiltonian aristocracy in the northern industrialism. Perhaps the important consideration is that industrialism was expanding faster than was agriculture. In their analysis of the undercurrents of early nineteenth century thought, R. W. Horton and H. W. Edwards explain: "To have stopped with the simple security of Jeffersonian mediocrity would have seemed mere sloth; to have concurred with Jackson's distrust of the fruits of capitalism would have been economic sabotage." [42] Avery Craven translates this industrial evolution into antislavery sentiment outside the South: "Lincoln's attitude and actions were also the product of certain great changes that were gradually transforming his part of the nation. . . . For the realization of the American democratic

[42] Rodney W. Horton and Herbert W. Edwards, *Backgrounds of American Literary Thought* (New York, 1952), 106.

ideals, the Union had to be preserved, and slavery had to be put on the road to ultimate extinction. There was no other choice." [43]

The Fire-Eaters represented a point of view antipodal to that of Lincoln. Not only were they born and bred in the intensely aristocratic slave culture of the South; they were born too late to share the love of the Union held by C. C. Pinckney, James L. Petigru, and John C. Calhoun. According to U. B. Phillips, the "central theme of Southern history" always was a determination "to keep assurance doubly, trebly sure that the South shall remain 'a white man's country.' " [44] This central theme did not exist, however, until tobacco, indigo, rice, and cotton brought black men to parts of the South in far greater numbers than the white men. And this idea did not have force until the free economy of the expanding northern industrialism threatened to turn the black men loose to dominate the few whites. The Fire-Eaters undertook to lead their states and region faster than the majority of constituents were prepared to go in meeting this danger. The citizenry could not be prodded into action until they were able to sense the reality of the components of the crisis. Nevertheless, the Fire-Eaters were either unwilling or unable to content themselves with riding the crest of a wave of public opinion which they thought was too slow for safety. Thus, they appeared to sacrifice themselves for a cause. The most they were able to accomplish by this rigid consistency was to hurry along the processes of group decision by providing ready-made arguments for people to use when the conditions made the arguments palatable. Their hundreds of speeches gave continuity and credibility to conditions which the South was reluctant to accept.

The Fire-Eaters did not—contrary to the claims of many

[43] Craven, *The Growth of Southern Nationalism*, 391–92.
[44] Phillips, "The Central Theme of Southern History," 151–65.

of their contemporaries—lead the South into the Civil War. Not one of them was in a position of high political leadership when secession began. Ruffin had not held political office since 1826. Quitman, after his resignation as governor of Mississippi in 1851 and subsequent withdrawal from the race for reelection, had served in the United States House of Representatives from 1855 until his death in 1858. Rhett had been in "profound political retirement" from 1852 to 1859, when he resumed public appearances in his Grahamville address. Yancey had not held political office since his resignation from the United States Congress in 1846. Their extremism and violent proposals had discredited these four leading Fire-Eaters so thoroughly in their own states and throughout the South that they were not acceptable for public leadership even after the southern states followed the secession course which those partisans charted ten years before. Doubtless, however, their years of agitation on the platform and in the press contributed to the convergence of conditions that made the war possible.

These were men of strong conviction who refused to yield to the pressure of public opinion. They were not demagogues; they were not opportunists—except in their consistent exploitation of fear of northern rule of the South. Their speeches and writings were highly logical in tone and format, with strong emotional undertones. Although their unyielding position and impatience with opposition sometimes produced invective and threats of violence, their language was predominantly calm and simple. For example, Ruffin in his so-called "maiden speech," in Columbia said: "I verily believe, the circumstances being as they are, that it is better that Virginia and all other border States remain quiescent for a time—but for a time—a barrier to the seceding States; and the first drop of blood spilled in South Carolina in defending her soil, will rally Virginia and every other border State with you [Applause]. If she does remain alone, which I do not deem possible, it is my full conviction that you will be able to defend yourselves against any power [Loud and prolonged applause]." [45]

Likewise Rhett in his test oath argument in 1834 argued typically:

The impression that sovereignty may be divided, has originated from confounding sovereignty with the powers that sovereignty may exercise. Sovereignty is not in power, but in him who possesses it. Power is an attribute of sovereignty; but it is no more sovereignty, than the actions or conduct of a man, are the man. All sovereignties, whether existing in the people, as in a republic, or in the will of a single man, as in a despotism, must exercise power in the business of Government, and these powers must be exercised by agents. The Almighty alone can will, judge, and execute his will. [46]

Advancing almost identical arguments in equally unornamented language Quitman said in his inaugural address in 1850: "Has the federal government power over all other powers? Not at all, sir. It is strictly limited; circumscribed by the most rigid limitations; forbidden by its organic law, over which it has no control, from exercising many of the most important attributes of sovereignty. It can exercise no sovereign powers by its own intrinsic force. It is merely a part of the machinery of government, through which, as through an agency, some of the powers belonging to sovereignty are put into operation." [47]

Even Yancey, despite his reputation as the "Demosthenes of fiery and impetuous speech," said in Cincinnati in 1860: "No part of the South proposes to resist if the Constitution

[45] Charleston *Daily Mercury*, Nov. 8, 1860.

[46] *The Book of Allegiance; or a Report of Counsel, Opinions of the Court of Appeals of South Carolina on the Oath of Allegiance* (Columbia, 1834), 94–95.

[47] Claiborne, *Life and Correspondence of John A. Quitman*, II, 341.

is preserved—if either Breckinridge, or Bell, or Douglas is elected. No part of the South proposes to withdraw from the Union in the event only that you prevent this great wrong of a party being put into power that shall endanger our domestic peace. The only threat of disunion is in the event of a party getting into power who will destroy the rights of the South if they get the army and navy and treasury into their hands." [48]

Despite Phillips' belief that much of Rhett's lack of "personal magnetism" was due to his love of reason, he was throughout his career the most violent of the Fire-Eaters in both his ideas and his language. Although he moderated his tone somewhat—after his outbursts advocating resistance and revolution during the nullification controversy from 1828 to 1833—he continued to threaten disunion frequently on the floors of the United States House of Representatives and the Senate.[49] Rather typical of what Laura White called his sophomoric rhetoric was his conclusion to the Grahamville address in 1859, when he said in part:

Shall we wait for this blissful consummation when the fires of insurrection will light up our homes and the North shall stand by to watch the conflagration? Such things will probably never be; because the South will not await their fearful coming but will anticipate them. When will she anticipate them and act out her redemption? When will her mighty heart beat free in the enjoyment of her rights, safe under the shield of her own protection; and casting off the incubus of ignorance and error and fear, which

[48] Cincinnati *Daily Gazette,* Oct. 20, 1860.

[49] See Benjamin F. Perry, *Reminiscences of Public Men* (Philadelphia, 1833), for complimentary comments on Rhett, though they disagreed on issues, and Charles Francis Adams (ed.), *Memoirs of John Quincy Adams,* (12 vols.; Philadelphia, 1874–77) for frequent severe criticism of his violent outbursts in Congress. Perritt, "Robert Barnwell Rhett: Prophet of Resistance" and Perritt, "Robert Barnwell Rhett: Disunionist Heir of Calhoun" detail his oscillation from violence to moderation, and back again.

now like a foul toad sits upon her bosom, rise up and command the liberation and independence of the South? [50]

Thus the Fire-Eaters were perhaps not as unemotional as Phillips implied, but they always attempted to keep their emphasis on logic. Worshiping at what they considered a shrine of reason, they had confidence in their conclusions arrived at through categorical syllogisms formed from indisputable premises of the region. Generally, southern slaveowners accepted without question the following premises: the institution of slavery has existed in all great democracies in history; it is natural for all nations to expand their borders; yielding to aggression only weakens the power to resist.

Doubtless the cumulative effect of their argument helped to crystallize the opinion in the South that the Union must be dissolved. Why then were the Fire-Eaters unable to persuade their listeners that they should lead the South in its hour of triumph? Why were they not able to win a more satisfactory immediate response? The answer lies partially in the force of their persuasion. Not having a strong desire to accept extreme conclusions, many persons were made uncomfortable by the self-assurance of the Fire-Eaters that they were right and that all who disagreed were either stupid or malicious.

Although they were essentially single-minded in their desire to preserve the culture and the traditions of the South, not one of these leaders seemed ever to take time really to enjoy the "good life" which they so stubbornly upheld. Despite frequent references by their families and friends to their warmth and sense of humor, these qualities were seldom demonstrated in their public utterances. Thus, whether they were really as amiable as their few close friends suggested was of little significance in their roles as speakers and politicians. Their reputa-

[50] Charleston *Daily Mercury*, July 6, 1859.

tions for being ambitious, arrogant, impulsive, intransigent, and doctrinaire contributed to their relative ineffectiveness.

No doubt, these men had the intellectual capacity, the energy, the vision, and the integrity to have achieved greatness in both politics and oratory. Their insistence that their states act faster than the people were motivated to act by social forces, and their stubborn appeals that the South heed their warnings only discredited them as conceited, ambitious, irrational alarmists. Whatever effectiveness they had as public speakers, therefore, resulted from their devotion to a cause, their consistency, their dignity, their intensity, their apparent learning, and their unquestionable honesty.

In their rhetorical and political practices, these men were, at the same time, both homogeneous and heterogeneous. They were remarkably homogeneous in their single-minded devotion to defense of agrarian slavocracy against encroachments by the expanding industrialism. Despite various economic and educational hardships in youth, they unanimously considered themselves of noble white Anglo-Saxon Protestant birth and, thus, endowed by nature with a mission to protect the South's peculiar institution from the ruthless invaders from the North and West. All, except Quitman, were at times associated with operation of large plantation holdings and mixed their public platform agitation with extensive journalistic endeavors. On the other hand, Quitman was the only military figure of the group—unless Ruffin's firing of the cannon at Fort Sumter qualifies him in this respect. At any rate, they were the self-appointed spokesmen for the southern slavocracy in the irrepressible conflict between agrarianism and industrialism.

This unity of purpose and orientation occurred despite wide differences in personal idiom. Ruffin, who repeatedly wrote of his "ineptness" in public speaking, was most unimposing in his appearances to talk on agricultural and political subjects—until his 1860 campaign for secession in South Carolina. Likewise, Quitman, despite his military accomplishments and early reputation in Mississippi legal circles, seems to have been regarded, even by his friends, as of only mediocre stature as an orator. On the other hand, Rhett was acclaimed by his friends as the "ne plus ultra" of South Carolina rhetoric—while his enemies seemed more likely to consider his rapid-fire rhetoric and mixed metaphors the rantings of an irrational extremist. Of the four, Yancey seems to be the only one who enjoyed a general reputation as an effective speaker, though sometimes disappointing to both friend and foe because of his personal mildness even when arguing for a fundamentally violent course.

Underlying many of the speaking practices of the Fire-Eaters was their apparent approach to the speaking situation. Their dogged defense of slavery somehow seemed inseparable from a tendency toward introspection and subjectivity. According to L. Sarett and W. T. Foster:

An effective speaker usually is objective. He thinks in terms of the audience; he studies the audience both in the preparation of his speech and as he speaks; he tries to understand its point of view, biases, prejudices and predispositions, its tendencies, instincts, sense of values, habitual modes of thinking, crowd characteristics, range of information, social background, and environment; in short, everything which may have some bearing on the task before him of eliciting the desired response. If the speaker's attitude is objective, he is likely to be a persuasive speaker. This is one of the basic principles of speech.[51]

If the Fire-Eaters were aware of this fundamental of persuasion, they must have generally thought their audiences believed as strongly in their altruism and unfailing reason as they did. They seemed to feel that they should be able to win public

[51] Lew Sarett and William Trufant Foster, *Basic Principles of Speech* (New York, 1946), 489.

255

approval of their points of view if they only explained their reasons for arriving at their conclusions. Furthermore, their attempts to develop ethos during their speeches almost invariably revealed a high degree of subjectivity. They frequently opened their speeches with explanations of their personal reasons for speaking and closed on equally subjective comments concerning their personal attitudes and actions on the matter under discussion. The cumulative effect of their many references to personal attacks on them, to their popularity in their home districts, and to threats of the dire results if the South did not resist only tended to reinforce the public impressions of their egotism.

On the other hand, credit them with their apparent willingness to sacrifice their personal advancement for principles, and the conclusion must be that they were singularly successful. Openly for nearly twenty years and by implication for over thirty years, they stood almost alone in advocacy of southern secession. N. W. Stephenson thinks that "as in Yancey, so in Rhett, there was something that fitted him to one great moment but did not fit him to others." [52] Ben Ames Williams believes that "Edmund Ruffin . . . and Rhett and Yancey and Pryor did more than any other four men to bring about secession." [53] Rhett's rival of many years, James H. Hammond, grudgingly gave the Fire-Eaters credit in 1861: "Rhett and Co., . . . brought on this great movement. They were instruments in the hands of God (as Judas was)—though it was denied me to see it then." [54] Charles Cauthen seems to have summed up the total influence of the Fire-Eaters most accurately: "Indoctrination in the principles of state sovereignty, education in the necessity of maintaining Southern institutions,

[52] Nathaniel W. Stephenson and Walter Lynwood Fleming, *The Confederacy and Reconstruction* (New Haven, 1919), 89.

[53] Ben Ames Williams (ed.), *A Diary from Dixie by Mary Boykin Chesnut* (Boston, 1949), 60n.

[54] White, *Robert Barnwell Rhett*, 182.

256

warnings of the dangers of control of the federal government by a section hostile to its interests—in a word, the education of the masses in the principles and necessity of secession under certain circumstances—had been carried on with the skill and success hardly inferior to the masterly propaganda of the abolitionists themselves." [55]

Thus, despite their unpopularity with most of their contemporaries, the conjecture seems safe that the Fire-Eaters would have been considered much more effective by both historians and rhetorical critics if the secession of the South had been successful. The "fathers of secession" would then have become "fathers of their country."

---

[55] Charles Edward Cauthen, *South Carolina Goes to War, 1860–1865* (Chapel Hill, 1950), 32.

IX

The Southern Unionists
1850–1860

JAMES L. GOLDEN

There were ominous signs on the political horizon as the members of Congress arrived in Washington in December, 1849. Both the Democrats and the Whigs of the North seemed determined to thwart the spread of slavery. To bridge the gap between these two irresistible forces Henry Clay presented an omnibus bill to the Senate on January 29, 1850. Although these resolutions, eight in all, balanced concession against concession, they failed to placate the militant leaders of the South. Senator Albert Gallatin Brown of Mississippi, in one of the boldest speeches of the session, warned his northern colleagues that if the legitimate rights of the South continued to be ignored the Union might be dissolved. Nor did all of the opposition come from the South. After Clay delivered a great defense of the compromise measures on February 5 and 6, a group of Pennsylvania and Delaware citizens sent a petition to the Senate, asking "the immediate and peaceful dissolution" of the Union.[1]

These threats of disunionism from the extremists of the

[1] Avery O. Craven, *The Growth of Southern Nationalism, 1848–1861* (Baton Rouge, 1953), 72.

258

South and the North aroused Sam Houston of Texas. On February 8 the "old Hero of San Jacinto" put aside the stick he had whittled so often and long during Senate debates on less crucial issues. Now the time had come to strike a blow for the Union, and no one, thought Houston, was better qualified than he to meet the challenge. He could not forget nor would he let his colleagues forget his exploits at San Jacinto, his services first to the republic and then to the state of Texas, and, most of all, the drops of blood he had spilled for his country. Dressed in his crude, panther-skin waistcoat, out of place in the dignified Senate, Houston delivered one of the most effective deliberative speeches of his career.

He called upon "the friends of the Union from every quarter, to come forward like men, and to sacrifice their differences upon the common altar of their country's good, and to form a bulwark around the Constitution that cannot be shaken." Then rising to his full height, which was well over six feet, he denied in ringing terms "the power of all the ultras on earth to dissolve this Union, or to rend it in twain."

But Houston and his Unionist colleagues knew that harmony could never be restored until the tongues of the radicals on both sides were stilled. He was quick therefore to counsel each section to remember its responsibilities in the controversy. Speaking first to the North, he said:

What will the North gain by disunion? Do not the productions of the South contribute to the employment of their moneyed capital? ... Sir, if the North does not refrain, if they persist in their threatened aggressions upon the South, and invasions upon their rights established under the Constitution, the sin must lie at their own door. ... And I ask of them now calmly to consider upon it, and to reflect that they have gone far enough; that the South has been sufficiently excited, and that expressions too passionate for reason have been indulged in on both sides.

Houston next directed his remarks to the South. After repeating his opposition to the Southern Address,[2] he denied the charge that he was a deserter who sought to curry favor with the North. "If I am of the South," said he, "can I not recollect the North? What is our country? It is a nation composed of parts, East and West, South and North. It is an entirety. There are no fractions in it. It is a unit, and I trust it will so remain." In language that anticipated Lincoln, Houston concluded: "A nation divided against itself cannot stand. I wish, if this Union must be dissolved, that its ruins may be the monument of my grave, and the graves of my family. I wish no epitaph to be written to tell that I survived the ruin of this glorious Union." [3]

There was little in Houston's speech to bring comfort to the two groups which he and other Unionists so vigorously opposed throughout the 1850's: the southern ultras and the northern abolitionists. But he had said much that the moderates of both sections could enthusiastically endorse. Writing from Hartford, Connecticut, Radcliffe Hudson observed that Houston had won "the highest esteem of all the North by his conduct in the Senate." Others from Rhode Island and New York viewed the speech as an able and powerful address designed to preserve "our glorious Union." [4] Equally important, in a Senate which placed great emphasis on oratorical art and apt retorts, Houston had now become an eloquent spokesman for Unionism.

Eleven years later, in February, 1861, as the floodtide of secession rolled over the Lower South, Houston sat helpless in

2 Following a caucus of eighty southern congressmen early in 1849, Calhoun with the help of a committee wrote a document directed to the people of the South. Subsequently it was signed by forty-eight members and became known as the Southern Address.

3 *Congressional Globe*, 31st Cong., 1st sess., Pt. 1, Appendix, 97–102.

4 Llernena Friend, *Sam Houston: The Great Designer* (Austin, 1954), 203. For other reactions to the speech, see M. K. Wisehart, *Sam Houston: American Giant* (Washington, 1962), 535–36.

the governor's chair while legislators on both sides of the house and senate in Texas opened the dike which had long held back the waters of disunion. Flaunting their power, they disregarded the wishes of Houston and called a state convention, which not only passed an ordinance of secession but declared the governor's seat vacant. When asked to take an oath of allegiance to the newly formed Confederate government Houston refused, arguing that the convention had derived none of its powers from the people. Courageously and defiantly he declared the ordinance null and void. But it was of no use. He was a governor without a state to govern.

Saddened by the prospect of a long civil war which he now believed inevitable, Houston left Austin for his home at Cedar Point. As he traveled by stage coach through the town of Brenham some of his old soldier-comrades and other friends asked him to express his views. At first he declined their invitation. But when he learned that a group of fiery secessionists had declared he should not speak because to do so would be treason against the Confederate government, Houston became aroused and gave a fighting speech on behalf of Unionism. Standing in a densely crowded courthouse, he began his impromptu remarks amid cries from excited hecklers: "Put him out; don't let him speak; kill him." But Houston was not without friends, and order soon was restored by a wealthy planter who leaped upon a table and brandished a revolver.[5] Undaunted by the threats on his life, the deposed governor then said: "I have heard the hiss of the mobs upon the streets of Austin, and also heard the hiss of the mobs upon the streets of Brenham, and friends have warned me that my life was in great peril if I expressed my honest sentiments and convictions. But the hiss of the mob and the howls of their jackal leaders

[5] Donald Day and Harry H. Ullam (eds.), *The Autobiography of Sam Houston* (Norman, 1947), 272.

cannot deter me nor compel me to take the oath of allegiance to a so-called Confederate Government." [6] With these brave words Houston ended his long and stormy political career.

In the years which lay between Houston's great Senate speech on the compromise and his valedictory remarks in the courthouse at Brenham, he and other gallant southern conservative political leaders used their oratorical talents and historical insights to emphasize to local, state, and national audiences the value of the Union and the Constitution. In doing so they often incurred the wrath of prominent citizens in their home states. But they did not scare easily. They came to believe, in the crises of 1850 and 1860, that the Union was in jeopardy, and no force, including their own political ambitions, could change their course. In state legislatures, in the House and the Senate, in national conventions, in lecture halls, and on the stump both above and below Mason and Dixon's line they led the fight for the compromise resolutions in 1850 and 1851, and, ten years later, combined their talents once again in an effort to prevent secessionism.

Of the southern Unionists whose careers paralleled that of Houston none were more attractive, colorful, and effective than Henry S. Foote of Mississippi, Henry W. Hilliard of Alabama, John J. Crittenden of Kentucky, Benjamin F. Perry of South Carolina, and John Minor Botts of Virginia. These leaders, long the forgotten men of history, were influential far beyond the recognition they have received from twentieth century historians and rhetoricians. Few senators played a more significant role than did Foote during the compromise struggle. It was he who offered the first resolution and the first bill for the organization of the territory acquired from Mexico. Behind the scenes in committee rooms and on the floor of the Senate he joined with Clay and Webster to help

[6] Amelia W. Williams (ed.), *The Writings of Sam Houston* (8 vols.; Austin, 1942), VIII, 296.

perfect each compromise resolution and to beat down opposition to it. Then he went to the people of Virginia, Louisiana, Mississippi, New York, and Pennsylvania to win support for the measures.[7]

At first glance it seemed incongruous to find Foote cast in the role of peacemaker. Although his small, pudgy frame and greyish-white hair and flowing beard gave to him the appearance of a patriarch and man of good will, he was by temperament a fighter. On the hustings in Mississippi he exchanged blows with Jefferson Davis and Governor John A. Quitman. On the floor of the Senate he engaged in personal vituperation with Thomas Hart Benton of Missouri. Often he was uncouth, belligerent, and sarcastic; sometimes he was inconsistent. But in his courage, which at times bordered on recklessness, he had few peers. Moreover, few could deny his devotion to the Union, his boundless self-confidence, and the galvanic effect of his oratory.

Equally colorful and perhaps more persuasive than Foote and Houston was another Unionist leader from the Lower South, Hilliard of Alabama. During the period between his congressional speeches favoring the compromise and his December, 1860, speech opposing secession, he achieved distinction both as a statesman and as an orator. The people of Alabama applauded him in 1851 as he stumped the Second Congressional District in joint debate with his perennial political opponent, William L. Yancey. The moderates of New York and Massachusetts cheered him as he preached his favorite doctrine of unionism on northern soil in the summer and fall of 1860.[8]

[7] For eulogies on Foote for his part in the compromise struggle see Washington *National Intelligencer*, December 6, 7, 13, 1850; New York *Herald*, December 10, 1850; and Greensboro (S.C.) *The Patriot*, July 13 and September 28, 1850.

[8] For an analysis of these speeches, see James L. Golden, "Hilliard vs. Yancey: Prelude to the Civil War," *Quarterly Journal of Speech*, XLII (February, 1956), 35–44; and Golden, "A Southern Unionist Speaks in the

Those who heard Hilliard were impressed with his digni-fied appearance. He was a slender man of average height. His complexion was dark, his temperament bilious. He had a quick and restless eye and a forehead which retreated rapidly on a small head. Elegant, commanding, and courtly, he was in the opinion of a contemporary "a man to stand before the king." [9]

If Houston, Foote, and Hilliard were the most colorful and eloquent Unionists in the Lower South, Perry was the most prolific. Called by Jefferson Davis, "the great Daniel Web-ster of the old Palmetto State," [10] he fought the Nullifiers in 1830, and in the 1840's opposed the strong southern rights ground taken by Calhoun. Moreover almost single-handedly he opposed the secessionists in the South Carolina legislature in 1850, founded a newspaper for the purpose of upholding the Union, and vainly tried to prevent the schism of the na-tional Democratic Party in the Charleston Convention of 1860.

Possessing none of the eccentricities of Houston nor the bantamlike qualities of Foote, Perry was not unlike Hilliard in dress and bearing. On his six-foot-two-inch frame rested a well-proportioned body. His prominent features were marked by a long nose, high forehead, hazel eyes, and thin lips. Some thought he looked "as Saul did, superior to all around him." [11]

In the border states the two leading unionists, Crittenden of Kentucky and Botts of Virginia, presented a dramatic con-trast. Crittenden, who inherited the mantle of Clay, was eru-dite, polished, friendly, and eloquent. Equally important, he was a peace-loving man who knew how to conciliate. Large-

---

North on the Eve of the Civil War," *Southern Speech Journal*, XX (Fall, 1954), 28–36.

[9] William R. Smith, *Reminiscences of a Long Life* (Washington, 1889), 219.

[10] Jefferson Davis to Benjamin F. Perry, December 23, 1883, in Mrs. Ben-jamin F. Perry (ed.), *Tribute to Benjamin F. Perry, Ex-Governor of South Carolina* (Greenville, S.C., 1888), 2.

[11] "Extracts from Governor Perry's Journal," in Perry, *Letters of Gov-ernor Benjamin F. Perry to his Wife* (Philadelphia, 1889), 146.

ly through his efforts and inspiration the Constitutional Union Party was born in 1860, and not a few, including Edward Everett, were disappointed when the venerable Kentuckian refused to accept the presidential nomination. Moreover it was primarily because of his talents and perseverance that the Blue Grass State made its choice to abide by the Union in 1861.

Whenever Crittenden spoke on great congressional issues the Senate galleries and lobbies were crowded, the press box was jammed, and the senators were in full attendance. To these groups, which sometimes included such dignitaries as Baron Stoeckel, Lord Napier, and Reverdy Johnson, Crittenden was an imposing figure as he stepped to the rostrum with notes and documents in hand. A man of medium height and small bodily structure, he had features that were warm, healthy, and flushed. These made a pleasant and picturesque contrast to the white hair which decorated his head.

The outspoken, roughly eloquent Botts possessed few of the traits which made Crittenden the most beloved Unionist in the South. Often violent, denunciatory, and distrusting, especially when attacking his lifelong target, the Democrats, he was described by his political opponents as the "unspeakable Botts," "the terrible Botts," and "the Great Groom of Gahanna." Yet despite the fact he was the most ridiculed man in Virginia, no one could deny that he was fearless and ruggedly honest. He prided himself on being as courageous as any man in the country; and through his words and actions he went far to prove the point. "Muzzles were made for dogs, and not for men," he told his Richmond audience in 1856, "and no press and no party can put a muzzle on my mouth, so long as I value my freedom. I make bold then to proclaim, that I am no slavery propagandist." [12] Such frankness prompt-

---

[12] John Minor Botts, *Political Issues of the Day*, speech delivered at the African Church in Richmond, August 8, 1856 (Richmond, Va., 1856).

ed a reporter for the Newark *Mercury* to observe: "He [Botts] does not stop to enquire whether a measure is *popular*, but whether it *is right*." [13] No cause was, in Botts's opinion, more right than that of Unionism. "The Union," he said at the close of the war, "was the god of my idolatry on earth, and from its preservation I never permitted my eye to be turned for a moment." [14]

These six men, along with many others who might be analyzed in a longer study—John Bell and Parson William Brownlow of Tennessee, Zebulon Vance and William A. Graham of North Carolina, John S. Carlile of Virginia, Benjamin H. Hill of Georgia, Judge William L. Sharkey of Mississippi, and Michael Hahn of Louisiana—wielded a strong moderating influence which often gave to the South and to the nation a salutary balance in political affairs. The part which oratory played in making this influence possible is the principal burden of this essay.

What generalizations may be drawn concerning the rhetorical practice of the southern Unionists? What characteristics of presentation made them tower above so many of their contemporaries? To answer these questions we must bring into focus their basic speech premises and the forms of proof, language structure, and delivery used to project their ideas.

Out of the stream of political thought which surged forward during the 1850's, the southern Unionists sifted three ideas which, to them, surpassed all others in importance. They believed that the preservation of the American Union, the protection of southern rights, and an adherence to the Constitution were questions which affected not only the United States but the entire Christian world. These three tenets, comprising a simple unity, constituted the core of their political philosophy

---

[13] Newark *Mercury* , September 14, 1853.
[14] John Minor Botts, *The Great Rebellion: Its Secret History, Rise, Progress, and Disastrous Failure* (New York, 1866), 67.

and value system in the decade preceding the war. With equal vigor they contended on the one hand that the Union must be perpetuated and on the other that the rights of the South must be upheld. As Perry put it: "Whilst I shall defend, at any and every hazard, the rights of the South and the honor of Carolina, I am also disposed, if possible, to preserve the Union of the States." [15]

As the North and South jockeyed for power, the Unionists came to believe that their first two premises were subordinate to the third. Unionism and southern rights, they argued in Congress, in state legislatures, and on the stump, could not be pushed beyond the limits of the Constitution. Thus they fought the secessionists and the abolitionists, both of whom held that there was a moral law which transcended the Constitution. "Come weal, come woe," Hilliard told his Newark audience in 1860, he was "bound to die in the Union." Then with his eyes upon the Fire-Eaters as well as upon the abolitionists, he declared: "The true way to begin would be by ridding the country of sectionalism and sectional men." [16] Foote likewise condemned the extremists on both sides. Speaking to the Young Democratic Association of Saratoga, New York, in July, 1860, he boasted that he had sent the old disunionist, Jeff Davis, to his home on the banks of the Mississippi. And there he would have remained, roared Foote, had it not been for the northern secessionist, Caleb Cushing, who brought him out of retirement. Turning next to the abolitionists Foote, with his right hand placed on his heart, solemnly declared, as did all leading southern Unionists, that Lincoln's election would lead to a destruction of the Union. He then

[15] Perry, speech delivered in the house of representatives of South Carolina, December 11, 1850. The text of the address appears in Benjamin F. Perry, *Biographical Sketches of Eminent American Statesmen* (Philadelphia, 1887), 111–43.
[16] Newark *Evening Journal*, September 8, 1860.

concluded by saying that if the North took care of Lincoln, the South would take care of Breckinridge.[17]

What concerned Hilliard, Foote, and their colleagues was the extremists' apparent disregard for the precepts of the Constitution. What right, they argued, do the abolitionists have to make inflammatory preachments on the moral evils of slavery, an institution endorsed by the founding fathers? But while the Unionists found it easy to condone a practice which by 1860 was buffeting the waves of advancing progress and civilization, they emphatically rejected the unconstitutional remedy of secession as a possible means to redress the wrongs committed against the South. This attitude stemmed in part from the belief that war would be an inevitable corollary of secession. "But does anyone suppose that so great a political event as the separation of these States," asked Perry, "can take place without some bloody wars ensuing?" And "if war follows a dissolution of the Union," he added, "the abolitionists will have an army on our borders, or in our midst, enticing our slaves to leave us, and to arm against us!" [18]

Nor did the Unionists' belief in slavery force them into the camp of those who argued that the African slave trade should be reopened. "To agitate the subject of repeal," observed Hilliard in his commencement address delivered at the University of Virginia in July, 1859, "is to present a question which will array us against each other at home, and weaken us in the face of the enemies of our institutions." In what is perhaps the most convincing analogy to be found in his extant speeches, he claimed that it would be better "for Holland that she should cut the dikes which shut out the sea, than that the South should re-open her ports to an unchecked inundation of barbarians." Not only did Hilliard oppose the measure on

17 New York *Herald,* August 3, 1860.
18 Perry, speech delivered in the house of representatives of South Carolina, December 11, 1850.

the ground that it was impractical but also because he deemed it unconstitutional.[19]

The Unionists seemed content therefore to draw their basic arguments from the important but somewhat general document written by the founding fathers. To the Constitution could be traced their faith in compromise, their belief in state rights, their defense of slavery, their support of Bell and Douglas in 1860, and, in the case of most of them, their ultimate loyalty to the Confederacy. Hilliard spoke for all moderates of the South when he said: "The Constitution is the strength of the government and the bulwark of personal liberty; it must be upheld. He who violates it is false to his country, to himself, and to his race." [20]

The forms of proof the Unionists used to substantiate their arguments, along with their language control and delivery, played an important part in their rhetorical effectiveness. Hilliard, always sincere, calm, and self-possessed, recognized the primacy of personal proof based on the speaker's trustworthiness and competence. At no time, he conscientiously told his congressional audience in 1850, had he deviated from the tenets of the Christian faith. His scholarly training also contributed to his appeal. While at Columbia College in the 1820's he developed an interest in the classics, English literature, and American history which remained with him throughout his public life. Whenever he spoke he displayed profound knowledge, and dignity and force of expression. Furthermore he made conscious efforts within the speaking situation to establish his own authority and character and to conciliate his listeners. Often he would say something to this effect: "If I am wrong in this Mr. Johnson is wrong; if I am wrong in that

[19] Hilliard, *The Spirit of Liberty*, an oration delivered before the literary societies of the University of Virginia, July 27, 1859 (Montgomery, 1860).

[20] Hilliard, speech on "The American Government," delivered in Philadelphia, January 3, 1851. The text of the address appears in Henry W. Hilliard, *Speech and Addresses* (New York, 1855), 357–82.

Mr. Clayton is wrong." Observed the Eufaula *Democrat,*
"This amiable weakness makes Mr. Hilliard . . . a very pleasant
gentleman; it polishes his manners . . ; it softens the tone of
his voice; it makes him a great favorite with the ladies." [21]

Hilliard's use of logical proof was similarly effective. Rarely
employing the syllogism, he worked mainly through examples,
quotations, comparisons, generalizations, and causal arguments. Of these types of support, proof from authority pre-
dominates. Again and again the papers of *The Federalist,* the
Constitution, the founding fathers, and Edmund Burke were
called to the witness stand to strengthen a point Hilliard
wished to make. Often he took to the platform documented
accounts of speeches which he hoped to refute. Through this
eclectic method of assembling examples, comparisons, and quotations to substantiate his views, Hilliard not only increased
the force of his reasoning but also the color of his style.

Arguments from cause to effect and effect to cause similarly were an integral part of Hilliard's proof. Throughout the
campaign of 1860 he and other southern Unionists prophesied
that the election of a 'Black Republican" [cause] would lead
to the dissolution of the Union [effect]. Moreover he never
failed to remind his hearers in the North that the state of un-
easiness in the South [effect] was a natural result of the abolitionist crusade [cause].

Hilliard in his public utterances showed clearly then his preference for constructing causal arguments and using evidence
drawn from history and literature which would appeal to the
understanding. Through this method he placed his speeches
upon a strong logical basis. Notwithstanding the fact that he
generally used solid reasoning and convincing supporting
details, Hilliard nevertheless sometimes offered inadequate solutions to the problems which he outlined. His role in the
1860 campaign, for example, was significant. Aware of the

[21] Eufaula (Ala.) *Democrat,* May 15, 1849.

danger which threatened the Union, he eloquently warned his northern and southern audiences to turn back the Republican crusade. Despite this accurate analysis of the crucial political questions confronting the Union, he looked, as did Botts and Crittenden, to the inept Constitutional Unionist Party as the remedy for the country's ills.

The source of Hilliard's power to arouse the emotions of his listeners was his ability to relate pathetic stories and describe battle scenes and to employ moving literary and historical allusions. The people of the Second Congressional District of Alabama, observed one contemporary, "have no need of an American historian. Even the flowery pages of Weems would seem tame and dull to him who has listened to the glowing eloquence of Mr. Hilliard." [22] And the glow always seemed especially bright when the occasion was important and the audience large. Thus as Hilliard spoke to the thirty thousand New Yorkers who crowded Cooper Institute and the surrounding area in September 1860 to hear a wide variety of anti-Republican orators, he was crisp, oral, vivid, and moving. In differentiating the 1860 presidential canvass from all the previous contests he solemnly declared:

Bodies of men—disciplined, drilled, marching to the sound of martial music, bearing not arms as yet, but torches—tread the streets of this great national emporium, and range their columns under the very shadow of the statue of Washington. What men are they? They call themselves Republicans, but they have lost the last element of that principle; they are truly sectional men. For what purpose are they trained? Against what enemy are they to march? One sentiment inflames the whole body. They are banded together for one purpose. They hate the South, and they will seek to overthrow the institutions of the South.[23]

Such emotional appeals produced a warm response. At one

22 *Ibid.*   23 New York *Herald*, September 18, 1860.

point in the speech, observed the New York correspondent for the Charleston *Courier,* "the whole immense assembly rose, cheered, waved their hats and handkerchiefs, presenting a scene that was startlingly grand and exciting." [24]

Cast in a similar rhetorical mold, though a less eloquent one, was Perry. In no sense a genius he was nevertheless intelligent and well read. Moreover he, like Hilliard, was surprisingly free from such habits as drinking and gambling which were all too prevalent in the 1850's. So convinced was Perry, for example, of the benefits of a well-ordered life and of knowledge for the sake of knowledge that he urged the ploughman to read while his horse was eating and the mechanic while he was resting from his labor or waiting for it to begin.[25] Nor was his own practice different from his theory. An extensive reader, he was an especially warm admirer of Shakespeare, Byron, Scott, Moore, Homer, and Virgil. History, biography, and natural philosophy also commanded his attention. His speeches were those of a man well versed in political affairs. Each argument he developed was well documented with historical and contemporary examples, impressive testimony, and valid statistics, and was expressed in language that was clear and forceful.[26]

But the primary source of Perry's power as a speaker was not his ability to construct a scholarly message. Rather it was his moral earnestness. Never was this trait more evident than in his Charleston speech during the Democratic convention of 1860. Angered and frightened by the reckless schism of the Democratic Party, he courageously refused to follow his

[24] Charleston *Daily Courier,* September 21, 1860.

[25] Perry, speech delivered before the merchants, mechanics and businessmen of Columbia, December 17, 1853. The text of the address appears in full in *Tribute to Benjamin F. Perry,* 80–91.

[26] Observe for example his discussion of the accomplishments of the South in his address delivered before the house of representatives of South Carolina, December 11, 1850.

South Carolina colleagues when they left the convention hall. Instead he remained to lead the fight to preserve the national party so that it, in turn, could save the South and the Union from the disruptive influence of the Republicans. On the eighth day of the convention he rose to speak and, despite the fact he stood on soil no man loved more warmly or served more conscientiously, he was greeted with loud hisses from the galleries. At once the chairman, Caleb Cushing, pounded the gavel and threatened to clear the galleries. But in "deep strong tones and deliberate manner always characteristic of him," Perry said: "Let them remain, Mr. Chairman. I would like them to hear what I have to say." When the noise subsided he began:

I stand before you, Mr. President, an old-fashioned Union Democrat, born and bred such, and such I have continued, consistently, without faltering or wavering in my faith, amidst the storms of secession and nullification which have swept over South Carolina. . . . It was as a Democrat and a Union man that I came into this Convention, determined to do all that I could to preserve the Democratic party and the Union of the States. I came here not to sow the seeds of dissension in our Democratic ranks, but to do all that I could to harmonize the discordant materials of the party.[27]

Few could dispute this earnest claim. Such sincerity caused the majority of South Carolinians to listen respectfully to him even when they could not agree with his arguments.

Notwithstanding Perry's overall effectiveness he could not, like Hilliard, be called an eloquent orator. Few of his passages reached the level of sublimity; few stimulated the passions. He seemed content to enlighten as a father counsels his son, and in this he was successful.

Although Crittenden used rational and emotional discourse with the ease of Hilliard, his principal strength as a speaker,

[27] Perry, speech delivered at the National Democratic Convention in Charleston, May 8, 1860. The address appears in Perry, *Biographical Sketches of Eminent American Statesmen*, 145–51.

as in the case of Perry, was the favorable image he conveyed. Learned, sincere, and warm-hearted, he was viewed as a scholarly, trustworthy leader, and a genuine emissary of good will. "A nobler, truer, and more patriotic man," observed Alexander Stephens in 1860, "breathes not in this broad land than John J. Crittenden." [28] On those rare occasions when he was attacked by a political opponent, he silenced his adversary by the force of his character. When Senator Green of Missouri expressed surprise at Crittenden's feelings and suggested that he had had bad schooling, the Kentuckian replied: "If my education is defective, it is on account of some defect in me, and not in the school. . . . Sir, *this* [the Senate] is the school in which I was taught. I took lessons here when this was a very great body indeed. . . . I learned from your Clays and your Websters, your Calhouns and your Prestons, your Bentons and your Wrights, and such men." Such a response prompted visitors seated in the gallery to ask who the speaker was and "a dozen voices, with some surprise and much gratification, reply, 'Crittenden of Kentucky.' " [29]

No name in the late 1850's carried more weight among the conservatives throughout the country than did that of "Old Man Eloquent," as Crittenden was affectionately called. More than any other single influence, thought Lincoln, the use of Crittenden's magic name gave Douglas his victory in the Illinois Senatorial contest of 1858.[30] So revered had the Nestor

[28] Washington *National Intelligencer*, October 18, 1860. Expressing a similar view, John Carlile told the Virginia Secession Convention in March, 1861, that "a nobler specimen of a man and a purer patriot than John J. Crittenden never trod God's free earth." John Carlile, *Speech delivered in the Virginia State Convention, March 7, 1861* (Richmond, 1861).

[29] John Savage, *Our Living Representative Men* (Philadelphia, 1860), 129. A strong element of ethos was also evident whenever Crittenden appealed to the Union and the Constitution. With arms that embraced the whole nation, he told his Nashville audience in 1860: "I would not part with one of you, for we are all one people by the Constitution." Nashville *Republican Banner*, September 26, 1860.

[30] Lincoln to Crittenden, November 4, 1858, in Roy P. Basler (ed.), *The*

of the Senate become by 1860 that some Unionists of the North believed a few well-placed speeches by him would enable Bell to carry New York and Massachusetts. "If you come to Boston," wrote Amos Laurence late in May, "you will have a welcome such as no other Constitutional Union man can receive. You will see old Faneuil Hall packed from top to bottom." Washington Hunt begged him to come to New York. "Even one speech from you in favor of union, for the sake of the Union, may turn the scale in New York, and thus insure the election of Bell and Everett." [31]

In retrospect, however, it would appear that Crittenden's popularity transcended his talents. Intellectually he was inferior to Clay, Calhoun, Webster, and Stephens; nor was he their equal in influencing antebellum history. Notwithstanding this fact, a great body of evidence suggests that as a spokesman for Unionism on the eve of the Civil War, Crittenden had no peers.[32]

Equally effective in the use of personal appeals to reinforce his arguments was Houston. Repeatedly he turned to his past military experiences to show his lifelong loyalty to the Union. He graphically described the drops of blood he had shed on the soil of the South, particularly on the plains of Texas. Note how he skillfully used this technique during the debate on the compromise resolutions:

Sir, when a stripling, I enlisted a private soldier in the ranks of my countrymen; I took my life in one hand—in my right hand I

Collected Works of Abraham Lincoln (9 vols.; New Brunswick, 1953), III, 335.

[31] Amos Laurence to John J. Crittenden, May 25, 1860; Washington Hunt to Crittenden, September 3, 1860. These letters appear in Mrs. Chapman Coleman, *The Life of John J. Crittenden, With Selections from his Correspondence and Speeches* (2 vols.; Philadelphia, 1871), II, 207, 217–18.

[32] See Albert D. Kirwan, *John J. Crittenden: The Struggle for the Union* (Lexington, Ky., 1962), 477–80.

grasped the weapons of war. We marched in quest of the Indian in his lurking place; we met the savage in his war path; we kindled our fires far in the land of our enemy; we sat by them until morning when the battle came; we met our enemies, they either fled or fell. There I offered the richest libation of my youth, the blood of my early manhood, to consecrate the soil to freedom and the Union. This was in the centre of the South. . . . With my gallant associates I have struck manacles from the limbs of a captive chieftain and restored him, with his vanquished comrades, to their nation and their homes, without ransom. I ask no recompense. Was not all this done for the South, and am I to be questioned of having a southern heart, when that heart is large enough, I trust, to embrace the whole Union, if not the whole world? [33]

By identifying himself with the triumphs of his state and country and expressing his ideas with intense feeling, Houston not only enhanced his personal prestige but he stirred the emotions of his listeners. An eyewitness gives the following description of a speech delivered in Austin in 1853: "The thick-coming memories of the past thronging upon him, his voice at one time faltered, and tears almost choked his utterance, while the moistened eyes of many of his hearers told how deeply they were affected by the evident emotion of the orator." James G. Swisher and Thomas W. Ward had come to the meeting determined to attack Houston, but as they heard his eloquent appeals and saw tears flow down his cheeks, they cried too. The man they had hated just a few minutes before now "looked like a prophet inspired by a vision unfolding the events of a thousand years to come." As Houston departed from the grounds at the close of the speech, Ward held one of his arms and Swisher the other.[34]

But Houston could make his listeners laugh as easily as he could make them cry. Whenever he was attacked by his po-

[33] *Congressional Globe*, 31st Cong., 1st stess., Pt. 1, Appendix, 102. Ten years later he made a similar vivid reference to his achievements. Washington *National Intelligencer*, October 26, 1860.
[34] Texas *State Gazette*, November 15, 1853.

litical opponents he told his favorite story about the sheep that relentlessly butted a maul. Eventually the game but persistent animal "butted itself all away except the tail." Even while in this apparently helpless condition, however, that part of the anatomy "was still in motion threatening the maul." With a sardonic smile Houston then made his point. "So whether or not my political enemies have butted themselves all away, except the tail, I grant they are still in motion." [35]

This ability to turn the faucet of his emotions and those of his listeners on and off at will and to silence his opponents with stinging invective clothed in humor impressed a New York reporter who came to Texas in 1860 to assess Houston's role in the presidential campaign:

He has a withering sarcasm . . . and a voluminous and crushing vituperation. . . . Besides this power of retort and invective, Houston has command of just the right kind of eloquence for his purposes. With no great logical or analytical faculty, he has the most absolute control over the passions and the feelings of his listeners. His forte as a lawyer is in the defence of criminals. And when, on the stump, he speaks of the dark and troubled times through which the state has passed under his guidance, of its early destitution and trials compared with its present prosperity, and, contrasted with the growing wealth of his neighbors, of his own honorable poverty after a life spent in the service of the community, every eye is filled with tears and the appeal is absolutely irresistible. There has probably never been a stump speaker—a field orator—in either England or America who was superior in this department to Sam Houston. He has also other faculties which enable him to excel all rivals as a canvasser. He never forgets a man's name or face, and hardly the names of any of his children, and is a most consummate master of the art of flattery.[36]

The rhetorical power which Houston demonstrated often

[35] Williams (ed.), *The Writings of Sam Houston,* VI, 210–11.
[36] New York *Herald,* July 22, 1860. For similar praise of Houston's dynamic style, see New York *Daily Tribune,* February 10, 1860.

produced a visceral rather than a cerebral response. He knew how to blend personal references and humorous stories with appeals to the passions that could modify the attitudes of his listerners. But frequently he failed in his attempts to construct arguments and use evidence needed to elucidate the issues. Sometimes his facts were inaccurate, even when describing the early history of Texas, and occasionally his organizational pattern was loose and rambling. With the slightest provocation he would drag into his addresses extraneous material. Whatever his subject or purpose he all too often made tangential references to the Indians.[37] These rhetorical techniques tended to reduce Houston's effectiveness in the Senate.[38] But his ability to play upon the emotions of his listeners with consummate skill made him a master of the stump.

The oratory of Foote, like that of Houston, was more suited to the hustings than to the Senate. The Little Bantam from Mississippi was too belligerent, too vindictive, and too sarcastic to impress his congressional colleagues—most of whom placed a premium on formality and dignity. This lack of restraint, however, added to his power as a stump speaker. No other southern Unionist except Houston could arouse such a wide variety of emotions in his auditors. As they listened to his irony and invective—clothed in vivid imagery and spoken in a rapid, urgent, and compelling manner—they experienced pity, shame, anger, humor, love, and patriotism.[39] He delighted his New Orleans audience in December, 1850, when he said: "Though our Governor [of Mississippi] has eaten lately of the insane

[37] Early in his career Houston spent several years with the Indians. This experience had a profound impact on the development of his political philosophy and rhetorical practice.

[38] Although Houston achieved distinction during the debates on the compromise resolutions and in the Kansas-Nebraska Bill, he was not, on the whole, an impressive congressional debater.

[39] A New York reporter found Foote capable of making "the very roof . . . to raise, in order to give vent to the tremendous and universal shouts of applause that broke forth." New York *Daily Tribune*, November 25, 1850.

root, and some of the juvenile members of the Legislature have largely partaken of the infection, I am gratified to state that the people *are sound*." [40] When addressing his own constituents in Jackson, Mississippi, a few days before, he also used his favorite rhetorical weapon—abrasive sarcasm and ridicule. Convinced that a state which seceded would no longer be able to maintain republican institutions, he painted a picture of the "future Emperor of Mississippi upon his imperial throne—John Anthony the First—arrayed in purple, and with the sceptre of command." Then he alluded "to the body guard of the new monarch, with their hands doubtless ready to be imbued in blood" as they greedily seek to confiscate the property of the Union men of the state.[41]

Nor had the asperity of his tone lessened by 1860. Still true to his nickname "Hangman Foote" he told the people of Mississippi, "We will hang every man who dares to dishonor himself by an effort to break up this glorious heritage of ours." [42] The oratory-loving people of the Lower South liked Foote for his "wit, sarcasm and inimitable delivery." But, added one reporter, "they, like the effervescence of champagne, must be enjoyed when first poured out, or not at all." [43]

Not only was Foote a master of colorful language, irony, and ridicule; he knew how to arrange extensive historical facts and deduce from them important political principles. Blessed with an orderly mind and always armed with convincing evidence, he spoke with authority on the leading issues of the day. In praising his role in the compromise struggle, Clay said of him: "Prompt, ready, and full of information, in debate he has

[40] Washington *National Intelligencer*, December 9, 1850.

[41] Natchez *Weekly Courier*, November 27, 1850.

[42] Percy Lee Rainwater, *Mississippi: Storm-Center of Secession, 1856–1861* (Baton Rouge, 1938), 139. This satire and ridicule, which for years had been the trademark of Foote's oratory, was also evident in his congressional speeches. See in particular the *Congressional Globe*, 31st Cong., 1st sess., Pt. 2, Appendix, 1391 and 1493.

[43] Natchez *Weekly Courier*, July 16, 1851.

sought with untiring industry and patriotic zeal, to heal and adjust the agitations and dissensions which unhappily affect our common country. Such a distinguished statesman deserves to be honored everywhere." [44] That the content of Foote's message rested upon an intellectual base far more substantial than that used by Houston seems clear. In the projection of an ingratiating personality and image, however, he was inferior. In all, they were equally effective as stump orators.[45]

The rhetorical practice of Virginia's leading Unionist, Botts, was in one important respect strikingly similar to Foote's. It was characterized by bold denunciatory language which often breathed defiance on the Fire-Eaters. Frequently Botts—displaying a bulldog ferocity, a biting sarcasm, and a clever sense of humor—impaled his opponents on the pole of intrigue. Why, he thundered during the 1860 campaign, did the Breckinridge Democracy propose a dissolution of the Union? Not because of the doctrine of squatter sovereignty nor because of their failure to secure a territorial bill for the protection of slavery. There was but one reason, he said, and that was to make "the election of Lincoln sure, and thus get up agitation and excitement in the South . . . for the purpose of reviving the African slave trade." With a feeling of contempt Botts angrily declared, in language which other border state Unionists expressed in private but dared not utter in public, that those who sought to restore this traffic to human misery were motivated by the most debased of all considerations, economic profit.

[44] Greensboro (S.C.) *The Patriot*, September 28, 1850. Similar praise may be found in Washington *National Intelligencer*, June 3, 1851; Natchez *Weekly Courier*, July 2, 1851; New York *Herald*, August 4, 1860; and Reuben Davis, *Recollections of Mississippi and Mississippians* (Boston, 1890), 101.

[45] See New York *Herald*, July 22 and August 4, 1860; Cleo Hearon, "Mississippi and the Compromise of 1850," *Publications of the Mississippi Historical Society*, XIV (University of Mississippi, 1914), 33; and Washington *National Intelligencer*, October 4, 1851.

They are impelled and are prepared not only to destroy the government, but to sell their liberty, and hopes of mankind, for gold, and for the purpose of introducing little negroes from the coast of Africa, into their cotton fields, in order that they may make cotton sell at 12 cts. a pound, to put into their breeches pockets. They do not ask us to unite with them, but we, the border states, are to act in the capacity of breakwater between them and the North—we are to do the fighting while they make the cotton. We are to do the fighting; they are to make the money.[46]

If Botts showed courage and skill in his use of epithets, he was even more effective in his use of striking and unusual analogies which both clarified and motivated. Speaking in New York before the Order of United Americans in the Academy of Music, he relied on this approach to show the value of political coalitions.

If I were at sea, one thousand miles from shore, and I found the ship had sprung a leak, and was fast going down—and whilst I was laboring with all my energies, to stop the leak, and any other passenger or person were to come up, and offer his assistance, I would not stop to inquire, what was his religion, what his politics, or what his profession; but I would take him by the hand, and say, go to work my good fellow; let us stop this leak, and save the ship, save our lives, save the crew and cargo—and if there is to be any quarrel between us, about the distribution of cargo, let us postpone that, until we get safely into port. . . . Our country now is in that sinking condition; it is traveling with rail road speed down on an inclined plane to destruction—and the only question for us to decide, and we must decide it quickly, is whether we shall apply the brakes, and the man who has the most power for the application is the *Brakeman* I want. . . . I will not ask what have been the politics of any man who will help me to do it.[47]

[46] Botts, *Union or Disunion,* speech delivered at Holcombe Hall, Lynchburg, October 18, 1860 (Richmond, 1860).

[47] Botts, *Speech delivered before the Order of United Americans in the Academy of Music, February 22, 1859* (New York, 1859).

Often Botts incorporated humor in his homespun analogies. In his Lynchburg speech, delivered in 1860, he emphasized the solemn nature of the compact between the states by drawing a parallel with sacred marriage vows.

The wife, on entering the marriage state, binds herself to obey her husband just as we bound ourselves to obey the laws of the country, and the Constitution of the United States. But she has an ugly, crabbed old husband with whom she becomes dissatisfied, and she claims that she reserves the right to destroy by poison, and withdraw in search of a more congenial partner. Some old man has an ugly old wife, and sees a handsome, rich young woman, and falls in love with youth, beauty, and wealth, and though he did bind himself perpetually to the marriage contract, yet, casting aside the marriage tie, and forgetting the sacred compact, he says, "Though I did enter into such an agreement, there were mental reservations of my own—certain reserved rights by which I can withdraw, and form another and more favorable alliance." Now I would advise all the secession men to go over to the "Free Love" party. There is where they belong, and there is where their doctrines should be appreciated.[48]

In using such illustrations Botts wanted his audience to laugh an idea to death. That he succeeded is evidenced by the number of times the word laughter appears in the printed versions of his speeches. In the above passage alone the audience responded uproariously on three different occasions.

Not content to rely on irony, ridicule, and colorful analogies, Botts also freely used causal reasoning substantiated by evidence drawn from primary and secondary sources. He was able to discover issues, trace events, and interpret historical facts. Although he was highly persuasive when addressing neutral and friendly audiences, he was too frank and outspoken when speaking to hostile listeners. Thus he was cheered by his sympathizers and threatened by his opponents.

[48] Botts, *Union or Disunion.*

In choice of appeals and in language structure the southern Unionists reflected their personalities and training. While all of them had essentially the same message in the 1850's, they varied widely in their use of the forms of proof. In adjusting their speeches to different settings and locales, however, they employed similar rhetorical strategies. While speaking in Congress and in the North, for example, they often used a strong aggressive-defensive approach which both highlighted the importance of southern rights and the adverse effect which slavery agitation had produced on the mind of the South. "I ask the North," Houston said in plaintive tones in 1850, "to reflect that they have gone far enough; that the South has been sufficiently excited." [49] To his New York audience in 1860 Hilliard said: "What had the South ever begged of the North? Nothing, nothing! All she asked, all she wanted, was her rights, and nothing more. But if these are denied her we will witness 'a country deluged in fraternal blood.' " [50] Not a few of the Unionists felt, with Hilliard, that Lincoln's election would lead first to a loss of southern rights and then to revolution. With his right hand placed upon his heart, Foote told the Democrats of New York in 1860: "If Lincoln is elected on the platform on which he is running, all the efforts of all the Union men, North and South, would not be sufficient to prevent the destruction of the Confederacy." [51]

Two reasons dictated this bold southern rights stand on northern soil. First, the Unionists of the South wanted their counterparts in the North to know the potential power and influence of the Fire-Eaters. No one knew better than they how wrong the *Atlantic Monthly* was when it said in 1860: "Mr. W. L. Yancey . . . threatens to secede; but the country can get along without him, and we wish him a prosperous career in

---

[49] *Congressional Globe*, 31st Cong., 1st sess., Pt. 1, Appendix, 98.
[50] Newark *Evening Journal*, September 8, 1860.
[51] New York *Herald*, August 3, 1860.

foreign parts. . . . His throwing a solitary somerset will hardly turn the continent head over heels." [52] Such a flippant prophecy, characterized by lack of insight into the southern mind and the rhetorical effectiveness of the secessionist leaders, not only far missed the mark, argued the Unionists, but did irreparable harm to both sections. They felt constrained therefore to point up in graphic detail the militant attitude of the southern people and the ability of Yancey and his followers to strengthen that attitude. Indeed, as Foote correctly pointed out, not even the patriots of the South could resist Yancey's influence if Lincoln were elected.[53]

A second factor which contributed significantly to the mode of adaptation used by the southern Unionists in the North was their belief that if they spoke aggressively in that area they would then be able to speak soothingly at home. To the people of the South therefore they were less inclined to point up what they believed to be the evils of the Republicans and the weaknesses of Lincoln. Even if the Republicans were victorious, argued the Unionists late in the campaign of 1860, there would be no just cause for disunion. For such a victory, however distasteful it might be, would be hammered out on the anvil of the Constitution.

In a further attempt to soothe the excited feelings of the South the Unionists sometimes appealed to fair play when addressing their constituents. "Our newspapers and orators," cried Perry in 1850, "must stop playing up Northern anti-slavery meetings and failures to capture run-away slaves, while at the same time ignoring the great unionist mass rallies in Philadelphia, New York, and Boston, and the successful attempts to return fugitive slaves. Nor do they have a moral right to describe in detail the speeches of the abolitionist leaders, unless they are willing to give more than passing notice to the cour-

[52] *Atlantic Monthly*, VI (October, 1860), 501.
[53] New York *Herald*, August 3, 1860.

ageous speeches of those gallant Northern men who consistently defend Southern Rights." [54] These were brave and forthright
words, not unlike those delivered by Webster on the seventh
of March. And they were in keeping with the Unionist strategy
to speak aggressively in the North and soothingly at home.[55]

The evidence pointed out thus far suggests that the southern
Unionists sought to gather high-compulsion, persuasive material from a wide variety of sources, arrange it in a clear, consistent thought pattern (except in the case of Houston), phrase
it in language that was simple, concrete, and vivid, and adapt it
to the interests and background of the particular audience. But
these were not their only sources of power as speakers. They
had the ability to deliver their arguments in an impressive manner. Possessing strong, resonant voices, they could be heard
clearly even by those who stood at the fringes of a large crowd.
And because they were animated and confident they generally
displayed pleasing vocal melody and free, properly motivated
bodily activity. "Rich and musical" were adjectives frequently
used to describe the voices of Perry, Hilliard, and Crittenden.
An enthusiastic contemporary observed that it was worth "going the full length of the state to hear him [Hilliard] pronounce
the word 'Alabama.'" [56] Whenever Perry, Hilliard, and Crittenden spoke their movements were easy, graceful, and energetic. They stood erect; they gestured freely with their heads
and arms; they did not walk or stamp their feet.[57]

[54] Perry, speech delivered in the house of representatives of South Carolina,
December 11, 1850.

[55] The Unionists were similarly effective in adapting their economic arguments to the locale. If sectional men were placed in power, argued Hilliard
in Boston in 1860, the days of the Republic would be numbered, for then
Southerners would feel that their financial interests would be advanced by
setting up an independent republic. Boston *Daily Evening Traveller*, October 26, 1860.

[56] Arthur C. Cole, *The Whig Party in the South* (Washington, 1913), 81.

[57] After hearing Crittenden denounce the sub-treasury bill, Philip Hone
observed: "I think it was the greatest speech I ever heard. His manners were

More crude and unorthodox, but similarly effective, in their delivery were Foote, Botts, and Houston. In their voice control and bodily movements they reflected their strong impulses and deep emotion. "It seemed," remarked one observer after hearing Foote attack Quitman, "as though he could not allow his words time enough to flow out, but they came rushing out in a burning torrent of eloquence that fell like lava upon his unfortunate victim." [58] What was true of Foote was also true, to a large degree, of Botts and Houston. In short, some of the Unionists were vehement, others calm; some polished, others rough, and, at times, crude; but each in his own way was conversational. Since their method of preparation was primarily extempore, they cultivated the habit of speaking in a sincere, direct, face-to-face manner. Such an intimate method of delivery doubtless increased the strength of their arguments.

What effect did the southern Unionists have upon the course of antebellum history? At first glance their record in 1860 and 1861 is unimpressive. Unable to silence the Fire-Eaters and the abolitionists, they could neither prevent the election of Lincoln nor the formation of the Confederacy. But if the Unionists could not prevent the disruption of the national government, they played no small part in delaying secession. Despite congressional approval of the compromise measures and a subsequent endorsement by the Georgia platform, the Unionists of Mississippi, Alabama, and South Carolina did not begin their contests with a strong advantage. Indeed, a considerable body of evidence suggests that the contrary was true. When Foote, for example, arrived home in October, 1850, fresh from his triumphs in the Senate, he soon learned that the opposition to the compromise was greater than he had expected. Arrayed

graceful and animated, his voice clear and distinct, his eyes alternately flaming fire and melting into tenderness." Philip Hone, *The Diary of Philip Hone, 1821–1851*, ed. Alan Nevins (2 vols.; New York, 1927), I, 305.

[58] Natchez *Weekly Courier,* July 16, 1851.

against him were Jefferson Davis, Governor Quitman, both houses of the legislature, the judicial officers of the state, his five colleagues in congress, and a majority of the press.[59] Moreover these groups, reinforced by support from other citizens who opposed the compromise, had recently formed the State Rights Party. They were ready to press the cause of secession in a campaign which promised to be as explosive as it was to be amusing.

Nor was Hilliard's opposition in Alabama and that of Perry in South Carolina less imposing. The Southern Rights Party of Alabama in the spring of 1851 rejected the compromise and, declaring that "the only issue before the people was secession," persuaded their most eloquent orator Yancey to meet Hilliard in joint debate.[60] In many respects Perry had a more formidable task than that which confronted Foote and Hilliard. So rampant was disunion sentiment in South Carolina during the spring and summer of 1850, for example, that moderates like James Petigru and Francis Lieber wrote Webster: "Almost everyone is for southern separation." [61] Perhaps even more significant was the fact that the governor had at his disposal $350,-000 for arming the state. Throughout every district noisy public meetings in opposition to the compromise were held in the fall. With unity of purpose the voters went to the polls in October and filled the legislature with secessionists. Perry and his two colleagues from Greenville were the only Unionists who were elected.

Against this background of opposition the Unionists were victorious, and they were pleased with their achievement. Foote gloated over the prospect of seeing his opponent Jefferson Da-

[59] Henry S. Foote, *Casket of Reminiscences* (Washington, 1874), 353.

[60] Joseph Hodgson, *The Cradle of the Confederacy* (Mobile, 1876), 304–305.

[61] Herbert D. Foster, "Webster's Seventh of March Speech," *American Historical Review*, XXVII (January, 1922), 248.

vis "wending his way to 'Briarfield,' on the bank of the Mississippi"; Hilliard took comfort in the fact that he had "crowded Yancey into silence"; and Perry smiled at Robert Barnwell Rhett's prediction that South Carolina was dead to the value of the Union.[62]

The Unionists, then, began the decade with triumphs they could not repeat ten years later. But while the tangible results of their speaking were less perceptible in 1860 than in 1850, it cannot be assumed that their overall rhetorical effectiveness had diminished. When the Breckinridge Democracy in 1860 heard that Foote, then called the greatest stump orator in Tennessee,[63] would return to his old stamping grounds on a mission of peace and patriotism, they immediately "resolved to send out their ablest speakers . . . to follow at a respectful distance after him and endeavor to rub out his marks." [64] While Foote gladdened the hearts of Tennesseans and Mississipians with the type of stump eloquence they had come to appreciate, Houston in the summer and fall of 1860 made the Texas prairies ring with a similar brand of rough oratory. The third member of the great triumvirate of stump speakers within the Unionist ranks, Hilliard, likewise had lost none of the rhetorical power which enabled him to defeat Yancey in 1851.[65]

If, then, the Unionists were as eloquent in 1860 as in 1850, what accounts for their ultimate failure to stem the tide of secession? The answer to this question lay in a changing public opinion. Despite their strong opposition from political leaders and newspaper editors in 1851, the Unionists had the support

[62] Foote, *Casket of Reminiscences*, 355; Avery Craven, *The Repressible Conflict, 1830–1861* (Baton Rouge, 1939), 3; Washington *National Intelligencer*, November 28, 1850.

[63] New York *Herald*, August 4, 1860.

[64] Natchez *Daily Courier*, October 10, 1860.

[65] So pleased was a New Jersey reporter in 1860 with Hilliard's speech that he declared it "had never been excelled in the prolific annals of the Newark stump campaigns." Newark *Evening Journal*, September 8, 1860.

of a large segment of the people. Following Lincoln's election, however, many voters shifted their loyalty from the moderates to the Fire-Eaters. No longer representatives of majority or strong minority sentiment, the Unionists suddenly found themselves on the side of forlorn hope. Their reactions to this challenge were not always realistic or creative. By continuing to preach adherence to the Constitution they gave an emotional thrust to their moderate position, but they were not responsive to the changing attitudes on slavery which led to a polarization of views in the 1850's. It is ironical that they correctly understood the potential danger of dissolution of the Union in 1860, yet tended to ignore the moral and economic implications of the central question of their time.[66] Thus, in a period when fresh analysis and new rhetorical strategies were urgently needed in evaluating the South's peculiar institution, they chose instead to eulogize the Constitution as a panacea. This unimaginative and simplistic solution was by late 1860 too sterile and evasive to blunt the abrasive attacks of the secessionists.

But if the Unionists failed to develop meaningful policies, they were not without influence in the crucial campaign of 1860. More than most of their contemporaries they kept the forum of the South and the North open to free, public discussion at a time when radical thought was attempting to close it. Their national message, unlike that of most of the orators of the sectional parties, transcended geographical lines. When a reporter for the Boston *Courier* heard Hilliard's Faneuil Hall address in October, 1860, he reminded the Republican orators of the North that if they, "like the distinguished and statesmanlike son of Alabama," would deliver speeches "worthy of an American citizen," the South would display toward them an attitude of good will.[67]

[66] C. Vann Woodward, *The Burden of Southern History* (Baton Rouge, 1960), 180–81.
[67] Boston *Daily Courier*, October 26, 1860.

As the southern Unionists spoke, their conservative audiences saw men who represented the type of thought they most wished to cultivate. Moreover they saw men who thoroughly understood the mind of the South and of the North and who had the ability to adapt their message to that mind. In short, they saw men who could effectively—and at times eloquently —project safe, middle-of-the-road ideas at a crucial moment in history. If their rhetorical commitment to sterotyped appeals to the Constitution marred their long-range historical influence, it did not prevent the Unionists from contributing significantly to the delay in starting the Civil War.

A Selected Bibliography

The listings in this bibliography have been selected on the basis of whether they discuss or throw light on the concept (image or myth) of southern oratory. Included are only those items which generalize about groups of speakers or reflect upon the class designated as "southern." Selections reflect upon the collective nature of the nouns "oratory" and "orators," not upon individual speakers. The bibliography includes collections of speeches, school readers, theses, dissertations, monographs, and critical articles.

Alderman, Edwin Anderson and Joel Chandler Harris, editors-in-chief, and Charles William Kent, literary editor. *Library of Southern Literature.* 17 vols. Atlanta, 1907–13. Supplement No. 1 (Vol. XVII) was issued in 1923. Editors-in-chief Alderman and Charles Alphonso Smith, and John Calvin Metcalf, literary editor.

    The seventeen-volume set includes, among its selections of southern literature, portions of more than one hundred speeches from forty orators. Among the "Fifty Reading Courses" is one entitled "The Orator," which is composed of twenty-six studies "for special use of literary clubs and classes in the systematic study." See Vol. XVI, Course IV, pages 20–31.

Braden, Waldo W. "The Concept of Southern Oratory: A Selected Bibliography," *Southern Speech Journal,* XXIX (Winter, 1963), 141–45.

Bibliography

This bibliography is an early version of the present one.

————. "The Emergence of the Concept of Southern Oratory," *Southern Speech Journal,* XXVI (Spring, 1961), 173–83.

The article reveals how the image of the southern orator was developed in school readers, anthologies, literary histories, and historical writings.

————. "Southern Oratory Reconsidered: A Search for an Image," *Southern Speech Journal,* XXIX (Summer, 1964), 303–15.

This article analyzes various formulas for determining who is a southern orator.

————. "Three Southern Readers and Southern Oratory," *Southern Speech Journal,* XXXII (Fall, 1966), 31–40.

The article discusses the contents of the Judge, Ross, and Sterling readers. See entries below.

Brown, William Garrott. *The Lower South in American History.* New York, 1902.

Francis Gaines (see item below, pp. 124–30) says that this book is "one of the most suggestive studies in the field." In his discussion Brown devotes one chapter, entitled "The Orator," mainly to a study of Yancey.

Byars, William Vincent (ed.). *Orators and Oratory of Texas.* Chicago, 1923.

Byars' book, part of the Lone Star Edition of the *World's Best Orations,* contains seventy-eight speeches and excerpts from fifty Texans, dating from 1835 to 1920.

Carleton, William G. "The Celebrity Cult a Century Ago," *Georgia Review,* XIV (Summer, 1960), 133–42.

In discussing the "Golden Age of Oratory," 1830–60, Carleton, a political scientist of the University of Florida gives a prominent place to southern orators who, he says, were "orators for oratory's sake."

Chistophersen, Merrill G. "The Charleston Conversationalists," *Southern Speech Journal,* XX (Winter, 1954), 99–108.

The author discusses the conviviality with which the prominent men of Charleston from 1790 to 1826 pursued discussions in their private clubs, particularly the Cossack Club and later the Literary Club. The article gives insight into the training of some of the South Carolina speakers.

Davis, Frank B. "The Literary Societies of Selected State Universities of the Lower South." Ph.D. dissertation, Louisiana State University, 1949.

The doctoral study considers the societies of the nineteenth century at the state universities of Georgia, South Carolina, Alabama, and Mississippi.

Dickey, Dallas C. "Southern Oratory: A Field for Research," *Quarterly Journal of Speech*, XXXIII (December, 1947), 458–63.

Dickey discusses the opportunities for research, indicating several speakers who should be studied.

————. "Were They Ephemeral and Florid?" *Quarterly Journal of Speech*, XXXII (February, 1946), 16–20.

Dickey takes issue with Merle Curti's statement that southern public address was "embroidered oratorical rhetoric." He offers several examples to prove that it was not ephemeral and florid.

Diehl, George West. *The Rise and Development of Southern Oratory*. M.A. thesis, University of Richmond, 1917.

This thesis (completed for a degree in history) discusses southern speakers from colonial times through the Civil War. Based mainly on secondary sources, it makes no attempt to discover the distinguishing characteristics of southern oratory.

Gaines, Francis Pendleton. *Southern Oratory, A Study in Idealism*. University, Alabama, 1946.

Gaines explains his "historical-thematic treatment" as follows: "The transcendence of political oratory in the South may be ascribed to the fact that this oratory related, for better or worse, to the great ideals by which men live and for which men, if need be, die. In particular, the chronicle of Southern oratory centers in the struggle for human freedom."

Graves, John Temple, Clark Howell, and Walter Williams. *Eloquent Sons of the South: A Handbook of Southern Oratory*. 2 vols. Boston 1909.

Bibliography

The anthology includes excerpts from sixteen speakers. The goal, according to the preface, is to preserve "representative examples of the work of the most widely known statesmen and publicists of the South."

Green, Fletcher M. "Listen to the Eagle Scream: One Hundred Years of The Fourth of July in North Carolina (1776–1876)," *North Carolina Historical Review*, XXXI (July, 1954), 295–320; XXXI (October, 1954), 529–49.

Gunderson, Robert Gray. *The Log-Cabin Campaign*. Lexington, 1957.

Chapter XV, "Whig Champions of the Old South," considers the efforts of Seargent S. Prentiss, William C. Preston, John Tyler, Hugh S. Legaré, William C. Rives, and Henry A. Wise.

Hergesheimer, Joseph. "The Pillar of Words," Chapter II of *Swords and Roses*. New York, 1928.

Francis Gaines (see above) says that this book is an "impressionistic treatment of phrases and figures of the Old South." Included in this chapter are many implications concerning southern oratory and a discussion of William L. Yancey.

Hesseltine, William B. and Henry L. Ewbank, Jr. "Old Voices in the New South," *Quarterly Journal of Speech*, XXXIX (December, 1953), 451–58.

A study of the orators who "lived through the war and raised their voices again in the post-war years when the New South was rising from the ashes."

Hillbruner, Anthony. "Inequality, The Great Chain of Being, and Ante-Bellum Southern Oratory," *Southern Speech Journal*, XXV (Spring, 1960), 172–89.

"Even though they did not mention the 'Great Chain,' an examination of the public utterances of Calhoun, Stephens and [William Andrew] Smith will reveal that this cosmological-social structure provided an important philosophical rationale for the institution of slavery in the South."

Holliday, Carl. *A History of Southern Literature*. New York, 1906.

In his consideration of southern literature, Holliday recognizes and discusses the speaking of several orators, including

Patrick Henry, John Randolph, Henry Clay, John C. Calhoun, Thomas Hart Benton, Robert Y. Hayne, Jefferson Davis, Robert Toombs, Alexander H. Stephens, and Zebulon B. Vance.

Jeffrey, Robert C. "Men, Movements and Materials for Research in Public Address in Virginia," *Southern Speech Journal*, XXIV (Spring, 1959), 154–61.

Jeffrey argues, "There are undefinable limits to the opportunities for research in public address in Virginia."

Judge, Jonathan J. *The Southern Orator; being a collection of pieces in prose, poetry and dialogue: designed for exercises in declamation or occasional reading in schools and families.* Montgomery, 1853.

This reader is made up of selections delivered at schools where the author taught. In the preface the author says that he hopes to develop "genuine, heart-throbbing, soul-stirring eloquence." One of the rare copies is deposited at the Vanderbilt University Library.

Kearney, Kevin E. "What's Southern About Southern Oratory?" *Southern Speech Journal*, XXXII (Fall, 1966), 19–30.

Kearney suggests that the criteria for identifying southern oratory are the speaker's place of residence, his motive, and the speech context.

McConnell, Joseph Moore. *Southern Oratory from 1829 to 1869.* Ph.D. dissertation, University of Virginia, 1907.

This dissertation, completed in the Department of English, possibly under the direction of Charles W. Kent, is now lost. It probably resulted in the publication listed next.

————(ed.). *Southern Orators: Speeches and Orations.* New York; 1910.

The anthology "chiefly from political oratory" is probably an outgrowth of the author's doctoral dissertation (see item above). It contains thirty-four selections from thirty-four speakers, ranging from Patrick Henry to Henry W. Grady. This small book was one of the Macmillan's Pocket American and English Classics series designed for use in elementary and secondary schools. The author was professor of history and political economy at Davidson College at the time of publication.

Lomas, Charles W. "Southern Orators in California before 1861," *Southern Speech Journal,* XV (September, 1949), 21–37.

Lomas makes a study of the impact which Southerners made upon politics in California during the 1850's. Special attention is given Henry S. Foote, Edmund Randolph, and William M. Gwin.

Moses, Montrose J. *The Literature of the South.* New York, 1910.

The author devotes a chapter to "The Voice of the Old South: Being a Consideration of the Literary Claims of Orators—Typified in Calhoun, Clay, and Hayne" and a second to "The Problems of Secession . . . ," which considers Yancey, Toombs, Davis and others. The critic strives to discover what is unique in the speaking of his subjects. The first listed chapter is one of the early critical treatments of southern oratory.

Oliver, Robert. *History of Public Speaking in America.* Boston, 1965.

Chapter VI, "Spokesmen of the Old South," discusses the speaking of Alexander Stephens, Robert Toombs, Howell Cobb, Robert Barnwell Rhett, Judah P. Benjamin, William L. Yancey, Seargent S. Prentiss, L. Q. C. Lamar, and Jefferson Davis.

Peterson, Owen M. "The South in the Democratic National Convention of 1860," *Southern Speech Journal,* XX (Spring, 1955), 212–23.

The author discusses the forces which disrupted the convention in Charletson. He gives special attention to William W. Avery, Ethelbert Barksdale, and William L. Yancey.

Phillips, Ulrich Bonnell. "The Course of the South to Secession: The Fire-eaters," *Georgia Historical Quarterly,* XXII (1938), 41–71.

In considering his main theme, Phillips discusses briefly the speaking of Robert J. Turnbull, Rhett, Yancey, Louis T. Wigfall, and several minor figures.

Reynolds, William Martin. *Deliberative Speaking in Ante-Bellum*

South Carolina: The Idiom of a Culture. Ph.D. dissertation, University of Florida, 1960.

Reynolds analyzes more than five hundred deliberative addresses delivered by Carolina speakers between 1820 and 1861. Abstracted in *Speech Monographs*, XXVIII (June, 1961), 86–87.

Reddick, Glenn E. "When the Southern Senators Said Farewell," *Southern Speech Journal*, XV (March, 1950), 169–97.

Reddick's article reports the farewell speeches of the southern senators in 1861. He devotes special sections to Toombs, Benjamin, Albert G. Brown, Alfred Iverson, and John Slidell.

Richardson, Ralph. "The Rhetorical Death Rattle of the Confederacy," *Southern Speech Journal*, XX (Winter, 1954), 109–16.

A study of the Confederate war speeches designed to stir morale and delivered in Richmond, Virginia, February 6–9, 1865. Richardson refers to the speeches of Judah P. Benjamin, Jefferson Davis, and William Oldham as "the last outburst of the Confederacy's rhetorical defiance."

Rives, Ralph Hardee. "Public Address in the 'Old Dominion,' 1820–1840," *Southern Speech Journal*, XXVI (Summer, 1961), 318–28.

"In every facet of Virginia life, the orator was ever present—in the law courts, at political meetings, conventions, and camp meetings, in the pulpit, and at commencements and barbecues."

Ross, D. Barton. *The Southern Speakers or Sixth Reader Containing, in Great Variety, the Masterpieces of Oratory in Prose, Poetry and Dialogue*. New Orleans, 1856.

This school reader contains 385 purple passages, usually one page long, from a wide variety of speakers, many of whom are revered Southerners. At the time of publication the author was associate principal and professor of elocution in Rapides Institute, Alexandria, Louisiana.

Rowland, Dunbar. "Political and Parliamentary Orators and Oratory of Mississippi," *Publications of the Mississippi Historical Society*, IV (1901), 357–400.

The author's purpose is to rescue Mississippi orators and oratory "from the condition of oblivion into which it has fallen."

He gives brief analyses for the following: George Poindexter, Seargent S. Prentiss, Robert J. Walker, Henry S. Foote, Jefferson Davis, Alexander K. McClung, Albert G. Brown, L. Q. C. Lamar, Edward C. Walthall, James Z. George, and James L. Alcorn.

Shurter, Edwin DuBois. *Oratory of the South: From the Civil War to the Present Time.* New York, 1908.

The book, compiled by a professor of public speaking at the University of Texas, presents mainly "extracts" from eighty-four speakers of the post-Civil War period (1865–1908). The selections were intended for use as declamations and for inspiration.

Smith, Charles Alphonso. "Southern Oratory Before the War," Chapter V of Smith, *Southern Literary Studies.* Chapel Hill, 1927, 83–93.

The above is adapted from an address which Professor Smith first delivered to the Louisiana legislature in 1895, and "he repeated it on many later occasions."

Smithey, William Royall and Calvin Hall Phippins. *Virginia Oratory, Containing Selections from native Virginians arranged in chronological groupings to illustrate outstanding epochs in Virginia History.* Charlottesville, 1934.

This volume was "designed for special use in high schools and colleges." It contains seventy-two selections from sixty-eight speakers, ranging from Chief Logan (1774) to Harry Flood Byrd (1932).

Sterling, Richard. *Sterling's Little Southern Orator, A New Collection of Original and Selected Pieces, in Poetry, Prose, and Dialogue, For Juvenile Speakers.* Macon, 1872.

The preface suggests that this selection is for "boys of fourteen or fifteen years of age. . . . Extracts have been taken from the speeches of our greatest orators, the thoughts of which can be understood by the youngest pupils, while the language and style are elevated and oratorical. It is vain to attempt to teach a child to speak well unless you furnish him 'thoughts that breathe and words that burn,' to excite his emotions and fire his heart. Besides, the effect of such pieces is to elevate the thoughts, and cultivate a taste for the chaste and elegant in language."

_____. *Sterling's Southern Orator.* New York and Greensboro, N. C., 1867.

In the preface the author explains that his purpose is to make available "a collection of short and spirited pieces adapted to school and college declamations. . . . The book may be also used as a Rhetorical Reader in the higher classes in schools and academies."

This school reader contains selections for recitation and memorization. The first thirty-nine pages consider elements of elocution: style, voice, delivery, and declamation. Part I includes 94 selections of prose (pp. 1–126); 60 of poetry (pp. 127–55); and 6 of dialogues (pp. 188–97). Part II has the following composition: 233 selections of prose (pp. 201–395); 167 of poetry (397–471); 10 of dialogues (pp. 473–97).

Over 240 authors are represented, including 129 Southerners. Favorites include Clay, Calhoun, Prentiss, John Randolph, Alexander Stephens. In the front of the book is an "Index of Authors," identifying the native state of each author.

The appendix gives a list of 144 propositions for debating.

Stewart, Joseph Spencer and Lucian Lamar Knight (eds.). *Georgia Oratory, containing selections from Georgians, arranged in chronological groupings to illustrate outstanding epochs in Georgia history.* Designed for special use of high schools and colleges. Athens, 1933.

This small paperback contains sixty excerpts from over forty speakers. The selections are intended for declamations and for "collateral reference" for history classes.

Trent, W. P. (ed.). *Southern Writers: Selections in Prose and Verse.* New York, 1923.

This literary historian includes many selections from the speeches of southern orators.

Watson, Thomas E. (ed.). *History of Southern Oratory,* Vol. IX of J. A. C. Chandler *et al.* (eds.), *The South in the Building of the Nation.* 13 vols. Richmond, 1909–13.

This volume is probably the most ambitious study of southern oratory which has ever been undertaken. In the role of the apologist, the editor declares his purpose as follows: "To select some of the more notable characters of Southern history and to reveal in their own public utterances the manner of men they were." The volume presents a history of southern oratory and an anthology. The first part traces southern oratory from colonial times to 1909. The chapters are as follows:

Chapter I, "The History of Southern Oratory During the Colonial Period, 1763," by Thomas E. Watson.
Chapter II, "Southern Oratory During the Formative and Revolutionary Periods, 1763–1788," by Thomas E. Watson.
Chapter III, "The History of Southern Oratory During the Federal Period, 1788–1861," by Edward K. Graham.
Chapter IV, "The History of Southern Oratory During the War Period, 1861–1865," by Edward K. Graham.
Chapter V, "Post-Bellum Oratory in the South, 1865–1909," by Clark Howell.
Chapter VI, "The Political Oratory of the South," by Thomas E. Watson.
Chapter VII, "The Oratory of the Bench and Bar of the South," by John C. Reed.
Chapter VIII, "The Pulpit Oratory of the South," by Benjamin F. Riley.
Chapter IX, "History of General Oratory of the South," by William Vincent Byars.

The last part of the book (pp. 169–514) is a collection of speeches. Thirty-two speeches from twenty-seven speakers are included.

Wauchope, George Armstrong. *The Writers of South Carolina.* Columbia, S.C., 1910.

This literary historian sees fit to include a section on "The Orators" (pp. 40–53). He discusses the speaking of John C. Calhoun, Wade Hampton, Robert Y. Hayne, George McDuffie, Benjamin Morgan Palmer, William C. Preston, and Robert Barnwell Rhett.

Williams, Ray Robinson. *Representative Ante-Bellum Oratory in South Carolina.* M.A. thesis, University of South Carolina, 1924.

Williams' thesis, directed by G. A. Wauchope, discusses

Hayne, Calhoun, Preston, and George McDuffie. Forty of the forty-eight pages are devoted to original material.

Wynn, William T. (ed.). *Southern Literature: Selections and Biographies.* New York, 1932.

This anthology includes a chapter entitled "Oratory." Excerpts from twelve speakers are included. The speech "Southern Oratory Before the War" by C. Alphonso Smith is reprinted here. See Smith entry.

Yeomans, G. Allan. "Southern Oratory and the Art of Story-Telling: A Case Study," *Southern Speech Journal,* XXXII (Summer, 1967), 251–60.

The article discusses mainly the storytelling of James Thomas Heflin.

Young, Bennett Henderson. *Kentucky Eloquence, Past and Present, Library of Orations, Afterdinner Speeches, Popular and Classical Lectures, Addresses and Poetry.* Louisville, 1907.

The editor declares his purpose to put "into one volume the best things spoken or written by the men of Kentucky." He has included eighty-four speeches dating from 1803 to 1906 and extracts from eighty-one speakers. He also includes thirty pages of poetry.

Contributors

Waldo W. Braden is Professor of Speech and Departmental Chairman at Louisiana State University, Baton Rouge.

Bert E. Bradley is Associate Professor of Speech at the University of North Carolina, Chapel Hill.

Merrill G. Christophersen is Professor of English at the University of South Carolina. He completed his dissertation under the direction of Dallas C. Dickey.

Ralph T. Eubanks is Professor of Speech and Departmental Chairman at the University of West Florida. He completed his dissertation under the direction of Dallas C. Dickey.

James L. Golden is Professor of Speech at Ohio State University. He completed his dissertation under the direction of Dallas C. Dickey.

Robert G. Gunderson is Professor of Speech and Director of the American Studies Program at Indiana University.

Lindsey S. Perkins is Associate Professor of Speech at Brooklyn College.

H. Hardy Perritt is a consultant in education and communication, Atlanta, Georgia. He completed his doctoral dissertation under the direction of Dallas C. Dickey.

Owen Peterson is Professor of Speech at Louisiana State University, Baton Rouge.

Contributors

Jerry L. Tarver is Associate Professor of Speech and Departmental Chairman at the University of Richmond.

Donald W. Zacharias is Associate Professor of Speech at the University of Texas.

Index

Index

Pierce, 147–48; speech at Volunteer Encampment, 166–67
Johnson, Reverdy, 130
Jones, James C., "Lean Jimmy," 106, 107, 138

Kelly, A. H., 46
King, Mitchell, 76, 81, 87; opposes nullification in Tennessee, 87
King, Thomas Butler, 106
Know-Nothing Party: campaign of 1855, pp. 227–29; in Florida, 225; in Kentucky, 223; in Louisiana, 222; in Missouri, 224; language, 229–30; leaders, 219; oratory, 232; patriotic appeals, 231; Philadelphia rally, 1855; pp. 226–27; records, 219n2; as a ritualistic response, 233; speaking, 225–27; tactics, 229

Lawrence, Abbot, 116
Lawrence, Amos, 275
Legaré, Hugh S., 33, 40–41, 77–78, 109, 113, 138, 140; to Forsyth, 103; to his mother, 80; on Nullifiers, 78; resolutions of Anti-Nullifiers, 79–80; speech, July 4, 1831, p. 84
Leigh, Benjamin Watkins, 137, 139
Letcher, Robert P., 122
Lewis, Dixon H., 60
Liberator, 144
Lieber, Francis, 108, 110, 138, 287
Lincoln, Abraham, 122, 155, 159, 218; denounces Know-Nothing Party, 218n
Literary societies: in Charleston, 75–76
Logic: use of, 160
Lumpkin, Wilson, 93
Lyons, James, 210

McBurney, James H., 171, 176
McDowell, Frances: comments on cousin James, 156
McDowell, James, 153–54, 157; styles, 159, 162, 168; plea for abolition in 1832, p. 145; rhetoric of, 162; speech on emancipation in 1832, p. 152; speech to Virginia legislature, 1832, pp. 146–47; speech on Wilmot Proviso, 147

McDuffie, George, 53, 54–55, 82, 102, 105
McWhiney, Grady, 105n6
Maclay, William, 235
Mangum, Willie P., 94, 105
Manufacturing interest, 25
Marshall, Alexander K., 224, 227
Marshall, Thomas, 227
Mason, James M., 236
Mazlish, B., 67
Meacham, James, 160
"Mediatory ground": of Nullifiers, 22
Memminger, C. G., 96
Meriwether, James A., 245
Metcalfe, Thomas, 122
Middleton, Henry, 81
Milling, Chapman, 30
Mills, Glen E., 171, 176
Missouri Compromise, 160
Missouri question (1819–21), 22
Mitchell, Thomas R., 84
Moderate Democrats: audience adaptation, 153–54; beliefs, 146; career goals, 151; delivery, 158; ethos, 156; lack of sophistry, 153; logic, 160; source of strength, 151
Morehead, Charles S., 107, 223
Morehead, John Motley, 107
Mud-sill theory, 30–31

Nashville Convention of 1850, p. 236
Nelson, Thomas A. R., 106, 107, 125, 137
Nichols, Marie Hochmuth, 4
Niles, Hezekiah, 29
North Carolina: population in 1840, p. 111; religion, 111
Nullification: as defensive act, 66; controversy, 21, 27; ordinance to enforce, 96–97; repeal in 1833, p. 97; political and rhetorical origins, 22–29; rhetoric, 56–57
Nullifiers: answered, 83–87; axiological ground, 29; Calhoun formulates propositions of, 36; conservatism, 66–67; dialectical ground, 66; final assessment of, 72; in Alabama, 60; in Georgia, 59; in Mississippi, 60–61; in North Carolina, 59–60; in South Carolina, 27–28, 48, 95–103;

Index